384

KV-419-033

THE BUILD

DERBYSHIRE

PEVSNER

NIKOLAUS PEVSNER

STOKE-ON-TRENT
PUBLIC LIBRARIES
CENTRAL
REFERENCE LIBRARY
HANLEY

The County of
DERBYSHIRE
YORKSHIRE
CHESHIRE
NOTT
A
B
C
D
E
1
2
3
Melandra Castle
Hadfield
Glossop
Charlesworth
Rowarth
Hayfield
New Mills
Whitehaugh
Bradshaw Hall
Whaley Bridge
Taxal
Chapel en le Frith
Ford Hall
Fairfield
Buxton
Burbage
Ladybower reservoir
Hope
Castleton
Peveril Castle
Hazlebadge Hall
Lt Hucklow
Wheston
Tideswell
Wormhill
Taddington
Chelmorton
Hartington
Biggin
Alsop en le Dale
Ballidon
Parwich
Newhaven
Monyash
Ashford
Bakewell
Haddon Hall
Thornbridge Hall
Longstone
Hassop
Cressbrook
Litton
Foolow
Highlow Hall
Brough
Bamford
N.Lees
Brookfield Manor
Hathersage
Carlwark
Offerton Hall
Hazleford
Padley
Eyam
Stoke Hall
Stoney Middleton
Curbar
Baslow
Edensor
Beeley
Chatsworth House
Rowsley
Youlgreave
Alport
Stanton in the Peak
Stanton Moor
Birchover
Elton
Wensley
Winster
Snitterton Hall
Bonsall
Cromford
Middleton
Brassington
Wirksworth
Darley Dale
Matlock
Riber
Tansley
Dethick
Crich
S Wingfield
Brackenfield
Ogston Hall
Edelstow
Ashover
Overton Hall
Norton
Gleadless
Beighton
Dronfield
Holmesfield
Unstone
Barlow
Cutthorpe Hall
Brampton
New Brampton
Wingerworth
Stubbing Court
Eckington
Renishaw Hall
Whittington
Newbold
Chesterfield
Hasland Hall
Sutton Scarsdale
N.Wingfield
Clay Cross
Tibshelf
Morton
Shirland
Alfreton
Carnfield Hall
S Normanton
Blackwell
Brookhill Hall
Pinxton
Killamarsh
Park Hall
Spinkhill
Barlborough
Barrow Hill
Staveley
Clowne
Elmton
Bolsover
Scarcliffe
Heath
Ault Hucknall
Hardwick Hall
Pleasley
Langwith
Steetly
Whitwell
Cresswell Crags

STAFFORDSHIRE
INGHAMSHIRE
LEICESTERSHIRE

Alsop en le Dale
Ballidon
Brassington
Wirksworth
S Wingfield
Crich
Alfreton
Brookhill Hall
Pinxton
Parwich
Carsington
Hopton Hall
Alderwasley
Pentrich
Somercotes
Tissington
Bradbourne
Riddings
Kniveton
Ironville
Thorpe
Hognaston
Kirk Ireton
R. Derwent
Heage
Codnor
Fenny Bentley
Idridgehay
Belper
Mapleton
Hulland
Denby
Heanor
Ashbourne
Bradley
Milford
Holbrook
Kilburn Hall
Osmaston
Hazlewood
Smalley
Snelston
Mugginton
Horsley
Stainsby House
Cotmanhay
Norbury
Edlaston
Shirley
Duffield
Morley
W Hallam
Ilkeston
Brailsford
Lt Eaton
Yeaveley
Kedleston
Quarndon
Stanley
Kirk Hallam
Kirk Langley
Allestree
Breadsall
Locko Park
Dale Abbey
Longford
Darley Abbey
Cubley
Mackworth
Lt Chester
Stanton by Dale
Marston Montgomery
Markeaton Hall
Chaddesden
Ockbrook
Sandiacre
Boylestone
Radburne
Spondon
Hopwell Hall
Risley
Somersal Herbert
Trusley
Mickleover
DERBY
Long Eaton
Barton Blount
Dalbury
Osmaston by Derby
Borrowash
Doveridge
Church Broughton
Sutton on the Hill
Littleover
Alvaston
Breaston
Sudbury
Etwall
Normanton
Boulton
Elvaston
Wilne
River Trent
Scropton
Hilton
Findern
Chellaston
Shardlow
Sawley
Marston on Dove
Twyford
Swarkeston
Aston on Trent
River Dove
Willington
Barrow on Trent
Ingleby
Weston upon Trent
Egginton
Repton
Foremark
Stanton by Bridge
Newton Solney
Ticknall
Melbourne
Bretby Park
Calke
Scale of Miles
0 1 2 3 4 5 6 7 8 9 10
Stapenhill
Brizlincote Hall
Hartshorne
Swadlincote
Smisby
Walton on Trent
Caldwell
Woodville
Church Gresley
Rosliston
Overseal
Coton in the Elms
Catton Hall
Lullington
Netherseal
N
W
E
S
A B C D E
3 4 5

STOKE-ON-TRENT
PUBLIC
LIBRARIES

THE BUILDINGS OF ENGLAND

Derbyshire

BY

NIKOLAUS PEVSNER

*

720.94251

WITHDRAWN AND
SOLD BY
STOKE-ON-TRENT
CITY ARCHIVES

PENGUIN BOOKS
MELBOURNE · LONDON · BALTIMORE

FIRST PUBLISHED 1953

CENTRAL
REFERENCE LIBRARY
HANLEY

2 DEC 57

The author and publishers would be grateful
to any user of this book for having any errors
or omissions pointed out to them
in as much detail
as possible

WITHDRAWN AND
SOLD BY
STOKE-ON-TRENT
CITY ARCHIVES

MADE AND PRINTED IN GREAT BRITAIN
FOR PENGUIN BOOKS LTD
BY WILLIAM CLOWES AND SONS LTD
LONDON AND BECCLES

STOKE-ON-TRENT
PUBLIC
LIBRARIES

CONTENTS

★

★

The map on pages 2–3 shows all those places, whether towns, villages, or isolated buildings, which are the subject of separate entries in the text. The index on pages 273–282 gives references to the map square in which each place mentioned will be found

TO THE MEMORY OF MONKSDALE

*

STOKE ON TRENT
PUBLIC
LIBRARIES

STOKE-ON-TRENT
PUBLIC
LIBRARIES

FOREWORD

The preparation of the data on which this book is based lay in the experienced hands of Dr Schapire, the compilation of the notes on prehistory and Roman antiquities in those of Mr Jon Manchip White. I am grateful to both of them for what they have done for this book. In addition I have had the valuable help of the Derby Central Library and the Derbyshire County Library, where both Mr E. Osborne and Mr Keith Mantell have taken great interest in my research. Moreover, the Ministry of Housing and Local Government, who have a statutory duty to draw up lists of buildings of architectural or historic interest, have with their customary kindness allowed me access to unpublished lists and much other information collected by the Chief Investigator of the Ministry and his staff (here abridged MHLG*). The National Buildings Record made it possible for me to use their photograph collection and for this I am indebted to Mr Cecil Farthing and Mrs Mary Parry. I have also to thank Mr H. S. Goodhart-Rendel for permission to use his manuscript card index of Victorian churches (marked here* GR*) and Sir Thomas Kendrick for permission to use his card index of Victorian stained glass (marked here* TK*).*

I have had to write to many rectors and vicars and have received much kindness from them. Some have gone to a great deal of trouble to satisfy my requests for specified information. The same is true of owners of houses. Here also everybody, with hardly any exception, has been most obliging both in showing me their houses and in answering questions. In return I wish to make it quite clear to readers of this Foreword that houses must not be supposed to be open to the public because they are mentioned or even described in this book.

In connexion with individual places I owe a special debt of gratitude to Mr Francis Thompson the Librarian and Keeper of Collections at Chatsworth, Colonel and Mrs Sandeman of Meynell Langley, Colonel R. B. Turbutt of Ogston Hall, the Reverend A. Hopkins, rector of Kirk Langley, Sir Osbert Sitwell, and Mr F. Ward of Torquay.

STOKE-ON-TRENT
PUBLIC
LIBRARIES

INTRODUCTION

DERBYSHIRE is a county of contrasts: flat and uneventful country towards Nottinghamshire and Leicestershire, and the forbidding grandeur of the High Peak towards Cheshire; hedges between the fields in the south, rough stone walls in the north, brick cottages in the south, stone cottages in the north, agriculture in the south, pasture and bare moors in the north; industry in four distinct areas: the NE towards Yorkshire with Staveley, Eckington, Bolsover, etc., the NW towards Cheshire with Whalley Bridge, New Mills, Glossop, etc., the E towards Nottinghamshire with Ilkeston, Stanton, etc., and the S towards Leicestershire with Church Gresley, Swadlincote, etc. These industrial regions lie all along the margins of the county; the centre, especially N of a line from Asbourne to Belper, is all country rightly popular with tourists, Dovedale, Derwent Dale, Miller Dale, the Hope Valley, Matlock, Buxton, the High Peak. Tourists come for scenery of many varied attractions, less for architecture.

Indeed Derbyshire does not possess a cathedral (All Saints, Derby, was raised to cathedral rank only in 1927), nor a large abbey in picturesque ruins, nor many parish churches as spectacular as those of East Anglia or the Nene Valley or the South-west. But instead of grand churches there are grand houses: Haddon, Hardwick, Bolsover, Chatsworth, Kedleston; and these, especially since they have all been made accessible to the public, are what both, the layman and the expert think of, when Derbyshire is mentioned. The architectural historian will derive more enlightenment from domestic than from ecclesiastical architecture, and, it must be added, not only from the major mansions but also from a large number of manor houses (such as Tissington and Eyam) and farmhouses, in the aggregate highly interesting. Far more of such houses are preserved in the N than the S, because the rougher climate of the Peak prevented an C18 and C19 prosperity which, in the S, destroyed more of value than it replaced. Or is this impression deceiving? Is it due to the fact that the brick house of the C18 in the S has less to arrest the eye than the gabled stone house of the N?

The dividing line between brick (and, before brick became popular, timber-framing) and stone runs roughly from W to E a few miles N of Derby. It has its reason in the geological structure of the county. This is relatively easily described: Carboniferous Limestone N of a line from Ashbourne to Duffield and right up to the N border from Glossop to Hathersage, Millstone Grit as a narrow band to the NW and the E of the Carboniferous Limestone, Coal as a narrow band to the NW and a broad band to the E of the Grit, Permian (Magnesian) Limestone E of the Chesterfield–Staveley coal areas, a broad horizontal band of Keuper from Ashbourne and Uttoxeter E to Derby and then to the E border and the S border (with the interruption of a narrow strip of Bunter E of Ashbourne and a patch of Bunter S of Foremark and the small coal and grit areas S of this from Swadlincote to Melbourne and Stanton). Building stones are in accordance with this structure, but, as in most other counties of England, no specialized literature exists on the building stones of the past. On the whole one finds mostly the rough sandstones of the Millstone Grit and the coal measures, and further S those of the Bunter (used round Derby and Ashbourne), then the sandy, honey-coloured Magnesian Limestone in the NE and the Carboniferous Limestone on the high lands in the N (the Hopton Wood quarries belong to this).

On these high lands the most important prehistoric remains of Derbyshire are to be found. The oldest evidence of human habitation, however, are the paleolithic caves in the Creswell Crags on the Notts border. Derbyshire in prehistoric times formed part of the sparsely populated Highland Zone, its terrain too bleak on the one hand and too densely wooded on the other to attract any but the hardiest individuals. Nevertheless in late Neolithic and Early Bronze Age times Derbyshire was traversed continuously by a succession of traders crossing the Pennines from East to West and back again, and a number of these traders made a permanent home for themselves at this focal point of their customary trade route. The neolithic Peterborough Folk (*c.* 2500 B.C.), influenced by the more progressive Windmill Hill Folk of Wessex, were early specialists in the carrying trade, and Derbyshire contains significant traces of their presence. These neolithic merchants brought to the territory some of the ideas of the megalith builders of Ireland and the West. The Peterborough Folk gave way before the incursion of the vigorous Beaker Folk (*c.* 1800 B.C.), who arrived in Derbyshire from the direction of Yorkshire and the Wash. They were intermediaries between Ireland, a leading exponent of gold and bronze-working in the Early Bronze Age, and its English and Continental emulators. The Beaker Folk formed a ruling aristocracy over the greater part of Britain, and were responsible for the introduction of both civil and religious unification. To them or to their immediate descendants may be attributed the impressive stone circles of Derbyshire. These lie mostly within an area of no more than 20 square miles and above 1,000 ft altitude. The most important stone circles are Arbor Low near Youlgreave, Nine Stones near Wheston, and the Bull Ring at Dove Holes. Arbor Low has a diameter of *c.* 250 ft and is thus one of the largest circles in the country, but unfortunately all the stones are fallen. Successive expansions of the Bronze Age populations of the North of England, particularly in Yorkshire, led to the emergence in Derbyshire of substantial Food Vessel and Urn Folk colonies. These people appear to have been descendants of the old Peterborough Folk who inherited some of the traditions of the vanished Beaker overlords. They were mainly pastoralists, although tillage was practised on a small scale and in a rudimentary fashion. Towards the end of the Bronze Age, when the Lowland Zone was receiving influxes of talented settlers from the Continent, Derbyshire and the Highland Zone in general had become something of a backwater. From 1000 B.C. onwards the Urn Folk maintained a peaceful existence in the fastnesses of the Peak District, untroubled by the alarms of the Late Bronze Age and the Iron Age. Both these ages left little imprint in the soil of Derbyshire. A simple Bronze Age economy persisted right into Roman times, during which Derbyshire was no more shaken by great events than it was in the prehistoric era. It subsisted within the framework of the Pax Romana, the frontiers and the battlefields being well to the North and West. Roman roads, however, had to be made across the county to enable troops to be moved swiftly to any possible centre of revolt among the Celtic tribes who had rejected the adoption of Roman ways. This was very different from the civil zone of SE Britain, where the Celts were gradually becoming romanized. Three auxiliary forts existed, Little Chester (Derventio) just N of Derby, Melandra Castle W of Glossop, and Brough near Hope. Brough measured 340 by 285 ft, Melandra 360 by 335. Little Chester was considerably larger: 615 by 540 ft. The chief value of the county to the Romans was its lead. Six pigs of lead with Latin inscriptions have been found, one bearing a date from the reign of Hadrian. The centre of the industry was round Wirksworth. The baths of Buxton were also known to the Romans. The chief roads in Roman times were the Icknield Way from Lichfield by Little Chester and Chesterfield to Yorkshire and a branch road from Little Chester to Buxton.

After the withdrawal of the Romans the county seems to have remained for more than a century in the hands of the Britons. The Anglo-Saxons gradually moved in during the later C6. They were Mercians, and so Derbyshire became part of the kingdom of Mercia. A number of Saxon crosses of Mercian character dating from *c.* 800 onwards have been found; the best of this early group are at Bakewell and Eyam. Their style depends on the C7 art of Northumberland. The remarkable panel from a stone coffin with scenes from the Gospels at Wirksworth also belongs to *c.* 800. It is one of the leading examples of figure sculpture of its date in the country. Later Saxon crosses are of two types: panelled with interlace decoration (Hope, Norbury, etc.) and circular (Brailsford). The former seem to be of the C10, the latter, dependent on such superior north country examples as Gosforth of the mid C11. Saxon architecture is best represented at Repton, where a C10 straightheaded chancel with the typical thin lesenes of the period, fragmentary indications of transepts and crossing, and the famous crypt survive. The columns with thin spiral bands around and the primitive groined vaults may be an C11 insertion. As a vaulted crypt with columns Repton is unique in Anglo-Saxon architecture, but represents a type familiar in France and Germany.

The Danes gave Derby its name and established the shire. Derby, and Nottingham, Lincoln, Stamford, and Leicester, were the five principal towns of their Midland territory. Reconquest by the Saxons took place in the early C10. The Normans quickly incorporated the county in their administrative system. William granted lands chiefly to William Peveril and Hugh de Ferrers. William Peveril had Peak Castle built to guard the mining of the Hope Valley and Bolsover, amongst many other manors, to Hugh de Ferres Tetbury just across the Staffordshire border and Duffield are due. The keep at Duffield, the foundations of which are known from excavations, was larger than any other in England save Colchester and London. Peak Castle is by far the best preserved and visually the most rewarding castle in the county.

Of Norman churches the first rank is held by Melbourne and Steetley, Melbourne is the unique example of a mere parish church with such cathedral motifs as a two-tower W front, and a wall passage at clerestory level. It has the unusual feature of an open gallery towards the nave between the towers and the even more unusual feature of an originally two-storeyed chancel. All the detail is robust to the verge of brutality. The tall very narrowly placed circular arcade piers with their stilted arches are specially impressive. Norman arcade piers in Derbyshire are without exception circular (e.g. Youlgreave). Capitals vary according to their date in the same way as in other parts of the country. Arches develop from a completely unmoulded section to one-stepped, one-stepped-one-chamfered, and finally double-chamfered sections. Keeling of circular piers appears already in the transitional stage between Norman and Early English (Barlborough, Youlgreave, Whitwell). Only one Norman church other than Melbourne was intended to be on so large a scale. Bakewell, where a two-tower front was projected and begun, probably before 1100, and then a towerless C12 façade erected instead. Otherwise Norman remains belong to smaller churches, and Steetley, by far the most sumptuous example in the county of C12 decoration, is in size no more than a chapel. It consists of nave, lower and narrower chancel, and yet lower and narrower apse, the only Norman apse in Derbyshire. The arches between the various parts, the S portal and the exterior of the apse are all lavishly adorned. Why such a display should have been made just at Steetley has never been explained. Minor Early Norman elements survive at Ault Hucknall and Wingerworth. Doorways, tympana, W towers are too frequent to be discussed here in detail. Sandiacre may be mentioned for its doorway and windows; Hognaston, Parwich, and Ault Hucknall for their tympana; Bradbourne for its W tower. Whitwell has its Norman clerestory preserved. Most Norman Fonts are plain. Amongst those decorated the most interesting is that at Ashover, because it is of lead made no doubt locally. It has figures in blank arcades. Similar arcades on stone fonts exist at Hognaston and Eyam, interlaced arches at Ockbrook, Kirk Hallam, and Somersal Herbert, interlaced rings and zigzag at Church Broughton, leaf decoration at Chesterfield, incised animals at Tissington.

Of the comparatively few monastic foundations of Derbyshire little is left. The Austin Canons had Gresley (early C12), Darley Abbey (1154), Repton (1172), and Breadsall (well before 1260); the Premonstratensian Canons Dale Abbey (*c.* 1160), the Knights Hospitallers Yeaveley (Stydd Hall, *c.* 1190–5). Of the Cluniac St James at Derby, the Benedictine Kingsmead Nunnery at Derby, the Dominican Friary at Derby, and several smaller houses nothing survives. Chief clerical landowners in the county were the abbeys and priories of Burton-on-Trent, Lenton in Notts, Dunstable in Beds, and Basingwerk in Flintshire.

The Early English style appears in Derbyshire at

Ashbourne, where the chancel was dedicated in 1241. The dedication plate, a brass plate, survives. With its twin lancet windows in each bay (very similar to the chancel at Southwell begun in 1234) it gives one a safe starting point for the dating of an uncommonly ambitious group of later C13 churches on the same cruciform plan as adopted at Ashbourne. They are Chesterfield, Bakewell, Tideswell, Wirksworth (begun in 1272), and also Darley Dale, Hartington, Kedleston, and Monyash. Ashbourne, Bakewell and Chesterfield are further enlarged by E transept aisles, a motif also present *c.* 1225–50 at Lichfield Cathedral. To the same group belongs the spacious chancel of Doveridge. It is very instructive to compare the details of piers, arches, windows, etc., in this group. They give a clear and fairly complete picture of the architectural development during the years in which they were designed. For windows Derbyshire in the late C13 clearly favoured the type with two lancet lights and a pierced spandrel and the three-light type with intersected tracery. They were apparently carried on into the C14. A spectacular Geometrical window must originally have existed at Dale Abbey. Only the barest indications of its former tracery remain. Pier shapes are, as in other parts of the country, of greater variety than in any other period. They are mostly developed from the quatrefoil section by the addition of shafts and also by keeling and filleting. The many possibilities can best be studied amongst the remains of Repton Priory and at Ashbourne, but also at Wirksworth, Hartington, Tideswell, Bakewell, etc. Weston-on-Trent has simple circular piers, unusually tall and slim, endowing this relatively small church with remarkable nobility. The best E.E. W towers are at Breadsall and Eckington. They combine elegance with concision, as no earlier or later towers do. In this they clearly represent the same spirit as the window tracery of the mid and later C13.

It is specially illuminating to watch how, about 1300, heralding the intricacies and capriciousness of the Dec style, tracery forms begin to abandon the Geometrical clarity and logicality of circles with inscribed trefoils or quatrefoils. Such minor demonstrations of caprice can be studied in the Ashbourne transept, the Hartington S transept, Whitwell chancel, and at Dronfield. Mature Dec tracery is not particularly interesting in Derbyshire. Little of the flights of fancy occur that one is used to in East Anglia, Lincolnshire, Yorkshire, and the neighbouring counties. Reticulated tracery is usual and remains so until after the middle of the century (Spondon, rebuilt after 1340);* flowing tracery is rare and comparatively simple, and also still in fashion *c.* 1360 and later (Spondon, Sandiacre, Chaddesden, Tideswell, Taddington). So-called Kentish tracery is to be found at Sandiacre and Chaddesden. The chancels of these churches belong to the most important monuments of the C14 in Derbyshire. As in Notts (Hawton, Sibthorpe, Woodborough, etc.) wealthy and pious men were especially inclined to devote their means to the enlargements and embellishments of chancels, and the dimensions and the lightness and airiness of the best in Derbyshire are indeed splendid. They are Sandiacre built by Bishop Norbury of Lichfield *c.* 1342–47, Norbury built by Henry Kniveton, the then rector, some time between 1349 and 1395, Chaddesden, built by Henry Chaddesden, Archdeacon of Leicester, *c.* 1357, Tideswell built by John Foljambe † 1383 about *c.* 1360–80 as the end of a truly spectacular rebuilding of the whole church from *c.* 1320 onwards, and finally Tideswell of about the same date and probably influenced by Taddington. The large parish church of Chesterfield also must have been entirely rebuilt during these years. It possesses the remarkable anomaly (from the English point of view) of a transept chapel ending in a polygonal apse. The N and S windows at Tideswell and Taddington are straightheaded, the tracery motifs at Tideswell and Norbury oddly conservative, i.e. neither Perp nor Dec, but rather developed from simple quatrefoil and pointed trefoil and quatrefoil motifs. A peculiar variety of such tracery occurs at North Wingfield and Whitwell.

Of church furnishings the earliest screens belong to this age, and their tracery is as elementarily geometrical as that just referred to. They are the stone screen of Ilkeston and

* It also occurs in straightheaded windows, e.g. at Breadsall.

the timber screen of Kirk Langley, both early C14. At Tideswell (as also at Sawley) a stone screen appears in an unusual position, immediately behind the altar and a short distance W of the E wall, probably to divide off a narrow sacristy space. The earliest stained glass in the county is at Ashbourne, Dalbury, and then (C14) Cubley. The earliest wall paintings (*c.* 1300) are at Dale Abbey. A fine piece of sculpture of the late C13 is the Nativity at Bolsover. Bakewell font, adorned with figures, is the best C14 font in the county, Ashbourne the best of the C13. A special Derbyshire curiosity of the C14 is stone book-rests built into chancel N walls. They occur at Chaddesden, Crich, Etwall, Spondon, and Taddington.

One more architectural feature must be referred to, the C14 spires. The dating of spires is hazardous. There is little historical evidence to go by. Plain and rather broad broach spires apparently come before the slimmer spires starting recessed behind the battlements of towers. The latter is the more typical Derbyshire form (also typical of W Notts). Examples of the former are Baslow, Breaston, Hope, Ockbrook, Old Brampton, Rosliston, and Taddington. Examples of the latter are too numerous to be listed. In neither case are more than very occasional dates recorded. The earliest may be late C13, the majority early C14 (Repton completed 1340). The biggest Perp towers have no spires, Tideswell of *c.* 1380, Youlgreave, and All Saints Derby of the early C16. Derby with its tall four-light bell-openings and big decorated battlements and pinnacles is the most ornate. On the whole Perp towers in the county are not specially interesting. Tall bell-openings are rare. One group of towers has eight instead of four pinnacles (cf. Notts, especially St Mary Nottingham). Tideswell and Youlgreave (also Elvaston, Barlborough, and four or five others) belong to it.

The tower of Tideswell is the earliest dated document of the Perp style in Derbyshire. Until then probably Dec forms were still in use. The earliest dated Perp window is the E window at Ashbourne put in between 1395 and 1399.*

* Tracery motifs which appear Dec occur as late as South Wingfield Manor, i.e. *c.* 1440–50.

STOKE-ON-TRENT PUBLIC LIBRARIES

The late C14 and C15 being a time of high commercial prosperity for the towns and villages of England, churches of the Perp style are in many parts of the country especially splendid and numerous. Derbyshire is disappointing in this respect. All Saints Derby has been replaced by *Gibbs's* church in the C18, and no other is comparable with Long Melford or King's Lynn or Newark or Grantham or Chipping Campden or Tiverton or so many others. Even such details as tracery lack interest. The huge many-panelled windows so typical of ambitious Perp church architecture are rare; piers are not specially inventive in their shapes, capitals are only rarely decorated (Beighton, Hathersage, Mugginton), and roofs are almost exclusivcly of the simplest types (nice but also simple tracery above the beams at Tideswell, Ault Hucknall, North Wingfield). A group of tunnel-vaulted porches with transverse arches may be singled out (Ault Hucknall, Brampton, Langwith, North Wingfield, Shirland, Stanton-by-Dale and Wilne; cf. more in Notts), also two porches vaulted otherwise (Denby, Tideswell), and finally a group of windows with straight-sided arches (Repton, Elvaston, Killamarsh).

Exactly the same scarcity of really good work is to be found in late medieval church furnishings. Rood screens and parclose screens have been carefully listed by Aymer Vallance. Not one of them is up to East Anglian or Devon standards. The majority have one-light divisions (e.g. Ashbourne). Two-light divisions at Ashover, 1518, and Fenny Bentley. Three- and four-light divisions at Chesterfield, 1504. Here and at Fenny Bentley the groining for the loft is preserved. The only surviving loft is that of Wingerworth, not resting on a screen but attached to the nave E wall. Stall ends (Chaddesden), bench-ends and misericords (Bakewell) are so scanty and of such indifferent quality that no summing up is necessary. The same applies to fonts and sculpture. The best stained glass is that from Dale Abbey now at Risley. It is dated 1482. The glass at Norbury is C14–C15. At Caldwell and Egginton are some fragments of *c.* 1400, at Ault Hucknall a Christ Crucified of 1527. The earliest church plate in the county are the C15 censer at Langwith and the Patens of Hartshorne, Shirley, and Dronfield. At Haddon Hall in the chapel some delightful wall paintings have been recovered, figure work as well as a kind of *mille fleurs* pattern.

Church monuments are on the whole less disappointing. There are, it is true, no outstanding examples of the C13 and the early C14. The most interesting are no doubt the stone slab to Matilda le Caus † 1224 at Brampton and the oddly sunk heads in quatrefoils of a knight and his lady in the floor of Kedleston Church. They must commemorate the founders of the church and according to their style belong to the late C13. Directly alabaster became a fashionable material for monuments, the importance of Derbyshire increased. The best quarry, Chellaston, was in the county. At first alabaster seems to have been used only for very special clients, the effigies of Edward II, John of Eltham, Archbishop Stratford at Canterbury, Bishop Edington at Winchester, etc. And indeed the earliest alabaster in Derbyshire is perhaps the best, certainly as good as any later. It is the delightful epitaph to Geoffrey Foljambe at Bakewell † 1376 and his wife, with erect demi-figures under an arch of fanciful shape, lively and very delicately wrought. Mr Gardner has worked out that amongst 342 alabaster monuments listed in all English counties only Yorkshire possesses more than Derbyshire, and Yorkshire is six times the size of Derbyshire. Yorkshire has 34, Derbyshire 29, Notts 20, Lincolnshire (again a very big county) 20. So Derbyshire and Notts are the centre not only of the trade but also of the clientele. The best alabaster tombs in Derbyshire are at Norbury, Youlgreave, and Ashbourne. They have recumbent effigies and, against the walls of the tomb-chest, standing angels, or saints, or members of the family in panels or under little canopies. Ashbourne, Bakewell, and Chesterfield contain particularly rich assemblies of medieval and post-medieval monuments. The fashion for alabaster went out about the middle of the C17. Specially noteworthy later medieval stone effigies on tomb-chests are at Radburne and Ashover. The best is the latest: Katharine Bebington † 1543 at Morley. The earliest brasses are of 1383 (Tideswell) and

1399 (Dronfield) the best in the county is perhaps that of Robert Eyre at Hathersage † 1459.

The great families for which these monuments were made, the Vernons at Bakewell, Cokaynes at Ashbourne, Foljambes, Eyres, and so on were also the builders of the castles and manor houses of Derbyshire. And while none of the churches in the county are of more than regional interest (except perhaps Ashbourne), the domestic architecture of the C14 to C18 of Derbyshire could not be left out of any history of English architecture. For the Middle Ages the chief relics are Haddon Hall and South Wingfield Manor. Both are large and both are fortified, though domestic features have precedence; also both are built round two courtyards. But Haddon has the advantage of an unbroken tradition over centuries and the ensuing illusion of still being lived in, whereas Wingfield is a ruin. Wingfield, on the other hand, is the outcome of no more than twenty years, and thus possesses a rare unity of style. At Haddon the gate tower, some masonry, and part of the chapel prove that the Norman predecessor of the house was of the same size. The Hall itself with its Offices and the Parlour are C14, much of the other apartments are C15 and early C16 and yet more is Elizabethan and Jacobean. The total visual effect of the large grey embattled complex of buildings in its green setting is unparalleled in England. South Wingfield was all built between 1440 and 1460, the most ambitious surviving structure of its date in the country. The Hall and the large state rooms by its side are on a truly regal scale.

Codnor Castle of which only the scantiest ruins are left was built on nearly the same scale (length 150 ft). Other military remains are few and not important (gatehouse Mackworth Castle *c.* 1500; fortified manor houses near Fenny Bentley and Ashover). Of domestic architecture the most interesting (though minor) remains are at Norbury (*c.* 1300) and Ogston Hall (*c.* 1350–1400). Somersall Herbert is easily the best timber-framed house in the county, extremely pretty and fanciful in the W country manner. This takes us right to 1564.* Much earlier is Prior Overton's

* Other half-timbered houses at Hilton and Idridgehay.

tower and study at Repton (*c.* 1440), one of the finest pieces of early brick architecture in England. The beams inside as those at Haddon, the screen in the Hall, the interior of the Parlour, Great Chamber, and Earl's Apartments, all also at Haddon deserve attention too.

The earliest appearance of the Italian Renaissance style in Derbyshire is again connected with Haddon. It is in some panelling in the Parlour dated 1545. In monuments that to Sir John Port, the founder of Repton School, at Etwall, is still Gothic, although he died as late as 1551; that to Anthony Lowe † 1555 at Wirksworth is completely in the new taste. The type of the alabaster tomb with or without mourners also remained acceptable as late as the excellent Foljambe Monument of 1585 at Chesterfield, and even later, 1598 (West Hallam), 1632 (Thorpe), 1656 (Morley). The Pursglove brass at Tideswell of 1579 is still medieval in composition too.

Similarly in church architecture the Gothic style was not given up until after the Restoration.

The Parish Chapel of Buxton of 1625 is purely Perp; so is the church of Carsington, allegedly 're-edified' in 1648. The church at Risley dates from 1593 to 1632 and is equally medieval, though its two-light and intersected three-light windows are now roundarched. The Willoughby Chapel at Wilne of 1622 is specially notable for its contemporary fittings, tiles, and stained glass.* Even the church at Foremark which was built in 1662 shows its late date only in a certain exterior symmetry and some ornamental details.

Elizabethan and pre-classical C17 church furnishings are not frequent, and not of special quality: much of the fitments in the Chapel of Haddon Hall, the family pew at Elvaston, pulpits at Chesterfield, Dronfield, Sawley (1636), and Foremark (1662), and bench-ends at Hope, Castleton, and Tideswell with dates ranging from 1587 to 1690. Plate of the most prolific Elizabethan years (1565-70) is at Findern, Wilne, and Taddington.

All this does not amount to much. Monuments, on the other hand, once again the true reflexion of the state of

* Good C17 stained glass also at Staveley (1676).

domestic architecture, are many, and some of the highest quality available in England. The most usual Elizabethan type, as in all counties, is that with husband and wife kneeling opposite each other separated by a prayer-desk. The children kneel below in a kind of 'predella' (Bakewell 1584, 1623, Chesterfield 1592, Youlgreave 1613, Tissington 1619 and 1643, etc.). The best monuments appear only towards the end of Elizabeth's reign and between her death and the 1630s. They begin with the Foljambe Monument of 1592 at Chesterfield with its uncommonly good allegorical figures, and the exquisite and mysterious anonymous Foljambe memorial put up by the same member of the family. The shrouded figure on this, completely bundled up so that no face appears, is repeated in two effigies at Fenny Bentley, also anonymous. All the other monuments of interest are later than 1600. Some are of the familiar type with effigy or effigies under an arch flanked by columns (Sudbury 1600, Bess of Hardwick Derby before 1607, Etwall 1610, Bakewell 1617, Wilne 1622), but others are more original, especially the singular, rather naive Bradshaw Monument at Duffield of 1610, the elaborate Cavendish Monument at Edensor ascribed by Mrs Esdaile to *Maximilian Colt* (who probably worked at Hardwick), the Sleigh Monument of 1634 at Sutton-on-the-Hill which has, instead of an effigy, a big black stone coffin realistically carved down to the handles, and the very Italian and thus decidedly novel monument to the wife of the first Earl of Devonshire of 1627. Here the new art connected with Inigo Jones and Nicholas Stone begins in Derbyshire.

In the great houses of the Elizabethan and Jacobean age sculpture also appears. The Venus Fountain at Bolsover shows how bad it can be, the Diana at Chatsworth and the relief with the Muses at Hardwick, what internationally good quality could be obtained, perhaps by purchases abroad.

As for these houses themselves there is a rare wealth of them in Derbyshire ranging from the small manor house to the splendours of Hardwick. On the whole many more survive in the N than in the S of the county owing to the greater recent prosperity of the S. The earliest of the grand Elizabethan mansions does not survive, the Chatsworth of Bess of Hardwick, begun in 1557 and replaced by the first Duke of Devonshire's country palace. When she began to build at Hardwick for herself, Bess was much older. She first reconditioned the existing old mansion and then, aged 70 began a new one close to the old. Her hard, able, proud character seems reflected in its uncompromising rectangularity, its regular pattern of extremely large mullioned and transomed windows, and the somewhat coarse grandeur of the decoration inside. How much more sensitive in its proportions and details is the Long Gallery at Haddon than the Gallery and Presence Chamber at Hardwick. Hardwick belongs to a group of clearly defined Late Elizabethan houses, connected with the *Smythson* family of mason-architects which starts with Barlborough in Derbyshire and goes on to Wollaton in Notts. Barlborough and Wollaton have their square compact plans (and besides some details) in common. Hardwick has the Great Hall in a position quite contrary to medieval and earlier Tudor custom, and this and much else the house shares with Wollaton. Then there is the so-called Keep at Bolsover, begun in 1613. Here the romantic attitude of a self-conscious continuation or rather revival of medieval precedent is matched at Wollaton. One member of the Smythson family lies buried at Wollaton, two at Bolsover.

Two more large houses must be mentioned: Sudbury begun *c.* 1613 on the usual E-plan but only completed, and completed very sumptuously, after the Restoration, and Longford Hall whose projecting Tudor chimneys give one an idea of what the house must have been like before the Georgian and later alterations. But just as rewarding as these large houses are the more modest ones. There is a bewildering variety of them, and they do not fall into easily defined groups. We have to start with Hazlebadge of 1549, still with horizontal, many-mullioned windows with pointed tops to the individual lights. The same window shape also still appears at Offerton Hall. This latter detail was soon to disappear, but the low horizontal mullioned window itself remained current in the county right down to the C18. Typically Elizabethan with some stout classical decoration are Snitterton, a real gem, Aston Hall of 1578, and Dudley Hall. For the early C17 the prize should probably go to Tissington Hall, but there are more houses than can here be mentioned: the tower-like North Lees, Hartington Hall of 1611, Holmesfield House of 1613, Bradshaw Hall of 1620, Holme Hall, Bakewell, of 1626, Old Hall Farm, Youlgreave, of 1630, Riber Manor House of 1633, Renishaw in its H-shaped original core, Brookhill Hall, Camfield Hall, and so on. To these must be added the Ashbourne Grammar School of 1586 as an outstanding example of scholastic architecture of the age (more ambitious, for example, than Harrow),* the Jacobean Café at Derby of 1677 as a typical ambitious town house, and two examples from that little investigated field of Elizabethan and Jacobean architecture, the plaisance: the Stand or Hunting Tower at Chatsworth and the odd so-called Grandstand at Swarkeston.

The style of the manor house and farmhouse remained essentially Tudor to an astonishingly late date, and it is well worth studying the minor changes by which later buildings betray the time when they were really built. Dated examples are frequent; there probably exist more of them than I have been able to see and register. Here is a list, not even complete as far as this volume goes: Almshouses, Ashbourne, 1640 and 1669, Old Hall, Hadfield, 1646, Rowdale Cottage, Longstone, 1647, Youlgreave Old Hall 1650, The Peacock at Rowsley 1652,† Hallowes, Dronfield, 1657, Offerton Hall 1658, Ogston Hall 1659, Little Hucklow 1661, Longlee 1663, Stanton Old Hall 1667, Elton 1668, Derwent Hall (now destroyed) 1672, Eyam Hall 1676 (one of the best), Green Farm, Newbold, 1678, Seven Stars Inn, Derby, 1680, Almshouses, Etwall, 1681, Matlock Farm 1681, Bagshaw Hall, Bakewell, 1684, Old Hall Cottage, Fairfield, 1687, Newton Old Hall, near Tibshelf, 1690, Elder Yard Chapel,

* Some of the windows have even here still arched tops to the individual lights.

† The semicircular pediment here appears again at Elton in 1668, Buxton Old Hall in 1670, and Rose Hill, Dronfield, in 1719.

Chesterfield, 1694, Bath House, Bakewell, 1697, Wormhill Hall 1697 (bigger than most of the others), Town Hall, Bakewell, 1709, Almshouses, Ashbourne, 1710, house at Elton 1717, Chiverton House, Dronfield, 1719, Rose Hill, Dronfield, 1719, houses at Litton 1723, Slack Hall 1727, Netherseal 1751, house at Litton 1768. All these have the predominance of the mullioned window in common, mostly still horizontal. Straight gables are also still the custom. Broadly speaking the development can be watched in terms of a more and more symmetrical placing of the windows, the introduction of string-courses and the attachment of the windows to them, and occasionally in the admission of doorways more classical than the windows and gables would make one expect.

We must now try to trace the coming of the new Italian motifs and of what corresponds in Derbyshire to the revolutionary classical buildings of Inigo Jones in London. Nothing so noble and restrained exists in Derbyshire. Here the style appears instead in a less disciplined, also less knowledgeable, more Baroque form, partly indebted to Serlio, Rubens, and other architectural pattern books, and partly still to Jacobean motifs, e.g. in the retention of window tracery and the playful, curly Baroque gables popular in monuments earlier than in architecture proper. The first example of this style is the lavish new buildings put up at Bolsover about 1630 and now in ruins. The insistence on all kinds of heavy rustication is characteristic too. After Bolsover followed the Derby County Hall of 1660* and then Nottingham Castle 1675. The work of *Sir William Wilson* at Sudbury between 1670 and the 1690s also belongs here, although Wilson was familiar with Sir Christopher Wren's more metropolitan and more reasonable style.‡ Sudbury contains the most splendid interiors of the date in Derbyshire. They overlap with the beginnings at Chatsworth.

* The only other public building of note in the later C17 is the small Town Hall at Winster.

‡ It seems possible that *Wilson* also worked for Bentley Hall, the Etwall Almshouses, and the chapel at Barton Blount.

Only with Chatsworth, built from 1687 to 1707, Derbyshire reappears on the truly national stage. The work first of *Talman* and then of *Archer* (and perhaps *Thornhill*) is among the essential documents of the English style of *c.* 1700, closely related to Hampton Court, where Talman was Comptroller of Works from 1689 onwards. Of the contemporary treatment of the grounds the grand Cascade, the ruined Aqueduct, and *Archer's* Cascade House remain. For the interiors a team of artists was called in, partly of London reputation, like the painters *Verrio*, *Laguerre* (who also painted at Sudbury), and *Thornhill*, *Cibber* the sculptor, *Tijou* the smith, and the wood-carver *Grinling Gibbons* (again also employed at Sudbury), and partly local men of an artistry unquestionably equal to theirs. That applies certainly to *Watson* the sculptor and decorator at Chatsworth, and to *Bradbourne* and *Chellifer* the plasterers at Sudbury.

The grand style of Chatsworth was emulated at Calke Abbey of 1703, a surprisingly unknown large mansion, and then turned more Baroque at *Smith* of Warwick's Sutton Scarsdale of 1724, now a ruin. Examples of the comfortable medium-size classical country house begin with the stone-built Holbrook Hall of 1693 and then, in the Gibbs style, Melbourne Hall of *c.*1723. Examples in brick, usually with very restrained exterior decoration and occasionally with more ambitious interiors, are Hopwell Hall of 1720, Catton of 1745, Radburne of *c.* 1750, and Markeston of 1755. A livelier, earlier variety on a smaller scale appears in a house of 1706 at Kirby, the extremely pretty school at Risley of 1718, and the almshouses at Mapleton of 1727. Brizlincote House of 1714 and Hopton House are crowned by large segmental pediments, a Baroque feature which might have appealed to so wilful an architect as *Archer*. Strict Palladianism makes its entry with the remodelling of Melbourne Hall about 1723 and culminates at Foremark in 1762, built by *David Hiorns*, and Kedleston, planned by *Brettingham*, begun by *Paine*, and completed by *Robert Adam*. In his grand Entrance Hall Adam keeps to Paine's scheme and thus achieves a splendour of giant Derbyshire alabaster columns rare in his *œuvre*. The decoration of the

State Rooms at Kedleston is rightly amongst the most famous of its date in the country.

In ecclesiastical architecture of the period between the Restoration and the end of the Georgian era the county is not rich, but it possesses at least one example up to the standard and the scale of the most ambitious in London: *James Gibbs's* rebuilding of All Saints Derby of 1723–5. It is with its characteristic window shapes and interior arrangement at once recognizable as the work of the architect of St Martin-in-the-Fields in London, but it achieves an added elegance by the delicious wrought iron chancel screen, the work of the ingenious local blacksmith *Robert Bakewell*. He as well as *Weston* and the others mentioned in connexion with Chatsworth and Sudbury show how very much alive the provinces still were at that time. The deadening predominance of London began only later in the C18. *Bakewell's* artistry can also be admired in the Silk Mill Gates at Derby, at St Werburgh in Derby (what remains of the church is of 1699), at Longford, Barton Blount, and Etwall, and in the lovely Arbour in the gardens at Melbourne Hall. These gardens, incidentally, are an authentic design of *London* and *Wise*, the Royal Gardeners at about 1700–25, i.e. just before picturesque gardening began. The grounds of Kedleston are the finest examples of the Picturesque in Derbyshire.

Other C18 churches need no more than a passing mention: Trusley of 1713, a modest brick building, Mapleton with its dome and lantern on the W tower, the little Halter Devil Chapel near Mugginton of 1723, the modernization of the larger church of Chapel-en-le-Frith also in 1723, the interesting octagonal church of Stoney Middleton of 1759, and so on to *Wyatville's* St John at Buxton of 1811 with its heavy Tuscan portico, the even heavier Tuscan portico of Hassop of 1818, St Matthew at Hayfield 1818, Hartshorne of 1835 with its cast-iron tracery, and Hulland of 1837 with its very completely surviving furnishings. Of other furnishings it is sufficient to refer to the organ case of 1756 and the delightful candelabra of *c.* 1760 at Chesterfield, the baluster fonts at Kedleston and Willington, and a number of church monuments. The number is small compared with, for instance, the Home Counties, and the great London names appear only here and there. In the N of the county there are hardly any monuments of note later than *c.* 1650. The exception is that NE corner where the Sitwell tombs at Elkington of 1658 and 1667 herald the new style to come, where *Gibbs* himself may well have designed the Cavendish Monument of 1727 at Bolsover and where two more provincial monuments of 1673 and 1734 remain at Brampton near Chesterfield. The only series of expensive family memorials is at Kedleston, and there also the earliest two, of 1686 and 1727, are relatively modest. Of 1684 is the Pole monument at Radbourne by *Gibbons*; it has no effigy. Grander are some monuments those of the C18 and especially that at Kedleston of 1763 by *Rysbrack*. *Rysbrack* also did one monument in All Saints Derby (1760), *Roubiliac* another (1735), and *Nollekens* (1793) yet another. *Chantrey*, a Derbyshire man, was commissioned to do one in All Saints (1821) and one in St Werburgh (1830). A bust of 1820 by him is in the County Hall. To return to the late C17, the earliest of the four monuments at Kedleston is similar to that of 1673 at Brampton, and one of 1662 at Morley. A type characteristic of the late C17 has no effigy and as its centre an urn (Sudbury 1675, Staveley 1682, Radburne 1684, Wilne 1688). Early C18 monuments not yet mentioned are at Newton Solney 1709, Morley 1714 (a very Baroque composition of several urns), and at Calke 1741 and Alfreton 1742, both of excellent workmanship. A monument of 1764 at Parwich is signed *A.B.*, a bust of 1786 at Hayfield signed by *Bacon*. The Penelope Boothby Monument at Ashbourne by *Banks* (1799) with the sleeping child is amongst the most popular of its age. *Canova* did a monument for Elvaston in 1829 and *Sir Richard Westmacott* monuments of 1805, 1823, and 1824 for Ockbrook as well as one of 1830 for All Saints Derby and one of 1835 for Belper. The usual and often very elegant late C18 and early C19 epitaphs with urns, in flat relief with mourning allegorical figures, are hardly ever signed in Derbyshire. Nor do we know the names of the rustic craftsmen who did the slate head-stones in churchyards in the S of the county.

Nonconformist places of worship are, needless to say, very much more modest than those of the established Church. By far the most interesting is the Moravian Settlement of 1750–2 at Ockbrook with its handsome chapel in the centre of the main range of buildings. Chesterfield has the Elder Yard Chapel of 1694, and the Friends Meeting House of 1770. A grander scale was achieved only with the former Methodist Church in King Street, Derby, of 1841, with its display of Greek Doric columns. Parallel is the increase in scale in Roman Catholic architecture; *see* the churches at Hassop (1818) and at Glossop (1836).

Prosperous town architecture can be studied well in Derbyshire, not so much in the form of public display as of private houses. Here the brick fronts in Friargate, Derby, and the main street at Ashbourne show an evolution easily followed, and its evidence is borne out by the scarcer examples from other towns such as Alfreton and from the larger villages. As for public buildings no other than the Assembly Room at Derby of 1770 need here be mentioned.

However, when the Assembly Room received its elegant stone façade and the houses in Friargate their pedimented doorcases and Venetian windows, a development had already set in at Derby which was to change fundamentally the character of the town and of certain parts of the county. I am referring to the building of the vast, tall, monotonous Silk Mill of John Lombe, which was put up *c.* 1717 and blocked the chief portion of the river front. This mill no longer survives, but it was followed from the 1770s onwards by other mills using the new spinning and weaving inventions of Arkwright and Strutt. They were water-driven and built of brick or stone with at first timber pillars and timber beams. The earliest is at Cromford and dates from 1771. At Cromford in the 1780s several more went up, at Belper building began in 1776, at Milford *c.* 1780, at Calver (Curbar) 1785, at Cressbrook in Millersdale *c.* 1785 and 1815, at Tansleywood 1799, at Darley Abbey *c.* 1800, etc. They are big utilitarian structures of four to six storeys, occasionally adorned by such Georgian set pieces as Venetian central windows or a cupola. Uvedale Price, the great pioneer of the Picturesque, was scathing on their effect on the wooded valleys in which they were built. In the first volume of his *Essays on the Picturesque*, that is as early as 1794, he wrote: 'When I consider the striking natural beauties of such a river as that at Matlock, and the effect of the seven-storey buildings that have been raised there and on the other beautiful streams, for cotton manufactories, I am inclined to think that nothing can equal them for the purpose of dis-beautifying an enchanting piece of scenery.' Our view to-day may be more tolerant. Architecturally the most interesting development in these early factories is the change-over to a fireproof construction by the use of cast-iron stanchions and beams and of hollow-brick arched ceilings. The Belper mill of 1797 is amongst the earliest in the country showing this construction. Another reminder of the arrival of iron as a structural and ornamental material is the Suspension Bridge at Milford of 1826 and the tracery of Hartshorne Church of 1835.

With this church we have reached the threshold of the Victorian age, and of Victorian churches hardly anything need be said. The two facing churches of St Mary (Roman Catholic) and St Alkmund in Derby are characteristic of Early Victorian design, the former by *Pugin*, the latter by *Stevens* who did much work in the county and beyond its boundaries, never cheap-looking and never in bad taste. Characteristic also of the first years of the Queen is a passing fashion for Norman imitation. This is represented in Derbyshire by Long Eaton 1837, Wonsley 1843, and Woodville 1846. *Butterfield* built the church of Bamford in 1861, *Street* largely rebuilt Long Eaton church in 1868, *Sir George Gilbert Scott* was responsible for St Andrew Derby (1866) and Edensor village church (1867).

Edensor village is a pre-Victorian conception: the artificially picturesque village of cottages in many selected styles, made solid and durable and thereby Victorian. Its date is mainly 1839. Its erection is connected with the work of the sixth Duke of Devonshire at Chatsworth, work which extended to all parts of the house and grounds but is visible most spectacularly in the new N wing with its big Belvedere, the work of *Sir Jeffry Wyatville* of 1820, etc. *Wyatville* appears here in an Italian mood; at Bretby in 1812–13 he had built a big Gothic mansion on a hill. The Gothic Revival in domestic architecture had, however, begun earlier still in the county. Its first document is Arkwright's house Willersley Castle at Cromford of 1788. The architect of this mansion was *William Thomas*. Its style was followed by the large addition to Renishaw carried out in the 1790s by a Sheffield architect, *Badger*, castellated outside but with fine classical interiors, Elvaston Castle begun by one Mr *Walker* only in 1817, but said to be designed by *James Wyatt* who died in 1813, and the specially picturesque Snelston Hall of 1827 by *Cottingham*. The fashion finishes with a flourish in Riber Castle of 1862–8, the folly-residence of Mr Smedley, the founder of the Matlock Hydro. *Pugin's* Burton Closes near Bakewell represented a soberer Neo-Tudor (1845), *Stevens's* Osmaston Manor the same style used for grand display (1846–9), and *Nesfield's* Lea Wood (1870–6) the coming of the so-called Domestic Revival, that is the return to an intimate scale and pretty detail of much variety of materials and treatment.

The C20 needs no place in this brief survey. There is nothing of note in the county.*

Not that the preceding pages can have succeeded in drawing attention to all things of note during the centuries prior to the present; I am fully aware of the inadequacy of the work presented in the form of the following gazetteer. In its preparation it was necessary to rely mostly on published information, and Derbyshire is not a county which is well recorded architecturally or very active in local research.

* Except perhaps the sound and sensitive churches of about 1900 by *P. H. Currey* of Derby, an architect worthy of being better known, and the most recent schools designed by the County Architect's Department and built of light steel on a standard grid and faced with brick (Infants' School and Secondary School, Littleover; Longmoor Primary School, Long Eaton; Alvaston and Boulton (Eastern) Primary School; Shelton Lock Primary School; and Charnock Hall Junior School, Gleadless).

Moreover, some printed sources will most likely have been overlooked, and my travels through the county have not been close enough to discover more than accidentally where such gaps might have been left. This must have a bad effect especially on the recording of farmhouses and smaller manor houses. But there are also whole sections such as church bells which are not included at all, and others such as church plate which have never been systematically listed anywhere and which I have not made a point of seeing myself. Otherwise I have seen every building here discussed. Where this is not the case, the fact is specially indicated by brackets.

The principal book used is J. C. Cox's *Notes on the Churches of Derbyshire*, 4 vols., 1875–9. This is old now and in many ways no longer up-to-date, but still the only fairly complete survey. Dr Cox also wrote the original *Little Guide* of 1903. This has since been re-issued but in its architectural parts hardly improved. The *Memorials of Old Derbyshire*, a symposium of 1907, was edited by Dr Cox too. In the *Victoria County History* (2 vols., 1905) the chief parts of importance for this book are those dealing with prehistory, the Roman period, and then medieval monastic foundations and schools. For the churches there is great value in the *Rawlins Manuscript* (3 vols.) at the Derby Public Library, the *Meynell Manuscript* at Meynell Langley (kindly placed at my disposal by Col. and Mrs Sandeman), and the *Browne Sketches* (at present at Kirk Langley Vicarage and there shown me by the Rev. A. Hopkins). All these record in more or less careful water-colours the state of the exteriors before Victorian restorations began. For houses nothing better exists than the irritating J. Tilley's *Old Halls, Manors, and Families of Derbyshire*, 4 vols., 1892–1902, a book singularly devoid of architectural information. Papers have been published mostly in the *Journal of the Derbyshire Archaeological and Natural History Society*, and also in the *Reliquary* (1860–1909), the *Nottinghamshire and Derbyshire Notes and Queries* (1893–8) and *The Derbyshire Countryside* (1931 etc.). *Country Life* is invaluable throughout and Mr Hussey's accounts of Haddon or Hardwick or Renishaw could not be improved. Two special papers deserve mention here: that on Screens, etc., by A. Vallance (*Mem. of Old Derbys.*), and that on Crosses by F. E. Routh (*Arch. J.*, vol. 94, 1937). Of books on special church furnishings, etc., E. Tyrell Green's *Fonts* (1928) contains much on Derbyshire, and A. Gardner's *Alabaster Tombs* (1940) is of particular importance to the county in which the chief quarries lay. Guidebooks to individual churches or houses cannot here be quoted, nor special literature on towns. The Derby Public Library has in 1930 printed an extremely helpful Select Catalogue to its Derbyshire Collections. But one book on one house must not be omitted from even the briefest bibliography: Mr Francis Thompson's *Chatsworth* (1950). Of the more popular guidebooks none is more attractive than Christopher Hobhouse's *Shell Guide* (1935), intelligently compiled and excellently illustrated. The more recent series *County Books* and *Vision of England* have each a volume on Derbyshire (by Crichton Porteous and Nellie Kirkham), and Derbyshire Countryside Ltd have published an excellent cheap guidebook called *The Derbyshire Guide.*

Finally the student will always find it useful to go from recent books and papers to older topographical literature, and there the most important are Lysons's *Magna Britannia*, 1819, and Glover's *History, Gazetteer and Directory of Derbyshire*, 2 vols., 1829–30 (only parishes A–D). Other *Directories* are Bagshaw's of 1846, White's of 1857, and then the various editions of Kelly. They have all been consulted and found useful.

DERBYSHIRE

*

ALDERWASLEY

ST MARGARET. The only interesting feature of the chapel is the lintel above the S doorway, with crude Perp motifs in square panels. A new church was built in 1850 in the grounds of the Hall.

ALDERWASLEY HALL. Main façade Georgian with seven bays, tripartite central window, and tripartite semicircular window above; very plain. Large additions at the back.

ALFRETON

ST MARTIN. The church stands at the W end of the town by the entrance to the grounds of the Hall. It is a big church as Derbyshire churches go: W tower with diagonal buttresses, battlements and pinnacles, nave and aisles of five bays, S porch, chancel, and N vestry. The W tower has a C13 ground floor (*see* the tower arch towards the nave) and Perp upper parts. The N nave arcade has circular piers, the S arcade octagonal piers; they may date from *c.* 1300 and *c.* 1325. The fifth bay on both sides was added in 1868. Most of the windows are Perp, the E and S windows of the chancel C19. The interest of the porch is its doorway with heads as label-stops (this is a feature characteristic of the church throughout) and the ogee-headed niche above; the interest of the vestry its stone-vault with broad unmoulded transverse arches (cf. porches at Ault Hucknall, etc.). – PLATE. Paten on Foot, London, 1704; Chalice, London, 1709; Paten, London, 1721; large Flagon, London, 1728. – MONUMENT. George Morewood † 1742, standing wall monument of exquisite workmanship. No effigy; urn on big pedestal against the usual dark pyramid. On the pedestal a relief of a stork. All the ornamental detail admirable. 32b

ALFRETON HALL. A core of *c.* 1730 with C19 additions. The core is of seven bays, stone, two and a half storeys high with giant rusticated pilasters at the angles and a top balustrade; square and not at all deliberately pleasing. Early C19 four-column Ionic porch and W addition; large E addition (larger than the original house) of 1900.

The town is more attractive than the other industrial communities of the neighbourhood in that it possesses a High Street running up a hill and broadening at the top, with the Georgian GEORGE HOTEL facing down, and an early C18 stone house (with quoins and moulded window surrounds) at the corner of Church Street, the short street towards church and Hall.

In the main street towards the E opposite the Post Office an Elizabethan house with central one-bay projection with porch on the ground floor.

ALLESTREE

ST EDMUND. The church is of 1866 (by *F. J. Robinson* of Derby), but has a good broad Norman S doorway. The inner jambs and inner arch have quadruple zigzag without intervening capitals. Then an order of colonnettes with beakheads biting into them and the same repeated in the roll-moulding of the arch. The outer label has partly upright stylized leaves, partly a kind of four-petalled flower with the petals of fern-like shape. The W tower is the other old feature, C13, with broad buttresses only at the foot, a treble-chamfered tower arch into the nave, and two-light cusped bell-openings.

ALLESTREE HALL. Plain five-bay, two-and-a-half-storey stone house of *c.* 1830.

ALPORT

Unusually rewarding houses of the C17 and C18, especially MONK'S HALL, of later C16 or early C17 date, situated where the stream that comes down in little cascades joins the river Bradford.

HARTHILL HALL FARM, ½ m. E. Gabled C17 house with mullioned and mullioned and transomed windows.

HARTHILL MOOR. Nine Stones Circle (1½ m. NW of Winster). Only four stones remain of this Bronze Age circle, but one of them, when re-erected before 1939, was found to be 11 ft 8 in. long, 4 ft 4 in. of this being buried. Except for Arbor Low, this circle, with its diameter of 45 ft, is the largest and most important in Derbyshire. Also a small earthwork called CASTLE RING.

ALSOP-EN-LE-DALE

ST MICHAEL. Norman nave with a S doorway with an unusual variety of zigzag (double zigzag) in the voussoirs. Norman also the imposts of the chancel arch. The W tower is imitation Norman of 1883.

ALSOP HALL. C17 pre-classical, with symmetrical front, much renewed.

VIATOR'S BRIDGE, Mill Dale, 1 m. W on the footpath to Dovedale. Packhorse Bridge of very rough masonry, two low segmental arches.

ALVASTON NR DERBY

ST MICHAEL. The church is of 1856, but a Saxon coffin lid with a big primitive cross, and an extremely pretty, if somewhat rustic, piece of wrought iron with a figure of an angel and lambrequins and scrollwork speak of the existence of the preceding village church. There are also a few village houses left in the middle of all the surrounding suburban Derby housing.

ALVASTON AND BOULTON EASTERN PRIMARY SCHOOL. One of the recent standard steel and brick schools of the County Education Department (*see* Introduction, p. 33).

ANCHOR CHURCH *see* FOREMARK

ANDLE STONE *see* STANTON MOOR

ARBOR LOW *see* YOULGREAVE

ASHBOURNE

ST OSWALD. Ashbourne church is one of the grandest churches of Derbyshire, although its position in a valley does not allow its tall spire the effect it would have in a more prominent place. That defect disappears as soon as one is close to the church; for it lies in a graveyard a little below the road at the W end of the town and can be seen well from all sides. The church is remarkable also in its dimensions: the spire reaches a height of 212 ft, and the length of nave and chancel is 176 ft. Moreover, Ashbourne has more than regional architectural significance. It consists of nave and S aisle, crossing with crossing tower and spire, transepts with E aisles as wide as the transept, and a long chancel. There was no doubt a church of some size at Ashbourne in Saxon times. For in Domesday Book the town appears already as a Royal Borough. The existence of a Saxon crypt was verified during excavations in 1913. Of the church now above ground, however, the oldest part is the chancel. This must have been ready when the church was re-dedicated in 1241. An original inscription in brass records this event (S transept S wall). The chancel has on its N and S sides three pairs of closely spaced tall lancet windows. Inside they are enriched by filleted nook-shafts. The chancel S doorway is of six orders of colonnettes (renewed), i.e. quite exceptionally sumptuous. The complex mouldings of the arch are also partly filleted. The Sedilia have filleted shafts too. Two important alterations were made to the chancel later on, both to add light. The fourth pairs of lancets on the S and N, closest to the crossing, were replaced by large three-light ogee-reticulated windows in the C14, and the E end, no doubt originally lit by a group of lancet windows, received some time between 1395 and 1399 its seven-light window (with rather harsh long Perp panels in the tracery).

11

The transepts open in tall wide two-centred arches into their E aisles which later became the chapels of the two leading families, the Bradbournes (S; chantry founded in 1483) and the Cockaynes, later the Boothbys (N). The N transept has to the E two groups of triple lancets. Above them, in grey stone as against the earlier pink stone, is an insignificant Perp clerestory. The addition of the clerestory here and in the other parts of the church dates from *c.* 1520. The N side of the aisle has a rather bleak large five-light window with partly intersected tracery. The way in which the intersection is broken off to receive, as its top effect, a quatrefoil, not in a circle is somewhat perverse and typical of *c.* 1300. The transept itself has at its N end a five-light ogee-reticulated window, i.e. a motif datable *c.* 1320–50. The S transept, on the other hand, has no E window at all, at the S end of the E aisle a big Early Perp six-light window (at the top of each half still a reminder of the Dec style), at the S end of the transept itself a seven-light intersected and partly cusped window and below it an asymmetrically placed doorway with dogtooth decoration in three orders, and on the W side two plain lancets. The N side of the nave has windows of the late C13 (three-light of stepped lancets and two-light of lancets with pierced spandrel), the S aisle windows are early C14. The W front is C19 in door and window.

The crossing tower is a spectacular piece. It has two two-light bell-openings on each side, long, with one transome and early C14 tracery. Instead of battlements there is a pierced quatrefoil parapet. On the SE side a stair-turret rises higher and ends in an octagonal spirelet. The spire itself is tall and has four tiers of dormer windows, in style not later than the tower.

Now for the interior. The nave, as one enters from the W, is disappointing. The lack of a N aisle which was no doubt projected is painful. It means that a big NW buttress of the crossing tower sticks into the nave and a skew arch opens to its N into the transept. The S aisle, on the other hand, is wide and tall, and the four arcade arches are of fine spacious proportions. The piers are of eight shafts, the four main ones filleted. They have good leaf capitals of *c.* 1300 (also heads, etc.) and head stops for short vaulting shafts never continued. The roof is Perp, 13 much repaired. The early C14 crossing tower rests on piers with a section incorporating S-curves. Above the arches is one tier of three separate blank windows on each side. The other storeys of the tower are not visible from inside. The arcades between N transept and aisle and S transept and aisle differ. The pier on the N side has triple shafts on each of the main sides and hollows in the diagonals and carries arches of many fine mouldings, that on the S side has four filleted main shafts and in the diagonals a group consisting of one filleted flanked by two keeled. The arches are more like those of the crossing. The capitals on the N side are of big nobbly leaves and the S respond has nailhead decoration. On the S side the capitals are finely moulded. The triple lancets of the N transept E aisle are enriched by fine polygonal shafts with concave sides.

What can be guessed from all these details about the building history of the transepts and W parts of the church? The E parts with their lancet windows came first, probably from the middle to the later C13. The leaves of the N transept arcade and nave cannot be earlier than *c.* 1300, nor can the N transept aisle N, and the S transept S windows. The nave and aisle windows follow immediately. The N transept N window must be an early replacement. The variety of pier sections is specially remarkable at Ashbourne. It corresponds and may well be dependent on Repton Priory.

FURNISHINGS. FONT. C13 with trefoil arches and small fleurs de lis standing between them. – SCREEN. N transept, with single-light openings with ogee arches and a minimum of panel tracery above them. – STALL ENDS. Two, late C15, said to come from Norbury (S transept). – STAINED GLASS. C13 grisaille fragments in a N transept N window. – Other chancel windows 1861, pretty, although they infuriated Ruskin who, in a letter to the Vicar in 1875, called them 'the worst piece of base Birmingham manufacture which . . . I have ever seen'. S aisle W window by *Burlison & Grylls*, 1872. – S transept S window by *Hardman*, 1874. – E window 1896, by *Kempe*.

– N side, easternmost window and W window also by *Kempe*, 1902. – PAINTING. One panel, perhaps from a screen, late C15, with a female saint on one side, St Michael and the Image of Pity on the other. Under strong Flemish influence. Not good. – SCULPTURE. Small fragments in the Boothby Chapel, e.g. stone with Saxon interlace, stone with Norman zigzag. – PLATE. Paten with Crucifixus, 1683; Flagon, 1685; Paten, 1686. – MONUMENTS IN THE BOOTHBY CHAPEL. The Boothby Chapel (N transept) is as full of monuments as St Denis Abbey. They are, starting from the entrance: Slab with a foliated cross. – Francis Cockayne † 1538 and wife, two brasses in architectural setting with children below; tomb-chest with stumpy standing angels with shields in panels with cusped curved head and cusped curved foot. – Sir Thomas Cockayne † 1537 and wife, incised slab on tomb-chest with foiled panels. – Sir John Cockayne † 1447 and wife, recumbent alabaster effigies on a tomb-chest with stiff standing angels with shields separated by panel-tracery fields. – John and Edmund Cockayne, 1404, on a low tomb-chest with quatrefoil panels, a fleuron frieze and battlements. – John Cockayne † 1505 and wife, badly defaced alabaster slab. – Sir Brooke Boothby † 1789, by *Joshua Evans*, a Greek coffer on a pedestal, with surprisingly naturalistic convolvulus trails, as if it were Victorian work. – Marie Elizabeth Boothby † 1805, of the same design but with ivy trails. – Ann Boothby, née Cavendish, † 1750, not in its original state, big urn with inscription. – Penelope Boothby † 1791, *Thomas Banks's* most famous work; white marble; the child, in the long frock of the Napoleonic fashion, lies asleep. Queen Caroline is supposed to have broken into tears when she saw the statue at the Royal Academy exhibition. There is an inscription from Dante (Lei che'l ciel ne nostra terra nasconde, etc.), one in French, one in Latin, and one in English, which says: 'She was in form and intellect most exquisite. The unfortunate Parents ventured their all on this frail Bark, And the wreck was total.' – John Bradbourne and wife, late C15, recumbent

33

STOKE-ON-TRENT
PUBLIC
LIBRARIES

alabaster effigies on the tomb-chest, angels below broad ogee arches. – Sir Humphrey Bradbourne † 1581 and wife, recumbent effigies, against the tomb-chest short standing figures with shields between them.

OTHER MONUMENTS. Robert de Kniveton † 1471, recess with broad ogee arch in the chancel N wall. – Thomas Cockayne † 1592, standing wall monument; rusticated pillars below, the figures lifesize and kneeling, facing each other across a prayer-desk; pilasters l. and r. with much strapwork; arch above the figures; the children in the *predella* below.

CHURCHYARD GATES. E exit; wrought iron, *c.* 1700.

THE TOWN

The perambulation starts from the church. To its SE the SPALDEN ALMSHOUSES, 1710. Three sides round a courtyard, the architecture very conservative, still with two-light low mullioned windows. Two-storeyed, with quoins and hipped roof.

CHURCH STREET is one of the finest streets of Derbyshire. It has a large variety of excellent houses and whole stretches without anything that could jar. The beginning is the GRAMMAR SCHOOL, 1586, an ambitious gabled stone building. The front is symmetrical with four small gables in the middle and two larger ones on the sides. Two doorways. On the ground floor mullioned and transomed windows. On the upper floor and in the gables low mullioned windows with arched heads to the individual lights. Opposite the MANSION HOUSE, early C18, of five bays and three storeys with projecting centre. Tuscan porch, Venetian window above, tripartite semicircular window above that. To the l. stables without windows to the street; tall blank arches. In the garden a handsome Roman Doric temple. The stables abut on the OWLFIELD ALMSHOUSES, founded 1640. These form one composition with PEGG'S ALMSHOUSES, founded 1669. The latter stand at r. angles to the street, the former face the street. The style is identical. Stone, four-centred

59a

doorways, low mullioned windows, plain gables.* Opposite: No. 49, plain three-storeyed five-bay house, late C18, with pedimented door. Again opposite: Ministry of National Insurance, four bays, three storeys, late C18, with segmental pediment to the door and rusticated lintels (as usual at Derby). The METHODIST CHURCH follows, a pretentious eyesore of 1880. Opposite another Victorian specimen, but a commendable one, the DERBY SAVINGS BANK, stone-faced *à la* Barry, *c.* 1840. Again opposite: No. 34, three-storeyed of three bays with doorway with attached Tuscan columns and triangular pediment; rusticated lintels. Back to the N side: No. 27, unfortunately roughcast. The ground floor windows with segmental, the first floor windows with triangular pediments, *c.* 1820. After that on the S side a big early C18 house, plain with shell-hood over the door, then Nos 24–26 with giant Ionic pilasters, also, alas, roughcast, and also early C18; and Nos 16–22, the CLERGYMEN'S WIDOWS ALMSHOUSES, Late Georgian, three-storeyed composition around three sides of a courtyard. On the N side Nos 15–7, a nice brick group of which only No. 7 deserves special notice (stuccoed doorcase).

From the E end of Church Street by Tigers Yard up to BELLEVUE ROAD. Here the plain two-window-wide LOCK-UP of 1844 (inscription above the door: House of Confinement). At the E end DOVE HOUSE, early C18, five bays, brick, with quoins, and stone window frames. In the MARKET PLACE not much, e.g. Nos 12–14, early C18, and the Market Fish Restaurant, timber-framed (the exterior not original). – In ST JOHN'S STREET, the continuation of Church Street, houses of the same type but more modest. Note the GREEN MAN HOTEL, mid Georgian of seven bays, with inn sign across the street and a picturesque little courtyard. Dr Johnson and Boswell stayed here several times. On the same side further down an early C19 house which looks as if it might have begun life as a Nonconformist chapel. Again

* The range facing Pegg's Almshouses is of 1848.

on the same side No. 54 with a broad tripartite doorway with Tuscan pilasters.

Outside Ashbourne, 1 m. NE, GREEN HALL, brick, two gables with balls and balustrade between, then five bays with quoins, doorway with segmental pediment, the centre bay distinguished by rusticated giant pilasters.

Also outside, 1¼ m. WSW, MAYFIELD BRIDGE across the river Dove, of five pointed arches with chamfered ribs. The roadway has been much widened.

ASHFORD-IN-THE-WATER

So called after the river Wye, crossed here by three BRIDGES. The one nearest the church, called Sheepwash Bridge, is still as narrow as it originally was. One of the two others dated 1664.

HOLY TRINITY, 1870. But from the medieval church remains the Norman S tympanum with a tree of life and facing it a lion on the r. and a hog on the l. The unbuttressed W tower may in its lower part be C13. The battlements and pinnacles Perp, renewed. – FONT octagonal, Perp, the bowl similar to Monyash. – PULPIT. Jacobean.

FIN COP, 1½ m. NW. Hill fort, possibly of the Iron Age, overlooking the river Wye at Monsal Dale. The N and E sides are protected by steep slopes, but on the S side is a double rampart 390 ft long, and on the W side a 940 ft long single rampart. These ramparts have outer ditches, measuring about 10 ft across, and being about 3 ft deep.

ASHOVER

ALL SAINTS. Finely placed in a churchyard flanked on the S and N by old trees. The general appearance of the church typically Derbyshire, i.e. tower with spire, and the rest of the church low and embattled. The W tower was completed by the Babingtons when they had come into the parish, which was in 1419. Angle buttresses, straightheaded bell-openings, still with Dec tracery motifs. Small ogee-headed W window, battlements, and recessed spire 128 ft high. The tall tower arch to the nave has a profile with two double curves. Of other features of the church the S doorway comes first, late C13. The chancel follows, *see* its two low pointed trefoiled recesses in the N wall (with unexplained brackets in the middle of the back walls) and also the ogee-headed S doorway and the pretty N doorway, cusped ogee with pierced spandrels. The windows are all later Perp and all straightheaded. The N arcade of the nave typical C14, the S arcade with very thin octagonal piers Late Perp. When it was built, four bays long, a fourth bay was added to the three-bay N arcade. Large squint from the S into the chancel. – FONT. The most important Norman font in the county. Of lead, which is interesting as there was so much lead-mining all around. England possesses altogether about thirty lead fonts. The one at Ashover is very small, the bowl only about 2 ft across. It has standing figures of 8 in. under arcades. In design the font at Dorchester is especially similar. – PULPIT. Plain panelled late C17. – ROOD SCREEN given by Thomas Babington who died in 1518. Two-light openings with the centre mullion running right up into the arch. Each light with crocketed ogee-arch and simple panel tracery. – MONUMENTS. Brasses to James Rolleston † 1507 and wife, figures of *c.* 34 in., the children kneeling below. – A priest, *c.* 1510, same size. – The alabaster tomb-chest with effigies of Thomas Babington † 1518 and his wife is the best of its date in Derbyshire. Against the chest walls small figures of saints, angels, and 'mourners' under crocketed ogee arches, one, two, or three in one panel.

17b

Several good houses in the village, e.g. one dated 1671. Just E of the church an earlier cottage and facing it the SCHOOL, very pretty, of 1845, stone, of three bays with projecting porch bay, shaped gable, and diamond-leaded window casements.

EASTWOOD HALL, 1 m. NE. Ruins of quite a sizeable fortified manor house, heavily garlanded with ivy. The recognizable features Elizabethan and older.

ASTON

ASTON HALL. Very interesting to the architectural historian because of its date: 1578, in an elaborate strapwork cartouche. The house is of five bays and two storeys, with a parapet rising in the middle into a steep gable. Inside the gable a three-light window with a pediment enclosing a small figure. Small figures also in gables on the other side of the house. The front has a central doorway with sturdy Roman Doric columns on tall pedestals and a broken pediment. The door-opening itself has a four-centred arch with leaf motifs in the spandrels. The windows are of two lights and symmetrically arranged, perhaps a later adjustment.

ASTON-ON-TRENT

ALL SAINTS. Norman W tower strengthened by a big diagonal buttress. Norman W door, W window above, and higher up Late Norman windows with nook-shafts and zigzag decoration of the arches. The upper part Perp, and the battlements with obelisk pinnacles post-Reformation. Inside, the tower arch also Norman. Nave and aisles later C13, of three bays, separated by short circular piers with broad elementary capitals. The clerestory Perp. The S aisle windows ogee-reticulated, i.e. Dec, the N aisle windows Perp. The N door with a pretty ogee-arched surround. The N chancel chapel with an arcade similar to the aisle arcades. The S windows of the chancel are the most interesting feature of the church, tall and straight-headed with a transome band of Dec tracery (the same motif as that of ogee reticulation). Chancel and clerestory are embattled. – FONT. Plain octagonal C13 on five shafts. – Old PEWS preserved. – CARVING. Saxon, with interlace, built into the outer E wall of the S aisle. – MONUMENT. Early C15 alabaster tomb-chest with angels holding shields. On it the recumbent effigies of a civilian and a lady holding hands.

ASTON HALL. Five-bay house with central Venetian

windows on both main façades. Also on both added early C19 one-storeyed Ionic porches. The original house is dated 1735 on a rainwater-head. Pretty staircase of that date. The house has been much enlarged.

AULT HUCKNALL

ST JOHN THE BAPTIST. In a lovely position just out of the industrial NE of Derbyshire with only one farm nearby and the square towers of Hardwick Hall in the distance. A typical Derbyshire exterior in that it is low and all embattled, but not at all typical in that it possesses a crossing tower, as only the most ambitious churches of the county do. This crossing tower is the most interesting piece of architecture. It rests inside on a W arch towards the nave and an E arch towards the chancel. The former is obviously Norman with an outer label consisting of jumbled up ornamental bits. The latter, however, is so narrow and low (hardly more than a doorway) that one would prefer to attribute it to a pre-Norman date, if its masonry were not un-Saxon in character; C11 anyway. Also Early Norman the nave and the N aisle. That is clearly visible in the W front, which has a blocked narrow doorway, a small N aisle W window with incised zigzag in the arch (again rather Saxon than Norman-looking), and a highly barbaric tympanum showing a centaur on the l. and the lamb and cross on the r. In the lintel a man fighting a big dragon. The main W window a C14 insertion (ogee-reticulated). The upper parts of the crossing tower and the porch with pointed tunnel vault and transverse arches Perp. Inside, the N arcade of two bays takes us back to the Early Norman period. Rectangular pier (like a chunk of wall) with the plainest capitals (like an arch impost) and unmoulded arches. The S arcade is C14, perhaps of about the same date as the nave roof with big tie-beams and coarse low trefoil tracery above (cf. North Wingfield). – STAINED GLASS. Crucifixion, in three lights (S aisle E window), grisaille and yellow, dated 1527. – MONUMENTS. Anne Keighley, wife of the first Earl of Devonshire, dated large 1627. Big, relatively low standing wall

8a

31

monument below the window of 1527. Big base with inscription and exquisite foliage decoration. Cornice and then a top like a hipped roof and, on corbels rising up from below the cornice, five free-standing allegorical figures. The whole is very Italian and not at all in the Jacobean Southwark tradition. – In front of the monument on the floor black slab with inscription. It commemorates Thomas Hobbes, the philosopher, a protégé of the Cavendishes who died at Hardwick in 1679.

BABINGTON HOUSE *see* BELPER

BAKEWELL

9 ALL SAINTS. Approached from the E and below. The picture one sees is typically Derbyshire, rather low and broad, embattled, and with a tower and spire. The plan is that of the most ambitious churches of the county, with crossing tower and transepts, the S one incidentally appreciably longer than that on the N. The scale in the case of Bakewell* is explained by the fact that the church was collegiate. King John in 1192 gave it to the Dean and Chapter of Lichfield. Its importance, however, must go back much further. For not only are there proofs of Norman building, but in the churchyard stands an uncommonly well preserved stump of a SAXON CROSS with vine scrolls and animals and very defaced human figures, which dates from the early C9, and in addition there is exhibited in the S porch and against the W wall of the N aisle a remarkably large number of ANGLO-SAXON FRAGMENTS, of interlace work and also figures. They are mixed up with even more numerous NORMAN FRAGMENTS, ornamented in many ways. Moreover, the W front of the church is essentially Norman; *see* the W doorway of two orders of colonnettes with, in the voussoirs of the arch, two orders of beakhead and a label with small saltire crosses. Above it a fragmentary blank arcade of intersected Norman arches, now broken by the later

* The total length of the church is about 150 ft.

window (of the C15, but with C19 Dec tracery). Inside the W front there are at the W ends of the aisles arches, now walled up, on the plainest imposts, and one-stepped and unchamfered. Excavations have proved them to be the former E entrances into projected but never completed W towers. So the Norman church was planned on the same ambitious scheme as Melbourne, and then during building reduced. The present outer W wall is part of the revised scheme, later than the tower arches and lying 15 ft further back than the façade was originally meant to be. Of the Norman period also the first bay of the arcades between nave and aisles, with unmoulded arches on imposts as plain as those of the W wall, except for a kind of billet motif. The masonry here may indeed be Saxon and only pierced by the Norman arches. The outer wall of the S aisle is largely Norman.

The next stage of the church (the C13) can be observed towards the E end. The S transept, with an E aisle just as at Ashbourne, was added *c.* 1220–40; *see* the tall separate W lancets with nook-shafts inside and the piers between nave and aisle (quatrefoil section with slimmer shafts in the diagonals, the latter with shaft-rings). Then came the chancel whose windows are of typical late C13 design (lancets of two lancet lights with pierced spandrels). Inside they have nook-shafts too. The chancel S doorway goes with the date of the chancel. So do the Sedilia and Piscina, the latter with a handsome twin arch with pointed trefoil cusping. The (renewed) N and S aisle windows are like those in the chancel. The widening of the N aisle must belong to this same period. So do the S and N doorways into the nave (dogtooth). The crossing tower rests on (rebuilt) C13 piers, with shafts filleted, moulded capitals and double-chamfered arches. One shaft of each pier rises higher and helps to carry the vault inside the crossing tower, a vault with diagonal as well as ridge ribs. It dates from *c.*1840. Outside only the lowest stage of the tower belongs to the C13. On it rises an octagonal stage with two-light bell-openings, and on that battlements and the spire. These upper parts were built *c.*1340, but taken down and rebuilt in 1841–52. At the same time the S transept was rebuilt. The shape of the piers and windows, however, is said to be a faithful reproduction of the originals. The E windows on that evidence must have been enlarged and modernized c.1325. They are big, of three lights, and have flowing tracery.* Of the nave nothing can now be said with certainty. Probably it belonged to the C14, but the arcades were 'rebuilt in a lighter style' in 1841–52. The chief Perp contributions are the S porch, the clerestory, the battlements, and the big three-light N window of the N transept, with one transome and panel tracery at the top.

FONT. Early C14, octagonal, without separate stem. Whole figures under broad crocketed ogee arches. One of them Christ seated. – ALTER PIECE with Crucifixion, word-carving of c. 1500, according to Dr Kamphausen probably North German – CHANCEL STALLS with misericords, six, C14, very restored. – AUMRBEY, S transept, with handsome frame with fleurons. – ROOD SCREEN. Of single-light openings, the upper part of the dado also pierced, C15. – TILES. A few in the S porch. – STAINED GLASS. S transept S window by *Wailes* (TK). – MONUMENTS. A great number of foliated crosses in the S porch. – Sir Godfrey Foljambe † 1377 and wife, an excellent and most unusual epitaph. The figures frontal, only down to their waists, no more than one foot long, with folded hands, under a capriciously shaped arch (i.e. the attitude of recumbent effigies, but upright), the whole an internationally remarkable monument. The material is alabaster. – The rest in the S transept E aisle (Vernon Chapel): Sir Thomas Wendesley † 1403, in armour, not well preserved. – John Vernon † 1477, small alabaster effigy on tomb-chest. On this small figures under ogee arches and plain panels and shields between. – Sir George Vernon † 1567 and two wives, recumbent alabaster

22

* On the other hand, it must be added that the Rawlins Manuscript does not show these windows in their present form. The whole E wall of the transept was incidentally pushed further E during the restoration, so that now it cuts into a chancel window.

effigies on tomb-chest with few figures. – Sir John Manners † 1584 and his wife Dorothy Vernon, standing wall monument with the usual kneelers facing each other across a prayer-desk, the children below; not good. – Sir George Manners † 1623, big standing wall monument of the same composition, but the kneeling children larger, in two tiers and under arches. On the arches verses from the Bible, e.g. above a baby in swaddling clothes: 'Mine age is nothing in respect of thee'; above the eldest son: 'Our generation passeth and another cometh'; and above two daughters: 'A prudent wife is from the Lord', and 'A gracious woman retaineth honour'.

THE TOWN

Its centre is the RUTLAND ARMS HOTEL of 1804, five bays, square, of stone, with a Tuscan Doric porch. It is the successor of an earlier inn. To its side across the street the stables, etc. From the square in front of the hotel BRIDGE STREET runs down to the river. In it on the r. the former MARKET HALL, late C17, but still with little gables and low two-light mullioned windows. The BRIDGE is of *c.* 1300, of five ribbed pointed arches with breakwaters (widened C19). At its town-end a solid, large, early C19 house. – From the Rutland Arms KING STREET goes up to the church. It is here that the old TOWN HALL lies. This was built as late as 1709 and yet has still three-light mullioned windows. It faces down the street towards the square. Opposite its side CATCLIFFE HOUSE, mid C18, ashlar, with door and window surrounds with intermittent rustication. Higher up, King Street skirts the S side of the churchyard. On the other side of the churchyard in Bagshaw Hill BAGSHAW HALL (Conservative Club) of 1684, facing E, down the hill, front with one-bay gabled side projections, the centre balustraded at the top, central door with segmental pediment. The windows still mullioned but of upright proportions, i.e. going more classical. Bagshaw Hill leads down to the Buxton Road. Off the Buxton Road in Bath Street, BATH HOUSE, built in 1697 for the Duke of Rutland. It still contains his bath (33 by 16 ft: MHLG), vaulted in 1705. The exterior of the house gabled and with low mullioned windows.

A little further out several worthwhile houses on their own. Across the bridge in Baslow Road CASTLE HILL HOUSE, late C18, stuccoed five-bay front, and off the road HOLME HALL, 1626, of three bays with central square projection, in which the blocked original porch. The sides have canted bay windows. The windows mullioned and transomed. The tops and the tops of the bay windows embattled. Several good C18 houses at HOLME.

Out on Haddon Road, still within sight of the town, BURTON CLOSES, *c.* 1845 by *Pugin*. The exterior quite a florid Early Tudor. The interior still in very good state a few years ago, but now derelict. The whole house scheduled for demolition.

On BURTON MOOR, 1 m. SW, a round barrow.

GRIND LOW, 1½ m. SW, a round barrow.

BALLIDON

ALL SAINTS. A chapel in a field near the small village. Its interest was its Early Norman parts, but they are so much restored that they can now hardly be taken as evidence: S doorway with simple imposts and an only slightly chamfered arch, chancel arch completely unmoulded on the simplest imposts, perhaps blocked N doorway; and possibly also the W window except for its new head. – FONT. Perp, octagonal, with simple shields, tracery motifs, etc., but most strangely, the majority of them upside down.

Two large round BARROWS below the crest of Minning Low hill, 2 m. NNE of Ballidon. The bigger is almost as large as Gib Hill and contains stone cists.

BAMFORD

ST JOHN THE BAPTIST, 1861, by *Butterfield*, with a typical spire similar in outline to Butterfield's All Saints, Margaret Street, London, if to no Derbyshire church. The tower is tall and slim and the spire needle-sharp and on a square, not an octagonal base. It stands at the W end of the N aisle. The aisle arcade is traditional Derbyshire. Its roof runs on with only a slight break into the steep-pitched nave roof. Fancy Dec rose window in the nave W wall.

BARLBOROUGH

ST JAMES. The church belongs more to the village than to the Hall. Its earliest feature is the N arcade of four bays. The date must be *c.* 1200 or a little earlier, i.e. the arches are still round but with two slight chamfers. The capitals have waterleaf or other upright leaves, the W respond is keeled, one pier is keeled, quatrefoil in section, the other octagonal. The S arcade is of 1899. The chancel arch (renewed stiff-leaf corbels, double-chamfered arch) and the W tower follow. The latter is unbuttressed, has lancet windows and a treble-chamfered arch towards the nave. The battlements and eight pinnacles are Perp. So are the chancel windows, especially the remarkably straight E window. – PAINTING. Small Crucifixion, Italian C14. – MONUMENT. Effigy of a Lady in sunk relief, said to be Lady Neville who died 1395.

BARLBOROUGH HALL. Dated 1584 on an overmantel. One of the not very frequent Elizabethan mansions of compact almost square plan. It has a small inner courtyard now glazed. The S front is tall (basement with kitchen and offices and two storeys), castellated with fancy battlements, and of only five bays, the central one projecting squarely, with a doorway with coupled columns. Inside the doorway is a miniature rib-vault. The angle bays have canted bay windows rising tower-like into third storeys. The sides of the house are asymmetrical, that on the E partly Georgianized; the back is like the front but with a middle projection coming forward in its centre triangularly. The house is crowned by a handsome circular cupola with mullion-and-transome-cross windows. Otherwise the windows have two transomes and several mullions. The only exterior decoration other than the doorway are medallions with busts below the main first floor windows. The house is plastered and was at the time of

40

writing not in good preservation. Inside, the Hall lies immediately to the r. of the main entrance and is no larger than the Great Chamber behind it. The largest room is the Long Gallery above. This faces the E and N and has a big fireplace with coupled columns and above them standing allegorical figures. In an adjoining room a big wooden fireplace with flanking bulbous columns and an overmantel of 1697. The kitchens and offices are banished into the basement. The architectural importance of Barlborough lies in the fact that it anticipates several features of Wollaton in Notts and Hardwick. Barlborough certainly belongs together with these two and was probably designed by one of the *Smythsons*.

A long two-storeyed later C17 house stands at r. angles to the S front on the l.

PARK HALL (*see* p. 199).

BARLOW

ST LAURENCE. Essentially a Norman church, and because of that provided in 1867 with a highly demonstrative Neo-Norman chancel towards the street. It is the Victorian way of putting it on thick: Mark, this is a Norman edifice! What else did Sir George Gilbert Scott do at Oxford Cathedral when he replaced a Perp by an imitation Norman window? The original church consisted of nave and short chancel. Both have Norman doorways (one blocked) without decoration. One N window in the nave also has its Norman reveals. The chancel has a late C13 window, the W window is Late Tudor or C17. Transeptal S chapel with an odd posthumously Perp five-light window with five separate ogee tops. – MONUMENT. Good incised alabaster slabs to Robert Barley † 1467 and wife.

BARLOW WOODSEATS (WOODSEATS HALL). Irregular gabled C16 to C17 house with mullioned and mullioned and transomed windows.

BARLOW WOODSEATS *see* BARLOW

BARROW HILL

N of Staveley

Factory housing, 'very neatly built', says Murray's *Handbook* in 1874. It dates from *c.*1863 and later.

ST ANDREW. An early work of *Sir Raymond Unwin*, 1895. Red brick with short pairs of lancet windows and a friendly interior with open timber roof starting low down on corbels. No tower.

BARROW-UPON-TRENT

ST WILFRED. The most remarkable feature is the N arcade with (much restored) mid C13 piers, especially one circular with four shafts in the chief directions, the shafts being provided with shaft-rings. The arches are double-chamfered. The base of the W tower and the N aisle windows are early C14. The S aisle has a C14 arcade with the usual octagonal piers and the only medieval window (E) is ogee-reticulated (in the N aisle E window). C15 the upper parts of the tower. These were altered in the C19 as was the clerestory. Squints into the chancel from N and S. – MONUMENT. Alabaster effigy of a Priest with long series of trough-like folds down the middle of the chasuble; C14.

BARTON BLOUNT

BARTON HALL. The C15 brick gatehouse encased in stone in the C19. Some old brickwork, however, survives exposed on other sides of the house which was otherwise rebuilt in fine ashlar stone in (it is said) 1741. At the back handsome early C18 brick chequerwork. On a terrace some wrought ironwork by *Bakewell* from St Mary-by-the-Bridge at Derby.

ST CHAD. Reconditioned some twenty-five years ago. The doorway surprisingly big with curly pediment, late C17 (by *Wilson*? *See* Sudbury). – MONUMENT. Lady wearing wimple. She is holding her heart in her hands.

BASLOW

ST ANNE. Beautifully placed with its steeple close to the river Derwent and the old bridge across the river. The tower has big angle buttresses, the spire big early broaches rising without battlements, and a tier of dormers between the broaches. Nave and aisles are embattled; so is the chancel, which was built in 1911. The interior much renewed in the 1850s.

BRIDGE. A tiny toll-house by the bridge with a doorway only 3½ ft high.

BUBNELL HALL. Apparently C17, with mullioned and mullioned and transomed windows.

BATHAM GATE *see* TIDESWELL

BEELEY

ST ANNE. Over-restored in 1882–4. Norman S doorway. Short W tower with battlements and pinnacles.

BEELEY HALL. Early C17. Two and a half storeys with porch on the l. The first floor windows mullioned and transomed, the others mullioned only. Straight hoods above the windows.

BEELEY HILLTOPS. Irregular early C17 house with gables.

Much Ducal Chatsworth housing of the Edensor date, i.e. *c.*1840–5.

HOB HURST'S HOUSE. This well-known barrow is beautifully sited on Bunker's Hill, 2 m. NE, overlooking Chatsworth House. Traditionally the home of Hob o' the Hurst. Formally a 'round' barrow, it is square with a square ditch and bank.

BEIGHTON

ST MARY. Perp W tower with diagonal buttresses, battlements, and eight pinnacles. The tower arch towards the nave has coarsely ornamented capitals, not a usual thing in the county. The nave arcade Perp too: octagonal piers and arches with a profile incorporating two wavy curves.

MANOR HOUSE. Five-bay Georgian with segmental pediment above the doorway and quoins. Adjoining farm buildings.

BELPER

SPINNING MILL. The importance of Belper lies in its large complex of mill buildings. They are connected with the two celebrated names of Strutt and Arkwright. Jedediah Strutt, a farmer's son and a wheelwright, in 1756 invented a machine for making ribbed stockings. Richard Arkwright at that time worked at Nottingham on the perfection of his water frame for spinning. Strutt who had acquired some wealth went into partnership with him. In 1771 they built the first water-powered spinning mill at Cromford (*q.v.*), in 1776 a first mill at Belper. The partnership came to an end in 1782. Cromford remained Arkwright's, and Strutt and his son William (born in 1756) became the rulers of Belper. The buildings grew there, and about 1780 a mill was added at Milford.*

The Belper Mill is now a large complex of buildings. According to the information available at the mill the oldest surviving range is that facing Bridge Foot to the N, close to the Green. It dates from 1797 and has slim cruciform cast iron columns throughout, cast iron beams, and hollow tile floors. The windows are slightly arched. The building has five storeys. According to Britton & Brayley, writing in 1802, however, the main mill was six-storeyed and 200 ft long. That seems to refer to the building the other side of Bridge Foot which was embellished by the brick and terra-cotta Jubilee Tower in 1897. So this also may be as early as *c.* 1800. A third early building is evidently the one between that of 1797 and the river, i.e. NE of the Jubilee Tower. To its NE is a big addition of 1912.

There is good early commercial architecture in other parts of Belper as well, e.g. GEORGE BRETTLE'S WAREHOUSE in Chapel Street, 1834, stone, in a dignified classical style.

* The Strutt mansion at Bridge Hill has been demolished.

ST JOHN THE BAPTIST, The Butts. The old chapel of the village of Belper. Nave and chancel only, small and with smallish lancet windows (renewed, probably incorrectly). No other distinctive features. The Rawlins Manuscript shows a date-stone 1683 on the porch.

ST PETER, 1824, by *Habershon*. Thin tall W tower with big pinnacles, the body of the church a parallelogram with tall lancet-shaped windows with Perp tracery and angle pinnacles. The E end with a pediment-like gable, all much in the Commissioners' style, but not at all cheaply done. A well preserved pleasant interior, white and spacious, without aisles, but with three galleries on cast iron columns. – MONUMENT to George Brettle † 1835 by *Sir Richard Westmacott*, a kneeling woman against a Greek *stele*, of the best workmanship.

TRINITY METHODIST CHURCH, Chapel Street, *c.* 1835. Stone, five bays with three-bay pediment and Tuscan porch; fine and dignified.

BABINGTON HOUSE (Workhouse), Derby Road, an early work of *Sir George Gilbert Scott*. Ambitious Neo-Jacobean stone front with a four-storey symmetrical centre, and three-storey ranges to the l. and r. projecting at the angles. The projections continued by lower ranges.

PARK FOUNDRY, 1949, by *Philip Gerrard* of *C. Howitt & Partners*, one of the very few buildings in a contemporary style in Derbyshire which are worth a mention.

MORLEY PARK FARM, 2 m. NE. S of the Heage–Ripley Road remain two early iron furnaces, one of the late C18 the other of 1818. They were built by Francis Hurt and are steeply pyramidal truncated structures.

64

BENTLEY HALL *see* CUBLEY

BENTLEY HALL *see* FENNY BENTLEY

BIGGIN

ST THOMAS. By *Shellard*, 1844–8 (GR).

BIGGIN HOUSE. Early Georgian stone house of five bays

and two storeys. Giant Tuscan angle pilasters and a metope frieze. The doorway also has Tuscan pilasters and a metope frieze.

BIRCHOVER

The Rev. Thomas Eyre was a great admirer of the Rowtor Rocks, a cliff with many oddly shaped blocks of gritstone. They were vaguely connected with druidical practices. Mr Eyre made of three of them seats, and he also built below the cliff ROWTOR CHAPEL (CHURCH OF JESUS) (chancel added *c.* 1869). This has been completely altered since. By the porch a number of Norman architectural fragments from an unlocated previous building on a different site.

DRUID STONES. Behind the inn called the Druid Arms are the Druid Stones, among them two 'rocking stones'.

BIRDHOLME HOUSE *see* CHESTERFIELD

BLACKWELL

ST WERBURGH, 1826, but in the N wall inside, one circular pier of Transitional style preserved, *c.* 1200 or a little earlier. Chancel 1870s. – Anglo-Saxon CROSS SHAFT in the churchyard, *c.* 5 ft preserved, in bad condition, with interlace patterns.

BLADON CASTLE *see* NEWTON SOLNEY

BOLSOVER

ST MARY. C13 W tower of light grey stone, with broad buttresses covering the angles, W door of one order of colonnettes, double-chamfered arch (one chamfer continued into the jambs without capitals), W lancet window, two-light bell-openings, a low, rather broad-shouldered broach spire with one tier of dormers between the big broaches and another high up. The rest of the church was gutted by fire in 1897 and restored by *Ambler*. The Cavendish Chapel added to the E end of the S aisle in 1624 remained intact. It is a square structure with a coved ceiling inside of wooden beams with stuccoed panels between. S chancel door Norman with odd treble-roll-moulded frame. The sculptured Crucifixion in the tympanum badly defaced cannot be earlier than the C13. – 12 SCULPTURE. Nativity, large relief of the late C13; originally it must have been of very good quality. – PLATE. Chalice of *c.* 1600. – MONUMENTS. Foliated cross slabs in the N porch. – In the Cavendish Chapel two sumptuous monuments about a hundred years apart: Charles Cavendish † 1617, standing wall monument, his recumbent effigy behind and a little above that of his wife. Kneeling children in the 'predella'. Arch between a pair of treble columns behind. The arch is coffered and in the tympanum is a rich strapwork cartouche. – Henry Cavendish, Duke of Newcastle, his wife and one of his daughters, erected by Henrietta Cavendish Holles Harley in 1727, a very civilized marble monument of reredos type, with a big black sarcophagus between large coupled Corinthian columns supporting a pediment on which lie two allegorical figures. The design may well be by *Gibbs*. – Buried in the churchyard are the masons John Smythson † 1634 and Huntingdon Smythson † 1648. They are probably both connected with the buildings of Bolsover Castle. John in addition worked for the Cavendishes at Welbeck Riding School 1622–3.

44b 45 BOLSOVER CASTLE. There are not many large houses in England in so impressive a position as Bolsover, stretching out along the brow of a hill which rises steeply out of a plain now all given to coal-mining. Torn-open ground, long flags of smoke from chimneys, soot and mist over the valley; such is the characteristic view down from the castle. Bolsover has a long history going back to the Conqueror who gave the site to William Peverel. In his time or somewhat later a keep was built, and the present Keep or Little Castle stands in all probability on its foundations. Yet that new Keep remains extremely puzzling all the same. For it was built in 1613–*c.* 1616, during a period, that is, which one does not connect with structures of such an appearance. There can be no doubt that

Sir Charles Cavendish, who leased the site from his step-brother the seventh Earl of Shrewsbury in 1613, meant to build in a medieval style for the romantic or chivalric attraction of it, a turn of taste rare but not unique in Elizabethan and Jacobean days (cf. Wollaton, Nottinghamshire Lulworth, Dorset; etc.). The block has angle turrets, and at one angle a broader turret for the staircase. The turrets rise above the top battlements of the walls just as had been usual in medieval times. On the other hand, the compact, almost square plan in itself, which strikes one as un-Jacobean is not really an anomaly. It corresponds to such houses as Barlborough or Chastleton Oxon., and the narrow front court with pavilions is also a familiar motif, made special only by the consistent use of battlements. Of individual motifs of the exterior the pretty cupola deserves notice with its posthumously Gothic tracery windows (cf. Wollaton), the windows which are upright with one mullion and one or two transomes, and the balcony in the projecting central bay of the SW façade on the first floor above the porch. The balcony rests on two animal corbels and a kneeling Atlas. The door is flanked by columns with intermittent square blocks all up their height. The columns carry a pediment. A similar but simpler balcony on the SE side.

As surprising as the exterior is the interior, and here even more the guest of the C17 must have felt transported into an Arthurian world, as he desired to be. The principal rooms on the ground floor (Hall and Pillar Room) are all vaulted, indeed rib-vaulted. The piers, it is true, are now columns, the bosses have scrolly ornamentation, the fireplaces with their highly unusual projecting canopy hoods have Jacobean decoration, and the ribs are panelled in the Jacobean taste. But the effect of venerable gloom remains all the same. More ornate panelling and more ornate fireplaces on the upper floor, especially in the so-called Star Chamber. As to the fireplaces it must also be mentioned that their arched openings include ogee arches, i.e. a form which must be regarded as a self-conscious quotation from the language of the medieval past. In the Elysium Room a mythological ceiling painting recalls the Palazzo del Té at Mantua, the most popular Italian prototype of such pleasure palaces. The quality of painting is poor, and poorer still in the Heaven Room. The quality of sculpture of the VENUS FOUNTAIN in the garden to the E of the Little Castle is beneath contempt. The Hall fireplace has a carved date 1616, the Star Chamber a painted panel with the date 1621.

Shortly after the completion of the Little Castle Sir William Cavendish, Earl of Mansfield, son of Sir Charles who had died in 1617, began a scheme to increase accommodation. He first built the long range of the Riding School some distance away to the SE, with a grand gateway to the outer bailey at its NE end, and then a large building connecting the Riding School at an acute angle with the neighbourhood of the Little Castle. This building has, facing the view towards the valley (SW), a Gallery 200 ft long. Stones with the dates 1629 and 1630 have been recorded on the W side of the Riding School. The Gallery range appears to be later, but was probably, with the great Reception Rooms behind the Gallery, facing the courtyard, also complete, when in 1634 the celebrated visit of Charles I and his Queen took place. The entertainment, at which a masque by Ben Jonson was performed, is said to have cost £15,000.

The Earl's buildings are amongst the most interesting of their date in England. They are of a very personal style, neither post-Jacobean Traditional nor influenced by Inigo Jones. They are on the one hand characterized by rows of dormer windows with curved gables carrying alternatingly triangular and segmental pediments, that is a motif typical of up-to-date yet not courtly architecture of about 1630 in England, on the other hand by an excessive use of fancy rustication for doorcases, gateways, and even fireplaces. There is quite a number of divers banded, diamond, and other varieties, derived presumably from such publications as Serlio's, Ducerceau's, and Rubens's. The pediments are mostly of the broken segmental type. The style – Baroque, not classical – corresponds to that of,

45a

say, the portal of St Mary at Oxford by Nicholas Stone and similar such decorative works. In the Midlands it has had a belated effect on Derby County Hall and Nottingham Castle. The architecture of Cambridge in the 60s and 70s also seems in some way connected with it. The oddest motif at Bolsover, however, appears in the façade of the Gallery towards the terrace. Owing to sloping ground the building which is towards the courtyard of one and a half storeys has a row of basement windows and above them two rows of upright rectangular windows. Outer staircases lead up from the terrace to the gallery level. Between the two rows of main windows attached shafts run up column-wise. But they are not columns. They start by being corbelled out of the wall, carry on banded and vermiculated, end without capitals, and die into the wall. I know no parallel or precedent in England or abroad.

BONSALL

ST JAMES. In a picturesque position on a steep hill above the village and Bonsall Brook. Perp W tower ashlar-faced, with diagonal buttresses, battlements, pinnacles, and an unusual and handsome spire with two ornamental bands around. The church is also embattled. The N side of the chancel tells of the C13. The three-bay S arcade has quatrefoil piers and simple moulded capitals, some with cable decoration. This also may be C13. The N arcade has later octagonal piers. The piers of both arcades are on uncommonly high bases. The E windows C19. – MONUMENT. Henry Ferne, wife, and daughter, † 1763. Oval epitaph with weeping putti.

The village possesses a fine CROSS on a circular base of thirteen steps. It stands in the little Market Place to the W and below the church. The KING'S HEAD was established in 1677. The house has the traditional low three-light mullioned windows, and two irregular gables. Higher up the Bonsall Brook, an unusually pretty view of village houses across a pond-like widening of the brook.

BORROWASH

ST STEPHEN, 1899, by *P. H. Currey*. Inside, an excellent wrought IRON SCREEN of C18 date, presented to the church by a member of the Pares family. It is probably the work of *Bakewell* of Derby.

BOULTON NR DERBY

ST MARY. Mostly C19, but the S doorway is Norman (one order of colonnettes, zigzag arch, tympanum almost completely defaced), the N chancel doorway also Norman (similar but smaller), the S porch has a nice cusped outer doorway of *c*. 1300, and a few small Perp windows survive.

BOYLESTONE

ST JOHN THE BAPTIST. The SW tower with a pyramidal roof with conical sides is C19. The chancel early C14 (but Perp E window), the S aisle windows and arcade also. In the chancel a finely moulded low N recess, also early C14.

BRACKENFIELD

ROAD NOOK FARM, ½ m. S. Smithy dated 1673, Tithe Barn dated 1683, the house chiefly 1840, but with old beams, etc., inside.

BRADBOURNE

ALL SAINTS. The N side of the nave is partly of Saxon masonry; *see*, for instance, the long-and-short work at the E end. W of this a C13 lancet window. A similar window in the chancel N side. Earlier is the square unbuttressed W tower. Its date is evidently Norman. The doorway on the S side has one order of colonnettes, two orders of voussoirs with animals, and the outer order with beak-heads stylized into no more than abstract tongue shapes. The twin bell-openings have zigzag arches and billet in the label. The corbel-table is also original, the battlements are later. Most of the windows of the church are renewed, but the S aisle windows show (*see* the label-stops) that the original windows were later C14. Inside, the Norman tower arch is broad and quite wide. The S arcade of three bays is low with keeled quatrefoil piers, i.e. *c.* 1300. The chancel arch seems to be later C14. The responds are castellated. – STAINED GLASS. Old bits in the chancel N window. – PAINTING. Large Adoration of the Shepherds; North Italian, early C17. – Primitive C17–C18 wall painting in the S aisle: Towers surrounding a black-letter inscription from Eccles. V.I. – CROSS SHAFT. In the churchyard, *c.* 800, with ornament typical of the date, and a scene of the Crucifixion.

BRADBOURNE HALL. Elizabethan, grey stone with three gables, the larger l. one later. The staircase good and simple Jacobean.

BRADLEY

ALL SAINTS. Nave and chancel, no aisles, no tower. C18 wooden bell-turret. The rest C14. The only noteworthy detail the two large corbel-heads inside l. and r. of the E window. – FONT. The bowl octagonal with trefoil arches and fleurs-de-lis between (cf. Bakewell). The foot of eight filleted shafts clustered together. C13; much restored.

BRADSHAW HALL

2 m. W of Chapel-en-le-Frith

Dated 1620 on the handsome garden gateway. The date and arms under a double-stepped hood-mould. The house is L-shaped, gabled, and has the usual many-mullioned windows with one transome, under straight hoods, not the earlier hood-moulds that come down on the sides. Most of the old windows are blocked.

BRADSHAW HALL *see* EYAM

BRAILSFORD

ALL SAINTS. Some distance away from the village, embedded in trees. In the churchyard S of the church the poorly preserved stump of a circular mid C11 SAXON

CROSS with interlace decoration, but also the figure of a man (compared by Collingwood with Penrith, Gosforth, etc., in the North, and Ilam and Leek in Staffs). The church possesses architecturally interesting remains of Norman date. The chancel arch rests on the l. side on a circular Norman pier with many-scalloped capital. The S arcade has one circular Norman pier with a similar capital and all the arches only slightly single-chamfered. The other piers are slimmer, one octagonal and one circular. The Norman pier stands one bay from the W end of the church and is connected by an arch with the W wall. This arch lies right in front of the S wall of the W tower, a proof that the tower was built into the width of the Norman nave. The tower is ashlar-faced and has diagonal buttresses, and a Perp W door and W window. The chancel also is narrower than the Norman nave; *see* the odd r. side of the chancel arch with its squint. The chancel arch is early C14, as is the chancel with its characteristic windows. The N and S windows of the church itself are Perp (S aisle windows C19). – REREDOS with built-in old linenfold panels and Flamboyant tracery panels. – BENCH-ENDS with tracery panels with shields in the main fields.

BRAMPTON

For New Brampton (*see* p. 190).

SS PETER AND PAUL. Broad W tower with later angle buttresses and one Norman S window. Norman also the S doorway into the church and the blocked N doorway. The tower-arch to the nave with keeled responds and a pointed arch of three steps of which only one is chamfered. Buttresses for the support of the tower stand out into the nave. The tower received a broach spire of the earliest type, with big broaches not behind battlements and one tier of low-placed dormer windows. Nave, S aisle, and chancel are embattled. Vaulted S porch with thick transverse arches (cf. Ault-Hucknall, etc.). The nave arcades of three bays have circular and quatrefoil piers, and double-chamfered arches, the last arches being gathered under one big relieving arch. Similarly the treble-chamfered chancel arch on three orders of supports is below a coarsely depressed rounded arch. The building history of the church needs more attention. – SCULPTURE. Small figures of St Peter and St Paul, the Angel and the Virgin of the Annunciation, and Christ Seated walled into the S aisle walls without any system. Their date seems to be *c.* 1300. – MONUMENTS. Stone slab to Matilda le Caus †1224, with Lombardic inscription. The figure is partly hidden by the inscription slab. Only her feet stick out at the bottom, and her head, shoulders, and hands holding her heart appear sunk in a quatrefoil at the top (cf. Kedleston). – Clarke Family, erected 1673 with two horribly badly carved angels holding curtains away from the inscription; a typical piece of folk art – Geoffrey Clarke † 1734, standing wall monument of reredos type with an urn against a grey pyramid in the middle. – Base of CROSS in the churchyard.

BRASSINGTON

ST JAMES. Essentially a Norman church. The S arcade is uncommonly fine: three bays, circular piers, capitals both many-scalloped and of waterleaf type and odd asymmetrically one-stepped arches (cf. Kirk Ireton). The W tower also is Norman, although it is ashlar-faced and has a diagonal buttress at the SW corner; *see* the tower arch towards the nave, the blocked W doorway, and especially the two-light bell-openings. The S porch is of the C13, as proved by its outer doorway. Some windows are Perp. The N aisle dates from 1881. But the most surprising feature is the S chancel aisle of two bays which, with its octagonal pier, coarse crocket capitals, and unmoulded arches can hardly be later than about 1200.

In the centre of the village a fine HOUSE of 1615: two and a half storeys, L-shape, with two gables, the projecting part having the larger of the two. The windows mullioned and in the projection mullioned and transomed.

BREADSALL

10a ALL SAINTS. The finest steeple near Derby, C13 tower and slim, elegant, recessed, early C14 spire. The tower is of four stages. On the ground floor a W doorway of two orders and a treble-chamfered tower arch to the nave, first floor double-chamfered lancets, second floor two-light windows under hood-moulds with dogtooth ornament, third floor two two-light double-chamfered lancets as bell openings. The battlements belong in date to the spire (grey stone, the older parts pink). Older than the tower is the Norman S doorway of two orders of colonnettes, a zigzag arch, and a simply decorated label. Again to the C13 belong the chancel (one N lancet window replaced Perp) and the N arcade (circular piers with octagonal capitals with nailhead decoration), or rather belonged; for the church was set on fire by suffragettes in 1914 and had to be very extensively restored. This was done well and carefully by *Caroë* in 1915. The nave S windows were of a handsome Late Dec variety, ogee-reticulated but straightheaded, with hood-moulds, the N aisle windows partly also Dec (intersected cusped tracery) and partly Perp. Squint from the N aisle into the chancel. Sedilia late C14 or C15 with ogee heads and shields in the spandrels; rather bare (cf. Horsley). – SCULPTURE. A Pietà, late C14, was found below the floor during the restoration of 1877. It is small, austere, and somewhat strident in expression; most probably of German origin.

HALL. Opposite the W end of the church. Medieval stonework, but very badly tampered with and added to.

BREADSALL PRIORY. On the site of the Augustinian Priory founded in the C13. Of this only an arch survives in the basement of the Jacobean mansion which has also been so much altered (early C19 castellated and late C19) as not to be recognizable in more than a few gables (S and N) and mullioned windows. Breadsall Priory was the residence during his last years of Erasmus Darwin. Inside, a large Neo-Gothic door made by *Mr Haslam* of Derby for the 1851 Exhibition.

BREASTON

ST MICHAEL. Unbuttressed C13 W tower, crowned by a short broached spire. S aisle also C13; *see* the blocked doorway with dogtooth ornament and the windows of three-lancet lights, the middle one higher than the others. The arcade of three bays to the nave has octagonal piers and double-chamfered arches. The date also late C13 or a little later; i.e. perhaps of the same time as the chancel E window which has Dec tracery. – FONT, 1720. No other furnishings of interest.

BRETBY PARK

Built in 1812–13 by *Sir Jeffry Wyatville.* An impressive castellated mansion overlooking extensive grounds and to the E a series of artificially contrived lakes. The building is of solid stone oddly tooled in a system of diagonal spots. The show (E) front has at the angles circular towers and in the centre a projection with angle turrets. In the S front a big gateway into the square courtyard. The windows are mostly rectangular, but also lancet-shaped with the characteristic early C19 revival of the C13 type with two lancet lights with pierced spandrel within the main lancet. The interiors as far as original are classical, especially handsome the room in the SE tower. 58

ST WYSTAN, 1877, has a good set of PLATE of *c.*1680, given to the church about the time of its rebuilding (Chalice and Paten on stem, and Flagon).

BRIZLINCOTE HOUSE

1¼ m. ENE of Stapenhill

1714. Brick, five bays and two storeys with quoins, pedimented doorway and alternating pediment of the upper windows. Hipped roof. So far nothing remarkable. But across the whole front extends a monstrous segmental pediment big enough to contain five windows, the outer ones small and circular. The shorter side elevations have also segmental pediments only slightly less gargantuan.

BROOKFIELD MANOR

1 m. N of Hathersage

Behind the romantic castellated house of 1825 in its picturesque position lie the remains of a fortified medieval house with a big gateway by the brook.

BROOKHILL HALL

1 m. NE of Pinxton

Originally probably a courtyard house. Now two ranges, L-shaped and a shorter range facing the E range. The building is essentially Jacobean; *see* the surviving mullioned or mullioned and transomed windows and gables. But the S front has been Georgianized (five bays, two storeys) and a fine drawing room added to the W range, *c.* 1770.

BROUGH

1¾ m. E of Castleton

ROMAN FORT. On a low hill in the valley of the river Noel, which flows 20–30 ft below it to the NE. It guarded the communications between S Yorkshire and Manchester. It was called Anavio. Built as a rectangle, with rounded corners, the sides measuring 285 by 340 ft. Gateway in the middle of each side. Constructed about the year A.D. 158. Brough is remarkable for its underground strongroom, 8 ft long and 6 ft wide, which was entered by eight steps. Similar to Melandra Castle at Glossop. A silver *denarius* of Severus (A.D. 193–210) suggests occupation into C3, i.e. longer than Melandra. Why the smaller fort should have been preferred to the larger, if this is in fact the case, the excavators have not explained.

BUBNELL HALL *see* BASLOW

BULL-RING *see* CHAPEL-EN-LE-FRITH

BURBAGE NR BUXTON

Now a suburb of Buxton.

CHRIST CHURCH, 1860, by *Currey*, one of the buildings

erected in connexion with the seventh Duke of Devonshire's plan for the development of Buxton. The church is atrociously ugly, with its tower which has twin circular bell-openings, a parapet which rises into a triangle in the middle of each side, and a pyramid roof. The aisles are separated from the nave by wooden piers and wooden arches of a fancy shape and with pierced spandrels.

BURTON CLOSES *see* BAKEWELL

BURTON MOOR *see* BAKEWELL

BUXTON

The waters of Buxton were known to the Romans. They were used in the Middle Ages and were much in favour in the Elizabethan Age. Mary Queen of Scots was brought here by the Earl of Shrewsbury, and the Earls of Leicester and Warwick made use of the springs. But the conversion into a spa is due chiefly to three later Dukes of Devonshire, the fifth, sixth, and seventh. The spa developed in the valley below the old town, and a division between the old market town (the highest in England) and the spa is still noticeable now. The old town strangely enough possessed no church of any size.

ST ANNE, tucked away behind the W end of the High Street. A church of chapel size, with no tower, no aisles, and no division between nave and chancel. Very low big tie-beams about 9 ft from the ground, low three-light mullioned windows. The date given is 1625.

No houses of that period are discernible, and the only buildings in the high town which need recording belong to the C18 and C19. In the MARKET PLACE the EAGLE HOTEL, a big Queen Anne house of nine bays and three and a half storeys, and the TOWN HALL, 1887–9, by *W. Pollard* of Manchester, rather poor with a thin tower in the middle of the façade.

The spa development began about 1780, when the fifth Duke of Devonshire as lord of the manor conceived the idea of making Buxton into a second Bath. So he obtained 61a the services of *John Carr* of York and had the CRESCENT built close to the original St Anne's Well at the foot of the rise of St Anne's Cliff in rather a cramped position. The Crescent is small compared with the Royal Crescent at Bath, completed less than ten years before. Its detail is more classical and elegant than the younger *Wood's*, giant Roman Doric pilasters in the rusticated arcades below, with metope frieze, cornice and top balustrade. Inside, the ASSEMBLY ROOM (now Buxton Clinic), a fine large room with giant Corinthian pilasters and at the end a shallow niche screened off by Corinthian columns. The Duke and *Carr* followed the Crescent by a large STABLES establishment behind to the N. This survives with additions of 1868 to 1882 as the DEVONSHIRE ROYAL HOSPITAL (cf. below). The original building was a square with chamfered corners and central pediments, of very restrained architecture. The centre was a large circular courtyard for riding exercise. The hospital added angle turrets, put a large iron dome on big Tuscan columns over the courtyard (1880), and a clock tower asymmetrically on the centre of the E side (1882). This was designed by *R. R. Duke*, the former alterations were due to the sixth duke's Buxton architect, the Londoner *Henry Currey* († 1900).

Also by *Carr* HALL BANK, the terrace of rising houses on the W side of the Cliff Gardens and THE SQUARE, also on arcades. The Square lies to the W of the Crescent and faces the later Pavilion Gardens. Between it and the Crescent at the corner OLD HALL, the oldest of the buildings of lower Buxton. It was here that Mary Queen of Scots stayed. But of the time of her sojourn nothing survives. The present building is of 1670 and altered. It has a five-bay front with slightly projecting angle bays, thick quoins, a door on Tuscan pilasters, and a window above it with a characteristic semicircular pediment (cf. the Peacock at Rowsley, 1652).*

* Between the Old Hall and the Crescent *Currey* built the Baths in 1853, but these have been altered completely.

The first work at Buxton connected with the sixth duke is the provision of a parish church for the spa.

ST JOHN THE BAPTIST, W of the Riding Stables, and at first quite isolated. Built 1811 by *Sir Jeffry Wyatville* whom, a little later, the duke was going to employ so extensively at Chatsworth. The exterior has an E portico of heavy Tuscan attached columns and a W front with Tuscan pilasters and above the pediment a tower rising to a domed top. The detail of the tower is remarkably free, and the domed top also has no parallel in the normal non-classical church types of 1810–20. The forms are rather Italian than classical. Interior without aisles, but with shallow transepts, the walls ashlar-faced with pilasters.

Wyatville is also said to have laid out the gardens up St Anne's Cliff (CLIFF GARDENS) facing the Crescent. The next layout job came a good deal later, *c.* 1845, and thus fell to the sixth duke's *confidant* and gardener, *Joseph Paxton.* THE PARK to the W of the Stables and St John was got ready for development, with a circular open space inside and houses around, somewhat on the pattern of Nash's original idea for Regent's Park. Only a few houses go back to *c.* 1845–50.

A larger scale of development started only after the sixth duke's death, when the railway finally reached Buxton. This event took place in 1867. In 1868 the seventh duke's architect *Henry Currey* built the PALACE HOTEL to the E and above the Devonshire Royal Hospital, i.e. the former Stables, and began the conversion of the Stables into the Hospital. More churches were also provided.

ST ANNE (R.C.), Terrace Road, 1861, by *Scoles.* Lancet style, no tower.

ST JAMES, Bath Road, 1869–70, by *M. H. Taylor* (GR).

HOLY TRINITY, Hardwick Mount, 1873, by *Currey.* Enlarged 1882 and 1894; tower completed 1900.

CONGREGATIONAL CHURCH, Hardwick Street, by *Currey,* 1861.

Finally, in 1871, Buxton established itself as a proper Victorian spa by the erection of the PAVILION and the pretty Pavilion Gardens in front of it. The Pavilion is a utilitarian, quite graceful iron and glass structure by *Mr Edward Milner* of Sydenham. It was enlarged by a CONCERT HALL on the W in 1875, a circular structure, heavier in the details.

The only later events which it is necessary to record are the building of the former EMPIRE HOTEL by *Thomas Garner*, *c.* 1906, to the NW of The Park, and of the OPERA HOUSE by *Frank Matcham* in 1903 at the E end of the Pavilion.

CALDWELL

ST GILES. Chapel consisting of nave with bellcote and lower chancel in the grounds of the house. The chapel is Norman though much renewed; *see* the small round-headed windows on the N side of nave and chancel and the S side of the nave. On the N side also a blocked round-headed doorway. In the W window two roundels of STAINED GLASS, probably *c.* 1400.

CALDWELL HALL. Eleven-bay brick mansion of two and a half storeys, plain with parapet. To the r. of the entrance a lower, pedimented range of seven bays with windows with one mullion and one transome. Date on a rainwater-head 1678. NW wing *c.* 1875.

CALKE

CALKE ABBEY lies in a dip, in extensive grounds, a large stone mansion dated 1703, all but unknown to architectural literature. It is very ambitious in scale, if somewhat coarse in detail. Low ground floor plus two large upper floors. Top balustrade. The entrance (S) front is eleven bays wide with a pedimented four-column Ionic portico above the ground floor level. The three bay angle pavilions project and are flanked by fluted Ionic giant pilasters. The same motif of pavilions with Ionic giant pilasters also on the W and E sides which are equally long. Inside, the Entrance Hall goes up the full height of the house. Also a grand Saloon with Corinthian pilasters and a large overmantel.

ST GILES, in the grounds of the house, but not near to it. Built 1826, with a narrow W tower and a castellated nave. – MONUMENT to Sir John Harpour † 1741 and his wife, of excellent workmanship (could it be by *Cheere*?). Inscription plate with lovely cherub's heads below. Above the usual pyramid, and to the l. and r. portrait busts.

CALVER MILL *see* CURBAR

CARLWARK

1¾ m. E of Hathersage

Superb hill-fort. The great fortress is built at an altitude of over 1,200 ft on a wild moorland summit littered with boulders and outcrops of millstone grit. Single well preserved entrance at SW. Its leading feature is a 100 ft long wall constructed of well chosen blocks of millstone grit bonded into a turf ramp. The turf ramp suggests that the fortress is not of Iron Age date, which is usually supposed, but that it may belong to the Dark Ages, as late as C5 or C6.

CARNFIELD HALL

1 m. E of Alfreton

Elizabethan stone mansion with Georgianized E front. The latter is of nine bays and two storeys, the three side bays on each side projecting somewhat. Central doorway with open segmental pediment. But Elizabethan twin gables appear above the projections to remind one of the real date of the house which is impressively obvious at the back. Here the side parts project more, and one of them is continued as a lower range. The windows are mullioned and mullioned and transomed. Opposite the back a stable range apparently of the early C18. Inside, the staircase is original and one upper room with panelling. More Elizabethan woodwork was evidently brought from outside

CARSINGTON

ST MARGARET. Nave and chancel in one, embattled with straightheaded three-light Perp windows. Yet the sundial in the S wall says 'Re-edified 1648'. It is an interesting, because specially complete case of Gothic Survival. Only the W end was altered in the C19 (pediment, bell-cote).

CARTLEDGE HALL *see* HOLMESFIELD

CASTLETON

Splendidly situated immediately below the steep-up Peveril Castle and with a view of the summits of the High Peak closing in to the W.

ST EDMUND. Broad Norman chancel arch of one order of colonnettes with block capitals. Big coarse zigzag in the arch. The rest essentially of the restoration of *c.* 1837. The aisles were then removed so that the nave has now the proportions of Commissioners' churches, and the windows given their lancet shapes and typical Neo-late-C13 tracery. Perp W tower, ashlar-faced with diagonal buttresses, battlements and eight pinnacles. – BOX PEWS. Excellently preserved throughout; C17, with various dates on (1661, 1662, 1663, 1676).

PEVERIL CASTLE (*see* p. 200).

MAM TOR, 1½ m. W. Hill-fort, probably of Iron Age date. It encloses 16 acres within 1,200 yards of ramparts. On three sides it is defended by a double rampart, but on the S side, where the entrance was situated, is a triple line of banks.

GREY DITCH. Three sections remain of this earthwork of unknown function, which may be Anglo-Saxon. It crosses Batham Gate N of Bradwell (which is 1½ m. SE of Castleton) and runs in the direction of Mam Tor towards Abney Moor.

LORDS SEAT, 2½ m. W. Round barrow on Rushup Edge.

CATTON HALL

A large, plain, but stately brick house, built in 1745. Nine bays wide with the outer three bays on the l. and the r. slightly projecting. The only decoration the main doorway. Sumptuously plastered Entrance Hall and staircase ceiling. Some fine original furniture.

CHADDESDEN

ST MARY. Rebuilt *c.* 1357 by Henry Chaddesden, Archdeacon of Leicester, encouraged probably by the immediately preceding work at Sandiacre. Important as a dated example of church architecture before the advent of the Perp style. Nave and aisles and tall and wide chancel. The high chancel N and S windows of three lights have a star-motif in the tracery, similar to so-called Kentish tracery, but with the three points of the star long and with concave sides (just as at Sandiacre). The E window is C19. The N aisle has also Dec windows (four lights in the E, three lights in the N). The S windows all new except the E one, but perhaps renewed correctly (flowing tracery). Some more windows re-done Perp, the W tower (ashlar, with angle buttresses, big W door and W window, and concave chamfering of the tall arch to the nave) also Perp. When the tower was built the aisles were extended to the W. The arcades inside (three bays) have tall octagonal piers with moderately finely moulded capitals and double-chamfered arches. At the E ends of the N and S aisles Sedilia and Piscina, with crocketed ogee-arches and stone reredoses to the altars, just long sunk panels no doubt originally painted. – SCREEN and STALL ENDS (with figures of a monk and a deacon). The screen has one-light openings with ogee tops rising into an upper part with panel tracery. Lectern of stone built into the chancel N wall (cf. Crich, Etwall, Spondon, Taddington).

Row of half-timbered cottages to the N of the church.

SECONDARY MODERN SCHOOL. By the *Architects' Co-operative Partnership* in collaboration with the *F. Hamer Crossley*. In course of erection. The building promises to become the most interesting example of the contemporary architectural style in the county. The plan is broadly speaking cross-shaped, heights vary greatly, in part owing to the sloping ground. In the centre of the cross low entrance hall, W of it smaller one-storey block with Assembly Hall and Gymnasium, to the E higher class-room wing, to the S yet higher and shorter block with class-rooms (four storeys). Construction is with a light steel-frame to a 3 ft 4 in module. The façades will be in large stretches completely of glass, constructed against other walls left entirely solid.

CHAPEL-EN-LE-FRITH

ST THOMAS BECKET. The first church was a chapel built by the foresters of the Peak Forest about 1225. Hence the name of the town (in-the-Forest). The present church is chiefly of the early C14, and quite large and wide. Nave and aisles of four bays, the piers octagonal of red stone with moulded capitals showing discreet nailhead decoration in the S arcade, and double-chamfered arches. The chancel arch appears of the same date. The chancel was much altered later and is over-restored. The W tower and the S front of the church altogether received new clothes in 1733. The architect of the modernization was *Platt* of Rotherham. The arched windows, the central one with alternating rustication, the S porch, and the tower with its parapet and obelisk pinnacles are all essentially in the medieval tradition. It is only the motifs which have been changed. – BOX PEWS, early C19. – PLATE. Flagon inscribed 1736; Paten inscribed 1747.

In the main street a few houses worth passing notice, chiefly the HEARSE HOUSE, dated 1818, and one a little further E with an uncommonly Baroque doorway.

BULL-RING, Dove Holes. Originally a Bronze Age sanctuary, associated with a cairn, just as Arbor Low. The mound with which the enclosure was connected stands 100 ft to the SW, and is 8 ft high. The sanctuary measures 160 ft across, and was surrounded by a stone circle, all the stones of which have vanished. A solitary monolith was in position at the end of C18. Around the enclosure a broad, shallow ditch beyond which an encircling rampart. Gaps in the ditch and rampart at the N and S mark the opposed entrances.

COMBE MOSS, 1½ m. W of the Bull-Ring. A promontory fort, dating probably from the Iron Age. It is defended on all sides by steep slopes except on the SE, where there are two ramparts, cut by entrance, 547 ft long and over 10 ft high.

FORD HALL (*see* p. 138).

GANTRIES HILL, 3 m. E. A round barrow.

SPARROW PIT BARROW, 3 m. E.

WHITEHAUGH (*see* p. 241).

CHARLESWORTH

ST JOHN THE BAPTIST. 1849, still in the pre-archeological lancet style. Big S tower.

CONGREGATIONAL CHAPEL. On the site of the original chapel of Charlesworth. Rebuilt for the Congregationalists in 1797. Big, with gable and central Venetian window on ground floor and upper floor.

CHATSWORTH

INTRODUCTION

Visitors to Derbyshire may argue whether Haddon or Hardwick or Chatsworth is the most impressive mansion in the county. Haddon is no doubt more romantic than either of the others, and Hardwick is, also undoubtedly, of an architectural unity which Chatsworth fails to achieve. The grounds of Chatsworth, on the other hand, are not matched by Haddon or Hardwick or indeed more than perhaps half-a-dozen of the country houses of Britain. The lack of unity of Chatsworth is not at once noticed as one sees the house from a distance and even as one approaches it quite closely. This is due to a relatively short main building period, that of the first Duke of Devonshire (1687–1707), and to the great tact and understanding with which the second main building period, that of the sixth Duke (1820–42) and his architect *Sir Jeffry Wyatville* treated the first, at least as far as alterations to the first Duke's palace went; for the sixth Duke added a highly palatial new wing which certainly lacks tact, even if it makes up for that by the rare combination self-assurance and sobriety of detail.

49a 49b

STOKE-ON-TRENT PUBLIC LIBRARIES

William Cavendish, fourth Earl of Devonshire (1640–1707), was made the first Duke in recognition of his share in the events of 1688 and the safe establishment of William of Orange. When he took possession of Chatsworth after his father's death in 1684, he found an ELIZABETHAN HOUSE no smaller than the one he was to build. It had been begun in 1557 by Sir William and his wife Bess of Hardwick. It was square, built around an inner courtyard, just as its successor, and had four storeys, square angle turrets and a tall gatehouse to the W with triangularly projecting turrets. Nothing visible to the eye survives of this house. However, of the smaller structures in its gardens and further away, two still exist: the HUNTING TOWER, or Stand, a look-out tower in the woods to the NE with four circular angle turrets with domed caps and windows with mullion-and-transome-cross, and QUEEN MARY'S BOWER, NW of, and close to, the N entrance of the house. The Hunting Tower was in all probability a summer-house or plaisance or gazebo of Bess of Hardwick, Queen Mary's Bower, with less probability but quite possibly, as the legend has it, a kind of open-air prison for the Queen during her periods of captivity at Chatsworth in 1570, 1573, 1577, 1578, and 1581. It is a low tower or platform surrounded by a moat and reached over steps which at the same time form a bridge.

EXTERIOR ARCHITECTURE

When the first Duke started building, he did not at first intend a complete replacement of Bess of Hardwick's house. That idea came only gradually. He began by putting up a new SOUTH RANGE (1687–9). This was designed by *William Talman* who had designed Thoresby for the Duke of Kingston shortly before, but was a relatively unknown architect to be entrusted with so big an enterprise. The artists engaged for interior work, on the other hand, were mostly men close to the court: *Laguerre* and *Verrio* for the painting, *Cibber* for sculpture, and *Tijou* for ironwork. All four also appear at Hampton Court, where the new King, for whom the Duke had done

CHATSWORTH

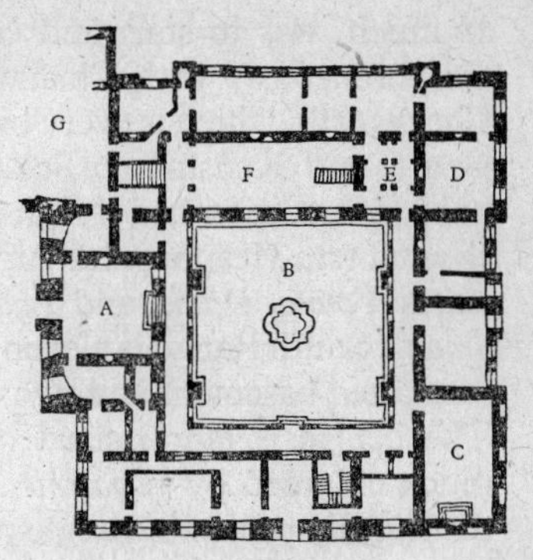

GROUND FLOOR

A. Entrance Hall
B. Inner Court
C. Chapel
D. Stag Parlour
E. Grotto
F. Painted Hall
G. North Wing

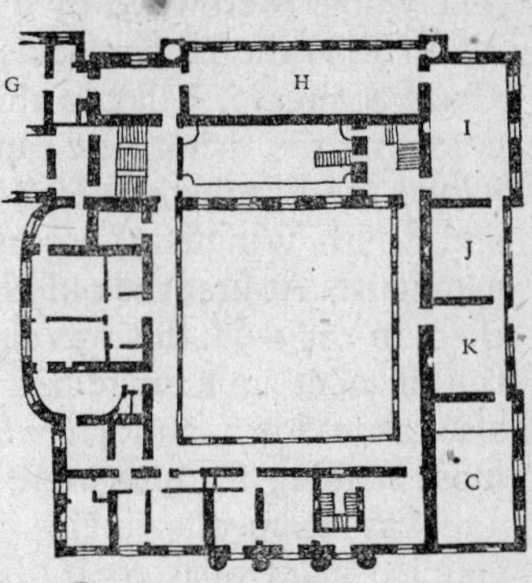

FIRST FLOOR

C. Chapel
G. North Wing
H. Library
I. Gold Drawing Room
J. Yellow Silk Drawing Room
K. Billiard Room

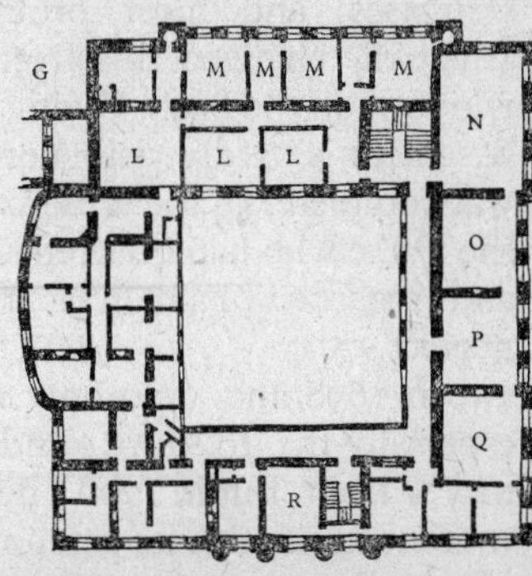

SECOND FLOOR

G. North Wing
L. Queen of Scots Room
M. Leicester Rooms
N. State Dining Room
O. State Drawing Room
P. State Music Room
Q. State Bedroom
R. Sabine Room

so much, was to start and carry on almost exactly contemporaneously with Chatsworth. But the woodwork at Chatsworth, which is every bit as good as that at Hampton Court, and Kensington Palace, is not by Grinling Gibbons, as tradition had it, but by the local sculptor *Samuel Watson* (*see* Heanor) and (up to 1694) his London associates *Young*, *Davis*, and *Lobb*.

Talman's South Range is eleven bays wide and consists of a rusticated basement and two upper floors of equal height. The centre is emphasized only by the outer staircase, much enlarged by *Wyatville*. The main emphases lie on the slightly projecting angle pavilions of three bays which have giant pilasters and some decoration in the frieze. The whole is crowned by a balustrade.

Early in 1688 the Duke decided to replace the Elizabethan Great Staircase. It lay in the S corner of the old W wing adjoining the rising new range. On the other side it adjoined the Elizabethan Hall placed as usual (*see* Haddon and South Wingfield) across the courtyard opposite the gatehouse. At first the old Hall was meant to remain, but then, in 1689–91, this was also replaced. Once so much of the Elizabethan E range had been destroyed, the rest was also taken down, and *Talman* designed a new E front. Its most striking features were the two narrow projections one bay from the angles which were decorated with coupled giant pilasters. Otherwise the front was plainly utilitarian, eleven bays wide. The projections hide spiral staircases, and most probably Elizabethan masonry. *Wyatville* changed this front by removing the top attic windows to the back. Owing to the rise of the ground the basement is hardly visible on this side. In 1696 this front was complete. In the same year *Talman* was dismissed by the Duke who had quarrelled with his London craftsmen and regarded Talman as partly responsible for their neglect.

Between 1696 and 1700 only minor additions were made, especially the TERRACE and Stairs in front of the future new W front. But in 1700 a new phase began, when Bess's W front itself with its gatehouse was demolished to make way for the grandest of the Chatsworth façades. This was built in 1700–3, and, strangely enough, it is not known for certain who designed it. The attribution to *Talman* had never been doubted, but recently Mr Whiffen has put in a claim for *Sir James Thornhill*, who is known to have been consulted on the architecture of other houses as well. The W RANGE is nine bays wide. It is the only one distinguished by a pediment and four all-round attached columns to carry it. The remaining six bays to the l. and r. have giant pilasters. The rusticated basement here has the height of a proper ground floor, and its centre was indeed the first Duke's main entrance into the house, a curiously insignificant entrance. This ground floor forms the base on which the giant pilasters and columns stand, a more crowded and more Baroque effect than that of the previous façades. There is a remarkably Baroque restlessness in the details of the design, the projections and recessions within the ground floor centre, the garlands round the central windows, the ornamentation of the frieze (taken over from the S range), and the carvings inside the pediment. The garlands are by *Newbould*, the decoration of the pediment is *Watson's* work.

In 1703–4 colonnades were added to the S range on the courtyard side to make communication easier. The idea may have come from Wren's colonnade in the Clock Court at Hampton Court. The colonnades were abolished by *Wyatville*. Finally in 1705–7 came the last stage in the reconstruction of the house, the new N FRONT. It is chiefly in the form of a shallow curve to connect the E and W ranges which differed in their extent to the N by as much as 9 ft. The bow has five windows and giant pilasters above the basement or ground floor. This wide centre part is raised, the only break in the continuity of the height of the balustrade. The motif goes well with the style of its designer who was almost certainly *Thomas Archer*. Archer spent some time at Chatsworth in 1704 or 1705 and was left £200 by the Duke in his will for 'his favour and his care and trouble touching the building of the house'.

In spite of this complex building history, Chatsworth as it appeared in Early Georgian days possessed a convincing unity of style. This was partly due to the square, compact shape of the block and partly, as has been said before, to the short intervals between the various phases. The next substantial addition was due to the fourth Duke who succeeded to the title in 1755. He employed *James Paine* to build a long low wing from the NE angle towards the N to house Kitchen and Offices. In the place of the previous main Kitchen, in the middle of the W bow, a new Entrance Hall was contrived (cf. below). Paine also designed extensive Stables to the NE. The Stables remain, but for the office wing a more substantial and infinitely more ambitious wing was substituted by the sixth Duke.

The sixth Duke (1790–1858) had succeeded in 1811. His first job was an internal adjustment, the conversion of the Long Gallery into a Library (1815; cf. below). He did not taste of the sweet taste of building until 1820, when work began on the new N wing and many more changes inside the house. His architect was *Jeffry Wyatt*, later *Sir Jeffry Wyatville*, who had made a name by his previous work for Longleat (1801, etc.) and Wollaton (1804) in the Elizabethan style, and Ashridge (1814, etc.) in the Gothic style. The main function of the NE wing, which is 357 ft long, was to provide a suite of representational rooms, longer, more easily accessible, and grander than the first Duke's State Rooms on the second floor of the S range had been. The architects of the Romantic period (and Wyatville was emphatically one of them, even where he used the chastest classical forms) disliked the symmetry of the Age of Reason. The Picturesque was their watchword, and so neither the Duke nor his architect was worried by the fact that the new wing destroyed the compactness of the old house. The length of the jutting-out new range seemed to add just what was needed, especially when, in 1827, an Orangery had been added at the N end as an afterthought and after that a Swimming Bath with a Theatre above. Finally, to top this achievement, the Duke out of his own mind finished the wing by the Temple

Attic, the big Belvedere storey at the N end. Its self-assertiveness hurts people, but as a symbol of the man who built it and of his time it could not be better. And it is besides in its somewhat Genoese Cinquecento character by no means offensive. It is to be hoped that purism will not prevail against it and that it will be allowed to assume a true Belvedere function for visitors to Chatsworth. Due to *Wyatville* also is the new outer Gateway in line and to the W of the N front of the N wing, a monumental overture in the Tuscan style to the N forecourt (with its fine weeping ash) and to the house.

INTERIORS

The interior of the house will be discussed in the order in which visitors (at the time of writing) see it. Parts not shown but architecturally of significance will follow after that, and then the outbuildings, gardens, and grounds. In accordance with the principles of *The Buildings of England*, neither furniture nor paintings will be mentioned, unless they can be considered fixtures and fitments.

The ENTRANCE HALL was contrived out of the first Duke's Kitchen by the fourth Duke *c.* 1755–60. The columns are copies of one by *Kent* in the grounds of Lord Burlington's Palladian villa of Chiswick, which had come into the possession of the Duke in 1753. The staircase was widened by *Wyatville* who also replaced the chimney-pieces by new ones and opened out the windows on the l. and r. of the stairs. The CORRIDORS in their present form are all *Wyatville's* work. To reach the Painted Hall and the main stairs the C18 visitor had to pass through the first Duke's open colonnade, an eminently inconvenient approach, even if one slightly more convenient than the original one, which from the low Entrance Hall in the middle of the W front had to be right across the open courtyard, as if the house had been one of the dark Middle Ages.

The PAINTED HALL is 64 by 26 ft in size. It was originally apsed at the W end, and two flights of stairs curved up against the apse to the first floor landing. This arrangement has been altered twice, first under the sixth Duke who also added as an easier access to the first floor the Oak Stairs N of the Hall with their domed skylight (1823–9), and again in 1911–12 when the present Hall Staircase and Galleries were built (by *W. H. Romaine-Walker*). The Hall has a ceiling and walls painted by *Laguerre* in 1694. They represent the Life of Julius Caesar. They are intended to be grand in the Baroque manner but do not succeed in this. Their colouring lacks fire and their compositions brio. It is particularly unfortunate that there is no framing with gilt and stucco round the ceiling painting. It makes the paintwork appear flat and just stuck on. The painted architecture on the walls has the same quality of flatness. *Samuel Watson's* stone-carvings, on the other hand, are superb.

The Great Stairs are approached by means of the staircase in the Hall. Originally they were meant to start from the ground floor. The change of plan left no function for the dark square space on the ground floor beneath the Great Stairs. So the first Duke decided to make it into a GROTTO, not really one with shell-studded walls and rockery, but at least a room the *point de vue* of which was a fountain. This, or rather the relief of Diana, was bought in London in 1692. It must be French work of *c.* 1600 and is of higher quality than contemporary figure work in England. *Watson's* stone-carving here is the most sumptuous he did inside the house. The ceiling of the Grotto is supported by four heavy Tuscan columns. If the room is less gloomy now than one might expect, this is due to the piercing of four openings by the sixth Duke and after.

From the Grotto visitors go by way of the Chapel Corridor
50 to the CHAPEL, the finest room at Chatsworth. It runs through two storeys, with a S (ritually W) gallery on the first floor. The walls are cedar-panelled with *Watson's* limewood carvings of garlands of fruit and foliage. Against the altar wall a magnificent reredos is erected of alabaster, with a niche immediately behind the altar, a broken pediment above it, and an upper storey with a

large painting of Doubting Thomas by *Verrio* flanked by two allegorical statues by *Cibber*. The top is a broken segmental pediment. In this work, completed in 1694, England is certainly as Baroque in the Continental sense, that is as magnificent and swaggering, as she ever was. *Laguerre's* walls and ceiling again fail to keep up this high pitch. They appear dull and slaty next to *Verrio's* painting and *Cibber's* sculpture. But even *Verrio* seems staid and somewhat phlegmatic if compared with *Sir James Thornhill's* early ceiling painting on the WEST STAIRS. It represents The Fall of Phaëton and shows that he owed as much to Rubens as to Italy.

Visitors go up the West Stairs straight to the second floor and enter the STATE ROOMS through the China Closet. To have the best suite on the second floor is an anomaly, explained by the fact that the ground floor was regarded as a basement, and owing to the fall of the site was indeed on the E side (where Hall and Great Stairs are placed) no more than a basement. The State Rooms (five in number) are of a type familiar from Hampton Court and Kensington Palace, with the doors in *enfilade*, made more impressive by continuing them at the E end with a mirror (costing the fabulous sum of £105) to double their length in appearance, with ceilings painted by *Verrio*, *Laguerre*, and *Ricard*,* and plenty of exquisite ornamental wood-carving by *Watson* and his companions. The rooms were decorated in 1689 to 1699. The so-called State Dining Room was of course never a dining room. Its original name was the Great Chamber.‡

Through the Leicester Passage one now returns to the GREAT STAIRS (1689–90). The ceiling here is by *Verrio*; the grisaille scenes on the wall by unrecorded painters. The statues are by *Cibber*, the alabaster doorcases prob-

* *Verrio* State Dining Room; all the others look like *Laguerre*: State Drawing Room Assembly of the Gods, State Music Room Phaëton praying to Apollo, State Bedroom Aurora chasing away Diana, State Dressing Room the three Goddesses dispatching Mercury to find Paris.

‡ The gilt tables in this room were designed by *Kent* for Lord Burlington's Chiswick villa.

ably by *Watson*. *Tijou*, the most famous artist in wrought iron ever working in England, did the stair balustrade and received £250 for it. The pattern is one (none too felicitous) of square balusters represented flat and in outline.

The next room shown to the public is the LIBRARY, seen from the Ante-Library. This is on the first floor and fills the whole E front except for one room with one window at each side. On the S this room is the one lying underneath the Great Chamber. The Library is 90 ft long and was originally the GALLERY. It was fitted by the first Duke in 1694–1700 and then refitted by the sixth in 1815. Of the original work only the ceiling remains, painted by *Verrio*. The panels are set in stucco work by *Gouge* of London. The walls had paintings by *Chéron* (who also painted the ceiling in the Ante-Library), and *Rambour*. The woodcarving (which has disappeared) was done by *Lanscroon*.

The redecorating of the Gallery started the sixth Duke on his much more ambitious scheme of creating a whole new suite of rooms, larger and grander than the old building could provide anywhere. So the new N wing (i.e. the wing projecting from the NE corner to the N) was designed by *Wyatville*, begun in 1818, and completed in the 1830s. It contained Kitchens and Offices on the ground floor, and the new State Suite on the first, with bachelors' bedrooms behind. The end pavilion had originally a Swimming Bath on the ground floor. Above this is the THEATRE, a complete piece of lush Regency or Early Victorian furnishing (neither name is strictly correct, as the date is 1830), enriched by the fitting up against its ceiling of the painted wall panels from the Library. Above the Theatre is the Duke's own Belvedere to which reference has already been made. Wyatville in his interiors kept to a grand classical manner and forgot about the fancies he was able to put into his Gothic work. The suite consists of an ante-room with lush columns of Pavonazzo and Giallastro and two slender vases of the rare Occhio di Paone, the Dining Room with its coved ceiling, the Sculpture Gallery with three square lantern skylights, and the Orangery, added in 1827 as an afterthought. In the

Dining Room the chimneypieces are by *Westmacott* and *Sievier*, in the Sculpture Gallery the very expensive ormolu capitals of the large columns by *Delafontaine* of Paris. It was a regally expensive job throughout.

Most of *Wyatville's* work inside the first Duke's block is not seen by the normal visitor. It comprised, for instance, the suite below the State Rooms, which became the principal living rooms for the family and are now used for larger scale entertaining (1827–33). It also comprised the introduction of more commodious corridors at the back of the S and W ranges facing the courtyard (1830s). Of private rooms on the ground floor only one needs mention: the OAK ROOM, next to the chapel, which was decorated by the sixth Duke with woodwork bought at a sale in London and coming from an unnamed German monastery: timber columns and the backs of choir stalls with figures in relief. The date may be about 1700.

Close to Wyatville's N wing is the big quadrangle of *Paine's* STABLES, built for the fourth Duke in 1758–63. The design is characterized by a free use of cyclopic rustication (on the pattern of Giulio Romano and Serlio). The front has a central triumphal arch motif with four attached columns and the usual clock-turret with open cupola above. The columns are given big blocks of heavy rustication at intervals. Inside the courtyard are four rusticated giant gateways, and an open ground floor arcade rusticated throughout. The walls above it are ashlar-faced.

The GARDENS and Grounds are basically due to the first Duke in spite of many later alterations. He did as much outdoors as he did to the house. In 1699 the house was reached from the W, not the N (cf. above). An unornamental bridge crossed the river and led to a forecourt with iron palisade by *Tijou* and the stables and outbuildings in line on the N. To the SW, S, SE, and E were formal parterres with fountains and statuary and the Bowling Green. The parterres were laid out by the King's Gardeners *George London* and *Henry Wise*, each in the taste of the time a separate rectangle. On the S side of the Bowling Green stood the TEMPLE OF FLORA (1693–5) with its four slim Roman Doric columns and top balustrade. Further away to the S was the LONG CANAL, an indispensable piece of French garden design, and to the E the most dramatic piece, the CASCADE coming down from the Wilderness. This was begun in 1694.* Water was brought along from the hill tops and led to an 51 AQUEDUCT, a piece of Baroque romanticism which no visitor should miss: four rudely rusticated arches in the woods ending abruptly. From there the water falls down to a lower level, where flat terraces lead it towards the house; accompanying it is a more natural (C19) sequence of smaller waterfalls. In 1702 the CASCADE HOUSE was built at the top of the terraces, no doubt from the design of *Thomas Archer*. It has a stepped little dome, corners with intermittently rusticated pilasters coming forward in a curve, two twisting dolphins flanking the entrance arch, and rockery and figures on the parapet.

The grounds remained in their state of 1707, until the fourth Duke began his improvements. They all belong to the less than ten years during which he held the title. Their purpose was to convert the first Duke's formal gardens into a landscape in the sense of *Capability Brown*, who was indeed called in in 1760. New lawns coming right close to the house and a new gracefully winding approach walk with a handsome new BRIDGE (by *Paine*, 1762) were made and thereby the character of the surroundings of the house created which we admire to-day.

Yet the sixth Duke's taste also appears in the gardens, as it does everywhere. As can be seen in the case of so many properties landscaped in the C18, the Victorian taste insisted on the restoration of a more formal layout near the house. So statues and clipped trees arranged symmetrically came back, even if no embroidery parterres. In addition large structures went up for horticultural pur-

*Not incidentally on the pattern of Wilhelmshöhe near Cassel, as the sixth Duke says in his *Handbook*; for Wilhelmshöhe was laid out only in 1701. The examples for both were the Roman villas and especially the Villa Aldobrandiui of 1598–1603 and Villa Torlonia of *c.* 1610–28, both at Frascati.

poses, due at first more to the Duke's gardener, the great *Paxton*, than to the Duke himself. The most impressive of these, the Great Conservatory (1836–40), 276 ft long, 65 ft high, 'the glory of Chatsworth and the most extensive in the world' (Murray's *Handbook*, 1874), was unfortunately demolished in 1920. In more than one way it was the immediate predecessor of Paxton's Crystal Palace. But Paxton's forcing wall survives running E from the Temple of Flora and the N end of Wyatville's new wing.

Finally a few buildings which the sixth Duke put up further out in the park must be mentioned: the GATE LODGES of the Beeley and Baslow Gates, the SWISS COTTAGE, by the Swiss Lake with rather wild fanciful bargeboarding on its three-dimensional gable (above a bow window!), the Emperor Lake not far from the Swiss Lake (and altogether the surprising lake scenery up on the hill to the E of the house), and the RUSSIAN COTTAGE in the woods W of Beeley Bridge and S of Edensor, a compliment no doubt to the sixth Duke's friendship with the Tsar.

CHELLASTON

Chellaston was famous in the Middle Ages for its quarries of alabaster which was used for figure carving chiefly by Nottingham and Burton artists.

ST PETER. Small church consisting of a W tower, rebuilt in 1842, a nave and S aisle and lower chancel. The three-bay arcade with the usual octagonal piers and double-chamfered arches. The window tracery mostly elementary late C13 (intersected in the S aisle E window). The chancel is Perp. – FONT. Norman, plain.

CHELMORTON

ST JOHN THE BAPTIST. Low broad W tower with battlements and recessed spire. The spire has one tier of dormers low down and a girdle high up. The rest of the church of a lighter stone. It has a three-bay arcade between nave and S aisle with plain octagonal piers and double-chamfered round arches, and a four-bay N arcade with fine capitals and pointed arches. At the time when the N arcade was built, the S arcade was lengthened by one bay to match its length. This fourth bay opens into the S transept. The E wall of this is not in line with the chancel arch. So the building history is complex. As to dating, the S arcade can hardly be later than *c.* 1200. The S transept has a genuine S window of three stepped lancet lights and an E window of two lancet lights with pierced spandrel, i.e. a date *c.* 1300. The N aisle doorway (blocked) has a plain steeply pointed trefoil head, i.e. again *c.* 1300. Regarding the date of the chancel, its Sedilia and Piscina look mid C14. Perp clerestory (altered C19) and porch. – FONT. Octagonal, Perp. – ROOD SCREEN. Stone, Perp, low, embattled, with blank ogee arcade, and below the battlements openwork quatrefoils. – STAINED GLASS, E window, 1880, by *Jones & Willis* (TK).

Round Barrows on Chelmorton Lows.

CHESTERFIELD

ST MARY AND ALL SAINTS. A big long church (173 by 110 ft) of sombre grey ashlar stone with a crossing tower, lying in the centre of the old part of the town. It is nationally famous owing to the freak that its timber and lead spire has warped into a comically twisted shape. It is 228 ft high and leans 7½ ft to the S, 10½ ft to the SW, and 3 ft to the W. The warping is due no doubt to the effect of the sun on the lead. It is made more peculiar to the eye by the lead plates being laid herringbone fashion so that the whole spire looks channelled although the eight sides are in fact perfectly flat. The church consists of nave and aisles of six bays, S and N transepts (the latter rebuilt and provided with a pediment in 1769), and an E end of unusual complexity. The chancel is flanked by two-bay chancel chapels as long as the chancel (St Katherine's N, Lady Chapel S), and to the S of the southern one follows a much shorter chapel with polygonal E end (Lesser Lady Chapel), an unusual feature in England though common on the Continent, and to the N of the northern a short rectangular chapel (Holy Cross) with the vestry E of it. This multiplicity of chapels is due to the wealth of guilds in the town. The earliest, the Guild of Our Lady and the Holy Cross, was founded in 1218.

The oldest architectural piece in the church is the PISCINA in the Holy Cross Chapel, trefoiled, E.E. The oldest major parts are the supports of the crossing tower, and the transepts with the piers separating them from an E aisle later converted into the chapels mentioned above. They date from the late C13 or a little later; *see* the S transept S respond (many slim shafts with shaft-rings) and N respond (three sturdier shafts with fillets) – the pier between was later converted into a semi-Perp shape – the W respond of the S chancel chapel, the beautifully stiff-leaf-decorated N respond and pier of the N transept (the latter octagonal and with ornamentation, including human heads), and the crossing piers, each facing the crossing with six big shafts, the two main axial ones filleted. The crossing arches are treble-chamfered.

Most of the rest of the church is Dec, or *c.* 1325–50. Walking around the outside the central W window is of seven lights with one transome and flowing tracery, the side parts chiefly ogee reticulated, the centre branching out in divers leaf shapes. The W door (and the great E window) date from *Gilbert Scott's* restoration of 1843. The N transept N window is original Dec, the S transept S window of 1875. All the aisle windows are simple three-light Dec, the tall slim windows of the Lesser Lady Chapel two-light Dec, the Lady Chapel S windows ogee-reticulated. Perp replacement windows appear chiefly at the W ends of the aisles and at the E ends of the chancel aisles, also in the clerestory. The main S doorway is typical C14 in its fine filleted shafts and arch mouldings. The S transept doorway and N doorway are C19; the N transept doorway dates from 1769 (with pediment). The upper parts of the crossing tower have two two-light bell-openings on each side and a parapet instead of battlements.

As to the interior architecture nothing has yet been 16a

said of the nave which is very different in feeling from the accepted Derbyshire types. The piers are quatrefoil with hollows in the diagonals and fillets on the main shafts, very tall and thin, the capitals moulded and the arches provided with two wavy mouldings. The date is apparently later than the rest, *c.* 1350–75 perhaps. A crocketed ogee-headed recess in the S aisle. – The only old roof is in the S transept, Late Perp. The W gallery is a reminder of the restoration of 1842–3, carried out by *Gilbert Scott*, an early work of his, not yet as archeologically competent as his later jobs.

FURNISHINGS. REREDOSES. High Altar by *Temple Moore*, 1898; Holy Cross Altar by *Temple Moore Jnr*, 1922. – FONT. Norman, tub-shaped with leaf decoration; also a foliated cross; badly preserved. – PULPIT. Uncommonly courtly work of Jacobean style; note the openwork plaited balusters of the stair. Perhaps by the carvers of the Long Gallery at Haddon. – SCREENS. S transept with original ribbed coving. Each section is of four lights with a depressed arched top; each light ends in a steep crocketed arch; no panel tracery. The date is *c.* 1500. – N transept, St Katherine's Chapel (not in its original position) with three-light sections and simple Perp tracery. This was originally the rood screen of *c.* 1475. – N transept, Holy Cross Chapel (towards choir vestry), Perp, originally belonging to the Foljambe Chapel (1503–4). The present rood screen is of 1918. – ORGAN. 1756, by *Schnetzer*, beautifully carved case. – CANDELABRA. S chancel chapel, presented in 1760, originally in the nave. It is in two tiers and has, above the upper tier, lovely wrought iron decoration nearly up to the very top. – SCULPTURE. Head-corbels in the N transept E and W walls, also in the Lesser Lady Chapel. – STAINED GLASS. Lady Chapel (1844) and St Katherine's Chapel by *Warrington*. – S transept by *Hardman*, 1875. – Nave W by *Hardman*, 1890. – Holy Cross Chapel E by *Sir Ninian Comper*, 1941. – St Peter's Chapel by the same, 1943. – Lady Chapel E and chancel E by *Christopher Webb*, recent. – PROCESSIONAL CROSS (at back of Bishop's Chair), said to be Italian, early C16. From Wingerworth. – PLATE. Two large Flagons, given 1735; large Almsdish of 1808.

MONUMENTS. Effigy of a Priest, two angels by his pillow, early C14(?), in the S aisle recess. – Members of the Foljambe family at the E end of the Lady Chapel: Henry 27 Foljambe † 1510 and wife, alabaster tomb-chest with recumbent effigies, made by *Harper* and *Moorecock* at Burton-on-Trent and paid £10. Against the chest walls standing figures of mourners under crocketed ogee arches, mostly two in one panel, under a twin arch. – On the top of this monument kneeling figure of a boy, probably Sir Thomas † 1604 (the head does not belong to the body). – Sir Godfrey † 1541 and wife, brasses, kneeling children below. – Sir Godfrey † 1585 and wife, big 28 Renaissance tomb-chest with recumbent effigies, of the best quality available, both in the portraits and the strap decoration of the chest. – George † 1588, damaged incised alabaster slab. – Godfrey and wife, 1598 (S wall), very cosmopolitan big standing wall monument. Two recumbent effigies on a straw mat. They lie not on a tomb-chest but on a bulgy sarcophagus with sirens and thick garlands. Back-wall with two Sansovinesque standing allegorical figures between columns to the l. and r. of the inscribed tablet, and above in the scrolly pediment two reclining allegories and more ornament and fruit bunches. – The same Godfrey was responsible for the erection of the large epitaph with kneeling figure to Sir James Foljambe who had died in 1558. It is unusually flat and as delicate as Godfrey's own tomb. Note especially the fine representation of the children below. To the l. and r. of the kneeler are panels with fruit, etc., and to the l. and r. of these thin caryatids. – Finally there is, arranged symmetrically with the previous monument, that of another ancestor left without any inscription. This was also commissioned by Godfrey. It has the figure all bundled up in a shroud (as at Fenny Bentley). Above, a tripartite 'reredos' with fine fluted pilasters and Death in the middle and Old Age and Childhood l. and r. Bones, shovels, and hoes in the 'predella' below – a mysterious and extremely fascinating monument.

HOLY TRINITY, Newbold Road. Of elephant-grey ashlar, lancet windows, W tower with pinnacles. 1838, by *Johnson*, altered 1889 (GR).

ANNUNCIATION, R.C., Spencer Street, 1854, by *Joseph Hansom*. Quite big, the most impressive part the *Westwerk* as the Germans call it, i.e. the big broad tower-like erection at the W end. This was added in 1874.

METHODIST CHURCH, Saltergate, 1870. Big, of brick, seven bays long, with spectacular Renaissance front with attached portico of giant Ionic columns and pediment.

CONGREGATIONAL CHURCH, Rosehill, 1822, formerly Independent Chapel. Much re-done. The Tuscan doorway is original.

ELDER YARD CHAPEL, Unitarian, Elder Way, 1694, but altered. The front has quoins, plain horizontal string-courses, a central door, and two low mullioned windows.

FRIENDS' MEETING HOUSE, Saltergate, 1770. It lies back from the street, with the little graveyard in front. Red brick with door on the r., three-window front, and hipped roof.

TOWN HALL, Rosehill. By *Bradshaw, Gass, & Hope*, 1937–8. In a fine position overlooking the valley, with ample lawns around. It is of a scale quite different from the Chesterfield of before, and it has the ostentation-cum-gentility so favoured for such buildings. Brick and stone, with a central portico of six giant columns.

MARKET HALL, Market Place,, 1857, by *Davies & Sons*. The crudest show of High Victorian provincial prosperity. Brick, symmetrical with a tall tower with slated ogee top.

GRAMMAR SCHOOLS FOR BOYS AND GIRLS, Sheffield Road. They form a contrast characteristic of many schools, the boys (1846 plus 1860 and 1862) in a gloomy rock-faced Tudor, the girls (1911) in brick, bright with a cupola and a cheerful mixture of Baroque and Tudor motifs.

THE TOWN

Chesterfield is singularly poor in noteworthy houses of any style. A detailed perambulation is not called for. It is sufficient to enumerate half-a-dozen houses in the town and another half-dozen in the vicinity.

The only worthwhile survivor of the timber-framed architecture of the C16 is the ROYAL OAK just E of the Market Place, tidied up and a little embellished, but essentially sound. The C18 is represented by two houses in the MARKET PLACE, facing each other and very similar to each other. Both have three bays, three storeys, and arcaded ground floors. The date may be *c.* 1770. More ambitious a terrace in SALTERGATE (Nos 69–79), late C18, brick, with doorways with recessed Roman Doric columns and a four-bay pediment. In NEW SQUARE, W of the Market Hall the Food Office, a late C18 house with pedimented doorway and two symmetrical central bays. In ST MARY GATE (No. 42) a Late Georgian five-bay, three-storeyed stone house with quoins. Special mention must be made of the ruthless Chesterization of KNIFESMITHGATE, i.e. the recent erection of a number of big half-timbered shop and office buildings with arcades on the ground floors.

Testimony of early industry at Chesterfield is the former SILK MILL of *c.* 1757 (now Messrs Harrison) in MARKHAM ROAD and some buildings incorporated into the large factory of MESSRS ROBINSON in Wheatbridge Road: at the W end Walton Corn Mill, C13, three-storeyed with four-storeyed r. end with shoot, and Gampee Tissue Room with cast iron columns and arched brick floors; in the main group of buildings, S of Wheatbridge Road C18 Blacksmith's Shop in Mill Road and one small building of *c.* 1830 across Mill Road.

Outside the town proper the C17 with mullioned windows and gables is represented by HASLAND HALL, Calow Lane, symmetrical with two projections, and BIRDHOLME HOUSE, half-way to Wingerworth and the dower-house of Wingerworth Hall, partly early and partly late C17 (the late part has the mullioned windows tied to a string-course above to systematize them). The stables are Georgian. PARK HALL, Back Lane, Walton, also looks late C17. SOMERSALL HALL, ¼ m. N of Park Hall, is a three-bay house of 1763 with pedimented doorway and unusually attractive outbuildings, partly of the C17 and partly Gothick. Close to the back of Somersall Hall lies the remaining portion of the old Hall, gabled, of the C17. Larger and of brick, also C18, TAPTON HOUSE, ¾ m. NW of Chesterfield, on a hill. It is of *c.* 1800: seven by five bays with a three-bay pediment, once the residence of George Stephenson the engineer. Finally RINGWOOD HOUSE, 2½ m. NW, early C19, with verandah of coupled Ionic columns and entrance porch also of coupled Ionic columns.

CHURCH BROUGHTON

ST MICHAEL. Mostly early C14, but the NE arcade respond semicircular with scalloped capital, i.e. Norman. Of external early C14 features note the windows of the lower parts of the tower (with angle buttresses; the upper part with C19 pinnacles and big gargoyles beneath the battlements), the S aisle S doorway and windows, and the chancel windows. The N aisle E and W windows look a little earlier. Inside, the arcade on circular piers and the tower arch on semicircular imposts are clearly early C14. The first pier of the arcade from the W is wider than the others, consisting, as it were, of two imposts and a piece of wall between. At capital height the wall-piece has a head and a demi-caryatid instead of a capital. The arches two-stepped and only slightly chamfered. Good Sedilia and Piscina group in the chancel, ogee-headed, i.e. also early C14. C15 clerestory and roof. – FONT. Norman, of tapering tub shape, with a large zigzag motif and, superimposed on it, large intersected circles.

CHURCH GRESLEY

ST GEORGE AND ST MARY. A priory of Austin Canons was founded here in the early C12. Of this only the slightest remains can be seen E of the present parish church. This also incorporates the tower of the conventional church. In its E wall inside is a blocked treble-chamfered arch. The rest of the church and the top parts of the tower date from *c.* 1820 (chancel 1872). Nave and N aisle with the typical lancet windows of two lancet lights. The arcade looks as if it might be old and only heavily restored (octagonal piers, double-chamfered arches). – MONUMENT. Thomas Gresley † 1699, lifesize kneeling figure with two standing putti to the l. and r.

CLAY CROSS

ST BARTHOLOMEW, 1851, by *Stevens* (GR), with broach spire. Chancel altered and vestry added by *G. E. Street*.

WINDTHORPE HALL. Small manor house, Elizabethan or somewhat later.

PITHEAD BATHS. By *J. W. M. Dudding*, one of the many exemplary structures put up by the Miners' Welfare Commission.

CLOWNE

ST JOHN THE BAPTIST. Outside the industrialized village. Perp W tower with diagonal buttresses, battlements and pinnacles. Nave and chancel essentially Norman. S doorway with an order of colonnettes; the capitals have spiral decoration and the arch one roll-moulding. Norman chancel arch on imposts with three shafts, capitals with several volute and similar varieties. To the S of the chancel arch a Norman recess, perhaps in connexion with the altar at the E end of a former S aisle. Norman chancel doorway plain and narrow. In the S wall also one big lancet window. The E window Perp.

MARKLAND GRIPS. Earthwork ¾ m. SE of Clowne church, sited somewhat surprisingly in flat terrain. Rampart 600 ft long, 7 ft high.

CODNOR

ST JAMES, 1843, by *Robert Barker* (GR), quite pretty. Stone with narrow W tower, the body of the church an aisleless parallelogram with lancet windows, white inside, and with a W gallery on cast iron columns.

CODNOR CASTLE, 1 m. E. Visually impressive, with its cliff-like fragments of masonry rising to a height of

18 ft, but archaeologically not very telling, unless one is provided with a plan of the results of excavations. Codnor Castle was built by the Lords Grey of Codnor and later belonged to the Zouche family. It was surrounded by a park of 1,500 acres. It consisted of a Lower and an Upper Court. The former lies W and NW of the present farmhouse. It was separated from the Upper Court by a wall with two circular towers at the end and two circular turrets flanking the gateway. In the middle of its W side were two slightly projecting rectangular turrets. The Upper Court contained the most important living quarters, a three-storeyed structure. Masonry dates from two periods, the early C13 and the early C14. The Lower Court was an addition to the earlier Upper Court.

COMBE MOSS *see* CHAPEL-EN-LE-FRITH

COP LOW *see* HAZLEBADGE HALL

CORK STONE *see* STANTON MOOR

COTMANHAY NR ILKESTON

CHRIST CHURCH, 1847, by *Stevens* (GR). Small, of stone, with lancet windows and a polygonal bell-turret of the restraint typical of Stevens.

COTON-IN-THE-ELMS

ST MARY, 1844–6, by *Stevens*. Narrow W tower with recessed spire. The nave (unaisled) is wider than the tower. Two-light lancet windows with Dec tracery. The stone diagonally tooled; Stevens liked all kinds of tooling of his walls.

CRESSBROOK

CRESSBROOK MILL. The main building of twelve-bay width with a four-bay pediment and a lantern on the hipped roof is still entirely Georgian in appearance. Inside it has the typical early slender cross-shaped cast iron columns but timber beams. The date is 1815. Behind it a derelict yet older building with a narrow Gothick front towards the mill-stream: turrets, lancet windows, etc., similar in style to Castle Mill, Popplewick, Notts. This seems to have been built after a fire had consumed the first mill in 1785. It was the Apprentice House.

CRESWELL CRAGS

Grey cliffs of magnesian limestone (Permian); trees and shrubs overhang the rocks. The scale is small. The caves in the cliffs of this gorge ('the Cheddar of the North') are famous as the dwellings of Old Stone Age huntsmen. The inhabitants of the Pinhole, Mother Grundy's Parlour, and Robin Hood's Cave killed their reindeer, wild horse, and bison with flint-, ivory-, or bone-tipped lances. The caves were occupied during the rigours of a late glacial climate for a span of no less than a hundred thousand years, from Middle Palaeolithic to early Mesolithic times. The artefacts of these ancient huntsmen have been dignified with the name of the Creswellian Culture.

CRICH

ST MICHAEL. Quite an important church. The N arcade of three bays Norman with circular piers, round unchamfered arches of two steps, scalloped capitals to the E and W responds, and extremely elementary moulded capitals to the piers. N arcade with slightly more detailed capitals and single-chamfered arches, Late Norman. At each end a narrower pointed arch was inserted to connect the earlier work with the C14 chancel. This has ogee-reticulated (renewed) windows, i.e. *c.* 1320–50, and plain ogee-headed Sedilia. The N and S aisle windows are partly Dec and partly Perp. The Perp W tower has angle buttresses, a handsome parapet (with a wavy band with trefoils) instead of battlements, and a recessed spire with two tiers of dormer windows. In the outer wall of the N aisle as well as the inner wall are low ogee-headed tomb recesses. In the chancel N wall one of the rare built-in stone bible rests (cf. Spondon, Chaddesden, Etwall). – FONT. Plain Norman. – Two BENCH-ENDS with poppy-heads (one in the vestry). – MONUMENTS. In the N aisle recess good late C14 effigy of a bearded man in a long frock, presumed to be Sir Roger Bellairs † 1380. – Godfrey Beresford † 1513, carved figure of knight, chancel S side. – Incised slab to Jermane Pole † 1588 and wife, the inscription below, and the slab upright in the chancel wall. – Below it incised slab on tomb-chest to John Claye † 1632 and his two wives, kneeling children against the tomb-chest. – Ephraim Shelmardine † 1637, brass memorial to a baby, with portrait, the plate 5 by 8 in. in size. – An epitaph of 1857 by *Mannings* of London still completely in the classical tradition.

CROMFORD

It was at Cromford that Richard Arkwright started the first cotton spinning mill worked by waterpower. The foundation date is 1771, and the OLD MILL still stands, close to the Bridge (now a colour works and a laundry): stone, of three storeys, with a higher part which is probably the one that was in course of erection in 1777 (Bray). Towards the road the old buildings have no windows on the lower floors. The inside is an irregular courtyard. It all looks rather grim now and must always have looked forbidding. Bray tells us that 200 were employed, 'chiefly children. They work by turns, night and day.' The buildings have timber beams, i.e. they are not fireproof like Strutt's mills (*see* Belper). The water was supplied partly by Bonsall Stream and partly by the stream of an adit for draining mines called Cromford Meer Sough. The same stream is the chief source of the Cromford Canal which was built by Arkwright in 1793 and accompanies the view from Cromford downwards. In 1783 Arkwright built a second mill a little higher up, the MASSON MILLS. These have developed into a big modern building, but in their middle is still the original six-storeyed building with the staircase in a projection and a top cupola. The projection has the odd rhythm of small semicircular between Venetian windows on each floor. This second mill is of brick and also still with timber beams. Of brick also the Nonconformist CHAPEL to its S (1777), to which is attached a quite ambitious late C18 tall brick house (the

63

mill manager's?) with a Tuscan porch and a canted bay to the S. Behind this towards the river a lower range with carriageway and Venetian window above.

Between the two mills the dramatic break through the limestone rocks which is called Scarthing Nick. Behind this, away from the river, at r. angles, Cromford Village, one wide street with, on the r., the GREYHOUND INN, a fine mid Georgian house, like a minor Town Hall, five bays with a three-bay quoined and pedimented centre.

Past the Old Mill the church of Cromford, ST MARY, is reached. This was built by Arkwright in 1797 and gothicized in 1858. It has now the old narrow W turret, but in front of it a three-bay open Perp porch. The windows Perp lancets. An apsidal chancel was added. – The WALL PAINTINGS and the STAINED GLASS inside by *A. O. Hemming*, 1897. – MONUMENT to Mrs Arkwright, 1859, by *H. Weekes*.

By St Mary CROMFORD BRIDGE. This is C15 like Matlock Bridge (three pointed arches). At the Cromford end first an early C18 FISHING PAVILION, square, with pyramidal roof, and the inscription 'Piscatoribus sacrum'. Then, attached to the bridge, a C15 CHAPEL, recently restored (W doorway and one two-light mullioned window to its l.). Across the bridge BRIDGE HOUSE, partly Jacobean and partly Georgian, and a little nearer the bridge the Lodge (square and classical, but with two blank quatrefoils) to Willersley Castle.

WILLERSLEY CASTLE was Sir Richard Arkwright's residence. It was built in 1782–8 by *William Thomas* of London, an ambitious seven-bay stone structure of two and a half storeys with lower side wings facing the sheer face of the cliff across a sloping lawn and across the river. The house is entirely classical in conception, but romanticized by semicircular turrets flanking the broad centre bay and smaller circular turrets at the angles of the side wings. Torrington in 1790 called it 'an effort of inconvenient ill taste'. The interior was burnt out in 1791 and redone. The finest room is an oval hall with galleries on both upper storeys and a skylight.

57a

CUBLEY

ST ANDREW. Late Perp W tower with angle buttresses, large W door and large W window, and tall tower arch towards the nave. – Nave and S aisle have C17 windows with one mullion and one transome; they are much larger on the S side. The chancel is C13 with a broad five-light E window. The chancel arch has semicircular responds with rude faces. The arch is double-chamfered. The interior shows, however, that the earliest part of the church is the nave arcade, with circular piers, unchamfered arches, and one capital with a rudimentary leaf motif. The W respond rests on a head bracket. – FONT. Plain Norman. – PAINTING. Yellow and black ornamental painting on the chancel arch and the last arcade arch to the E. – STAINED GLASS. Fragments of C14 figures in the chancel windows. – MONUMENTS. Alabaster tomb-chest to Sir Nicholas Montgomery † 1494, the effigy defaced, the four angels holding shields who stand against the tomb-chest are in better preservation. – Alabaster tomb-chest without effigy but with good figures against the chest, e.g. one saint in amply draped mantle. The weepers hold shields. The monument is ascribed by Mr Gardner to *Harper* and *Moorecock* of Burton (cf. Chesterfield), i.e. 1500.

BENTLEY HALL, 1 m. E. Elizabethan or Jacobean brick and stone building with flat quoins. The front has a central canted bay window (the conversion of the ground floor into a porch in C19). Added on the W side is a late C17 wing with rusticated quoins and a centre that has a doorway with a scrolly pediment, two giant pilasters, and a segmental top pediment. The style is so similar to Sudbury Hall that it may well be by *Sir William Wilson*.

CURBAR

ALL SAINTS, 1868, by *Salvin Jnr* (GR). Nave, chancel, and bellcote; rockfaced.

LOCK-UP. Circular with conical roof. At the top end of the village, S of the village street.

CALVER MILL, ¼ m. W. The main six-storeyed stone block dates from 1785. It has circular cast iron pillars but originally the floors were of wood. Wheel House with segmental arches. 62b

STOKE HALL (*see* p. 225).

CUTTHORPE HALLS NR CHESTERFIELD

(OLD HALL with the main rooms in three storeys above each other and the staircase in an attached wing, probably early C17. The NEW HALL, ½ m. away, is the product of growth, C17 and C18 parts, it seems.)

DALBURY

ALL SAINTS. Small with embattled bellcote. The only noteworthy old feature the small lancet on the S side. In it a blackened STAINED GLASS figure of St Michael. The other lancets, however, also occur already in drawings of the 1820s. These show the bellcote in its present state too.

DALE ABBEY

DALE ABBEY was a house of Premonstratensian Canons founded about the year 1160. Little of it remains now on its delightful site below the sandstone cliffs, where a Derby baker whom a vision had compelled to abandon his worldly goods and live as a recluse, had made his hermitage. The chief surviving architectural fragment of the abbey is the great arch of the chancel E window (over 17 ft) with indications of ripe geometrical tracery, similar probably to Newstead Abbey and the Angel Choir at Lincoln, i.e. late C13. Excavations have shown the church to have possessed transepts 100 ft in length, a crossing tower, S chancel chapel, a cloister 85 ft square, and a nave of unknown length. The Chapter House on the E side of the cloister is still recognizable. It has a doorway of four orders of colonnettes and two piers along its centre. It is now the museum of the scanty finds made on the site (many foliated cross slabs, floor tiles, the effigy of a canon). To the S of the cloister the N wall of a cow-house 10b

STOKE-ON-TRENT PUBLIC LIBRARIES

indicates some vaulting of the former Refectory, and further SW an end of a cottage is locally connected with the monastic Kitchen. Still further away, to the NW of the site of the Abbey are the remains of the Gatehouse.

ALL SAINTS, the present church of the village of Dale Abbey, is in no provable way connected with the Abbey. It is one of the smallest and oddest of English churches. Its size is 26 by 25 ft and it is under the same roof with a dwelling house. The interior is cram-full of box pews, has a gallery, a pulpit of 1634 to the l. of the altar high up, an altar fitted with doors and drawers for communion plate and some interesting wall paintings (Annunciation, Visitation, Nativity, N wall, all late C13). There is also a badly preserved incised slab. The masonry of the nave is Norman (perhaps the Chapel of Depedale, mentioned in the late C12), the aisle was added soon after. Most of the details are Perp, especially the addition of the upper storey with its open timber roof.

CAT AND FIDDLE MILL. The only working windmill in the county.*

DARLEY ABBEY

DARLEY ABBEY was an Augustinian Priory moved to Darley from St Helen's, Derby, in the C12. Very little of it survives, mainly part of one corner house at the foot of Old Lane. The house now called Darley Abbey is a school in a Derby public park, early C18, seven bays, brick, with bays 1 and 7 slightly projecting. The central door up a pretty staircase with iron balustrade has a Gibbs surround. The projections are flanked by giant brick pilasters. The top is parapeted. The S front is simply Late Georgian, uncommonly well proportioned, with widely spaced windows. Outside the park the former Stables and other contemporary housing. This is probably connected with the MILL (Messrs W. Evans & Co.), a complete group of which the oldest part (No. 15) is five-storeyed, of brick, and has segmentheaded Georgian windows. It may well be as old as *c.* 1800.

* Information kindly supplied by Rex Wailes.

ST MATTHEW, 1818, by *Moses Wood* of Nottingham. Stone, unaisled, of Commissioners' type with tall slender windows with Perp tracery and angle pinnacles. The W tower is pinnacled too. The chancel is Victorian.

DARLEY DALE

ST HELEN. A cruciform church (cf. Ashbourne, Wirksworth, Hartington). The S transept has lancets on its E side, and the chancel has a S lancet. The N arcade inside (three bays) goes with that: circular piers, moulded capitals, double-chamfered arches. The chancel arch of the same design.* The S arcade is a little later: octagonal piers. Its date may be that of the tall steep three-light Dec S window of the S transept and identical N window of the N transept. The S aisle windows are C19. Perp E window of five lights, Perp N aisle windows, Perp battlements on nave and transepts, Perp nave roof with bosses, Perp W tower with angle buttresses and W door and W window decorated with head label-stops, etc. – FONTS. One circular, Norman, small, with ribbed edges, the other octagonal, Perp, with tracery motifs similar to Hartington. – SAXON CROSS. Fragment of a shaft, recently discovered and of great interest because of its remarkably antique geometrical ornament – PARCLOSE SCREEN, S aisle. Stone, single-light openings, plain Perp design. – STAINED GLASS. Ralph Gillum Memorial Window, S transept, † 1860, four tiers of three small storeys, in the most excellent early *Morris* style, no doubt by *Ford Madox Brown*, *Webb* and the others of the circle. – The window was made by *Powell's*. – MONUMENTS. Several coffin lids with foliated crosses. – Sir John de Darley *c.* 1330(?), cross-legged, bearded, and moustached knight, holding his heart in his hand (S transept). – Incised slab, ruinous, S aisle. – Incised slab to John Rollesley † 1513 and wife, incised slab to John Rollesley † 1535 and wife (S transept). 20

In the churchyard the battered remains of a huge yew tree,

* The S doorway into the nave is completely renewed, if not new. Its design is of C13 style.

one of the largest in girth in England (4 ft from the ground it is 33 ft in circumference).

THE HOLT, Two Dales, 1 m. NE. Very handsome three-bay, one-and-a-half-storey, stone house with extremely elongated main floor windows, and extremely elongated thin giant Ionic pilasters, coupled at the angles; *c.* 1800 probably. – In the garden 5 ft high stump of an Anglo-Saxon CROSS SHAFT, well preserved, with the usual interlace patterns of the C11 (cf. Hope, Norbury).

DARLEY BRIDGE, C15, two pointed arches with ribs.

DENBY

ST MARY. Small, the earlier parts of brown stone, the later pink and grey. C14 W tower with angle buttresses connected at the top by a horizontal band, and broach spire rising behind a parapet with a handsome frieze of pierced pointed trefoils. No W door, but an ogee-headed niche higher up on the W side. The chancel Dec with a characteristic three-light E window and equally characteristic two-light N and S windows. Nave with C15 clerestory and S aisle. The arcade is the oldest surviving part of the church: two bays, Transitional or earliest C13: circular pier with very plain moulded capital and double-chamfered arches. One of the responds with a little nail-head decoration. The Perp N arcade was removed in 1838 and a gallery put in. But the FONT may well be part of the pier. A special show-piece the S porch, not axial with the S door, stone-vaulted with the side walls divided into two panels by a vertical shaft.

DENBY OLD HALL, 1 m. N. The house consists of two parts, the r. one Elizabethan with mullioned windows, two gables, and a square central projection with round-headed porch, the l. one late C17 with somewhat projecting sides and a top parapet; no roof showing.

DERBY

INTRODUCTION

LITTLE CHESTER just N of Derby was a Roman station, Saxon fragments remain in St Alkmund's church. Under

Danish occupation Derby was one of the five boroughs of the Midlands. St Peter's has structural remains of interest proving the church to be the successor of one Norman. The tower of All Saints is one of the biggest Perp church towers of England; testifying to the trading prosperity of the town. Its staple goods were wood and lead. A Guild Merchant had been formed by permission of King John's charter of 1204. The extent of the old town of Derby can still clearly be seen from any map. It went roughly from Bridge Gate in the N by St Helen's Street and Ford Street to the W, on by Friary Street (where the Dominican Friary was) to St Peter's Street, the Castle and Morledge on the S. Surviving architectural evidence before the C18 is deplorably scarce. The Jacobean Café of 1677 in Wardwick is the chief domestic building, the County Hall of 1660 the chief – and indeed a very interesting – public building. The industrialization of Derby began with the erection in 1717 of John Lombe's Silk Mill, the earliest built in England. The wealth of the town in the C18 is obvious from the handsome Assembly Rooms, the many sturdy, massive, and matter-of-fact red brick houses in the centre replacing the half-timbered Derby of the past, and the only slightly more elegant dwelling houses *ante portas*, chiefly in Friargate. The C19 brought a gradual not very spectacular increase in population and area (1801 *c.*11,000, 1821 *c.* 17,500, 1841 *c.* 33,000, 1861 *c.* 43,000, 1881 *c.* 58,000, 1901 *c.* 69,000). It was only within the first third of the C20 that Derby suddenly grew from a provincial town to a city (population 1931 *c.* 142,000; since then more or less stationary). This at first slow and then rapid growth has not brought the town much addition of architectural character. The chief Victorian improvement in the centre was the filling in of the stream which ran through Victoria Street and the making of Albert Street about 1850. Neither the C19 and C20 public buildings nor the Victorian churches are in any way remarkable. Commercial architecture has on the whole been sober and dignified right through the C19. Abominations are absent, but also the pleasures of fancy and folly.

CHURCHES

15 CATHEDRAL CHURCH OF ALL SAINTS. Raised to the rank of a cathedral in 1927. Until then the chief parish church of the town. Its W tower dates from the early C16, the rest was rebuilt by *James Gibbs* in 1723–5 (builder: *Francis Smith* of Warwick). Both parts are of high architectural quality. The tower is tall, square, broad and stately, the one powerful accent in the skyline of Derby. It has three tall storeys, all highly decorated with friezes, canopies, etc. The buttresses nearly meet at the angles. The ground floor has a big W door, the second stage large blank three-light windows with four-centred tops and blank decorative niches. The bell-openings on the third stage are equally large, of four lights with panelled tracery. The top of the tower has ornamented battlements, and very big pinnacles. The body of the church appears low compared with the C16 work. It spreads out broadly, has only one storey of large roundheaded windows and is crowned by a balustrade. The E end has a central Venetian window and a big pediment across nave and aisles. Door and window surrounds show a surfeit of Gibbs's favourite motif of intermittent rustication. As the windows are all separated from each other by coupled pilasters, the rhythm of the sides is comfortably unhurried. The general view of the church is ruined from far as well as near by the insane idea of building a power station immediately to its E.

16b The INTERIOR also appears broad and relatively low. It is designed on the same principle as Gibbs's St Martin's-in-the-Fields. Nave and aisles separated by Tuscan columns on tall pedestals (to allow for box-pews). Each column carries its own separate piece of entablature. The aisles are groin-vaulted, the nave tunnel-vaulted. The arcade arches cut into the tunnel-vault. The vaults are rather poorly decorated with panels. – PULPIT with Tester on two columns, 1873, by *Temple Moore*. – ALTAR AND ALTAR SURROUND classical with much gilding by *Sir Ninian Comper*. – CHOIR STALLS by *Temple Moore*,

1894. – PANELLING and raised seat in the N chancel chapel (Consistory Court), from the time of the building of the church. – W GALLERY: 1732–3, on fluted Ionic columns, extended through the aisles in 1841. The old centre part curves back gracefully and carries the organ. BISHOP'S THRONE, C18, apparently of foreign workmanship. Said to come from Asia Minor. – CUPBOARD in N chancel chapel, early C18, richly carved, Flemish. – SCREENS: the most important possession of the cathedral. Wrought ironwork by *Robert Bakewell*, the brilliant local smith who died in 1752. Partly continued by his pupil *Benjamin Yates*. Also probably by *Bakewell* the COMMUNION RAILS and the STANDS for Mace and Sword belonging to the Corporation Pew. – STAINED GLASS: E window with Crucifixion by *Clayton & Bell*, 1863, surprisingly vigorous for its date, strong colours, good faces. – PLATE: Chalice and Paten 1693; set of two Chalices and Patens, two Flagons and one Almsdish, London-made, given by the Earl of Exeter in 1727; two tall Vases, given 1828, their shape and decoration already very close to the Victorian taste.

19b

MONUMENTS: Alabaster slab to Sub-Dean Lawe, C15, incised figure surrounded by architecture with smaller decorative figures; the workmanship mediocre (N chancel chapel). – Timber monument with decayed timber effigy, small figures of mourners and fragment of GISANT or cadaver below (perhaps Sub-Dean Johnson, *c.* 1527; S aisle). – Elizabeth Countess of Shrewsbury † 1607, better known as Bess of Hardwick (cf. Hardwick for her life). Standing wall monument. Recumbent effigy of alabaster, not specially good. Black columns to the l. and r. and between them a shallow coffered arch. Back wall with inscription and strapwork cartouche. Above the entablature two obelisks and a tall central achievement. The monument stands in the S chancel chapel which was the Cavendish Chapel. In the middle stood until 1876 the monument to the second Earl of Devonshire († 1628). In the vault beneath the chapel over 40 members of the family were buried between 1607 and 1848. – Richard

Crowshawe † 1631, epitaph with kneeling figures (N aisle). – William Allestry † 1655 and his wife † 1638, epitaph with sarcophagus and four columns; no effigies (N aisle). – Sir William Wheler † 1666 large epitaph with two busts high up (N aisle). – Thomas Chambers † 1726 and his wife † 1735, by *Roubiliac*, a tripartite composition with the centre filled by the inscription below a pediment; in the sides two fine busts in circular niches. – Caroline Countess of Bessborough † 1760, daughter of the third Duke of Devonshire, by *Rysbrack*, standing wall monument, seated allegorical figure with bust behind to her l. on a bracket, the whole against a black pyramid. – Will. Ponsonby Earl of Bessborough † 1793, by *Nollekens*, epitaph with bust above a sarcophagus. – Richard Bateman † 1821, signed by *Chantrey* (who was born on the Derbyshire border), 1822, epitaph with weeping seated female by an urn. – Mary Elizabeth Chichester † 1830, by *Sir R. Westmacott*, small epitaph with reclining figure on a couch in a gently recessed oval panel. – Innumerable minor epitaphs.

ST ALKMUND, Bridge Gate, 1846 by *H. J. Stevens*. An ambitious building marking the beginning of Victorian prosperity. Ashlar stone slightly rock-tooled, tall nave with openwork balustrade, aisles, tall C14–looking piers inside, tall tower with spire supported by flying buttresses. – FONT. C14, octagonal, with two simple blank arches to each side; badly preserved. – SCULPTURE. In the S porch high up two small Anglo-Saxon panels, rudely carved, one with the Virgin and Child in an arcade, the other with two little men in narrow arcades. In the churchyard Saxon fragments with interlace have been found and are now at the Museum and Art Gallery. – MONUMENT: John Bullock † 1607, alabaster effigy, very long figure and extremely small head; on the tomb-chest much strapwork decoration.

ST ANDREW, London Road, 1866, by *Sir George Gilbert Scott*, tower and spire after his death 1881. Big church in surroundings of no character. C13 detail, NW tower with broach spire, apsidal chancel.

ST AUGUSTINE, Upper Dale Road, by *Naylor & Sale*, 1897. Brick with a little flèche and no tower. Two W porches into the aisles.

CHRIST CHURCH, Normanton Road, 1839–40, by *Habershon*. Plain ashlar-faced parallelogram, W tower with spire supported by flying buttresses. Lancet windows.

ST JOHN THE EVANGELIST, Bridge Street, 1828, by *Francis Goodwin*, apsidal chancel 1871. Ashlar-faced parallelogram with aisles and galleries. Tall coupled side windows with a little geometrical tracery, tall entrance niche. No tower, but four angle-turrets and odd pinnacles with far projecting castellated tops.

ST MARY (Roman Catholic), Bridge Gate, 1838–9, by *Pugin*. Enlarged in 1853. Ashlar-faced. Tall rather narrow W tower (ritual W; in fact S) of four stages. The lean-to roofs of the aisles appear behind it, also rather tight. Tall narrow nave separated from the aisles by slender piers without capitals. Clerestory with twice as many windows as bays in the arcade. All the detail still Perp. Later Pugin preferred the late C13 and early C14 centuries. The finest motif is the slightly lower, vaulted choir with an apse, all glazed above the base. – The STAINED GLASS is in an *altdeutscher* style by *Warrington*. – The small RECTORY to the E, brick with Gothic details, is contemporary.

ST MARY'S CHAPEL, Bridge Gate. One of the few surviving chapels built on bridges. The original C15 chapel was of stone, and the springing of the first arch of the old bridge can still be seen below the E end of the chapel. It is a picturesque sight with the straight-headed Perp E window and a half-timbered gable above. Much repair work in brick. The most recent restoration was 1931. Small aisleless interior.

ST MICHAEL, Queen Street, 1858, by *H. J. Stevens*. Stone-faced with a curious horizontal ribbed rock-facing. Imitation C13 detail, the interior inspired by St Peter's. – STAINED GLASS. E window by *Lavers* (TK).

ST OSMUND, London Road, Osmaston, 1904, by *P. H.*

Currey. A pleasant brick church with lancet windows, transept and a flèche. Low circular piers inside and a very tall, well-lit clerestory. Sunk garden in front and a group of cottages on the N side of it as part of the composition.

ST PAUL, Mansfield Road, 1849, by *Barry & Brown*. Quite a nice group with a symmetrically placed tower and transeptal wings.

ST PETER, St Peter Street. The only medieval church of Derby, although the exterior, except for the E end, looks new. The W tower was rebuilt in 1898, the S aisle heavily restored. The S aisle windows are of five lights with strongly elongated, uncusped ogee-reticulation. The N aisle and the W parts of the chancel have normal ogee-reticulated tracery. In the E parts of the N aisle, however, is a pretty design of tracery, consisting chiefly of pointed quatrefoils. It must be early C14, earlier probably than the ogee-reticulated tracery. The E end has a five-light Perp window. The picturesque two-storeyed NE vestry was added after the completion of aisle and W parts of chancel (blocked windows). The interior reveals the E wall of the nave to be Norman. The responds of the nave arcades have scalloped capitals. The rest of the N arcade has slim circular piers with simple moulded capitals, of the S arcade octagonal piers. The arches are double-chamfered. The aisles are comfortably wide and have lean-to roofs of flat pitch. The bulk of the church is evidently an early C14 rebuilding. – STAINED GLASS. E window by *Barber* of York (TK) very yellow and with much heavy canopy-work. – Behind the church, facing the churchyard is the former CHURCH SCHOOL, now Parish Hall, with mullioned and transomed windows and gables. The date probably early C17.

ST THOMAS, Richmond Road, 1881, by *Peacock*. Rock-faced. In the Norman style, with a silly conical flèche. A low porch with 'dwarf gallery' across the W front.

ST WERBURGH, Friargate. The C15 tower collapsed and was rebuilt in 1601 (*see* the Gothic bell openings and the obelisk pinnacles). The church was rebuilt in 1699. Of that building only the chancel remains. The rest was again rebuilt in 1893–4 by *Sir Arthur Blomfield*. He changed the orientation so that the altar is now in the N, and the old chancel is a long side chapel. This still possesses its fine Reredos with carved Royal Arms above, and some other wood-work. – FONT COVER wrought iron, by *Bakewell*, 1718, with scrolly leaf motifs; very attractive.* – PULPIT. Wrought iron, designed by *Blomfield*, 1894. – STAINED GLASS by *Kempe*, 1894–9. – MONUMENTS. Sarah Winyates, by *Chantrey* 1832, kneeling female by urn, rather hard. – Many minor epitaphs.

METHODIST CHURCH, King Street, 1841. A fine, stately Grecian front with a one-storeyed Greek Doric porch, and an upper floor with Ionic pilasters, arched windows and a pediment. Lower projecting wings.

UNITARIAN CHURCH, Friargate. The building is late C17, brick, with stone quoins. What is now visible belongs largely to 1890. The church was originally Presbyterian.

FRIENDS' MEETING HOUSE, St Helen's Street, 1808. Plain stone-faced rectangle with arched windows and hipped roof.

CEMETERY, Uttoxeter Road, 1842. A stone chapel with starved lancet windows by the entrance.

PUBLIC BUILDINGS

COUNTY HALL, St Mary's Gate. A remarkably interesting building of 1660. It lies back from the road, with the County Library (formerly an Inn) on one side of the *cour d'honneur* and a brick building of 1811 on the other. The façade of the Hall is of five bays, with tall arched windows in the first, third, and fifth bays (the mullions and transomes are typical of the date) and ornate doorways in the second and fourth. These have scrolly broken pediments of a style similar to the C17 buildings at Bolsover and Nottingham Castle. The inside is one large room with sparing classical decoration. – MONUMENT to F. N. Clarge Mundy, with bust, by *Chantrey*, 1820. 59b

TOWN HALL, Market Place, 1841, by *Habershon*. Dark

* Probably also by *Bakewell* the GATES beside the church.

stone with tall central tower with domed top. The detail late classical. The inscription proudly calls it the Forum Municipale. *The Builder*, in 1897, said of it that 'the detail is largely tinctured with Greek influence, but where Greek precedent has not sufficed, the architect has resorted to a modification of Italian Renaissance, supplemented by a certain amount of originality.' Behind the Town Hall is the large MARKET HALL of 1864, by *Thorburn* (altered by *Thompson*). It is 220 by 110 ft and has a tunnel-vault of iron and glass.

COUNCIL OFFICES, Corporation Street, 1938–41, by *C. H. Aslin*. A poor design in an C18 style. Brick and stone dressings, L-shaped, with a giant portico facing the roundabout at the meeting of the two ranges.

60b ASSEMBLY ROOMS, Market Place, 1763–74. Handsome five-bay stone-faced front with raised pedimented three-bay centre. Charming hall inside with coved stuccoed ceiling.

LIBRARY AND MUSEUM, Wardwick, 1878, by *Knill Freeman* of Bolton. Brick, in a Gothic style with a Franco-Flemish central tower and much decoration by means of those moulded tiles with diapered leaf and similar motifs which were so popular in the seventies. At the back (facing the Strand) the ART GALLERY, 1883, by *Story* of Derby. To the r. of the front the IRON GATES of the old Silk Mill (*see* Perambulation below) have been re-erected (*Robert Bakewell* at his best).

SCHOOL OF ART, Green Hill, 1876, by *Waller* of Gloucester. Neo-Gothic. Additions 1899.

MECHANICS' INSTITUTION, Wardwick, 1881, by *Sheffield & Hill*, typical of the remarkably sober if somewhat gloomy style of city architecture at the time in Derby.

DERBY SCHOOL, St Helen's House, King Street. An excellent stone-faced Palladian mid C18 front of seven bays with a three-bay centre with an attached giant Ionic portico above a rusticated ground floor and crowned by a pediment. The main first floor windows have alternatingly triangular and segmental pediments. Staircase with fine wrought iron handrail.

BEMROSE SCHOOL, Uttoxeter Road, 1930, by *Macpherson & Richardson.*

GENERAL INFIRMARY, London Road. By *Young & Hall*, *c.* 1890.

ARBORETUM, 1840. Designed by *John Claudius Loudon*, and given to the town by Joseph Strutt. It is the earliest public park of any English town. The size is moderate, the style mildly picturesque, with plenty of artificial undulation. The chief importance according to the donor was the large variety of different trees. The original lodges (by *E. B. Lamb*) were Elizabethan. But there also was from the beginning a debased-Italianate pavilion. The equally flabbily Italianate Gateway towards Arboretum Square was added about 1850.

GENERAL POST OFFICE, Victoria Street, 1869. *The Builder* in 1897 said: 'An admirable piece of dignified and restrained design in Classical Renaissance – somewhat cold perhaps.' In its dark stone a characteristic example of mid C19 commercial architecture in Derby.

MIDLAND REGION RAILWAY STATION. Incorporated into the building are considerable remains of *Francis Thompson's* celebrated Trijunct Station of 1840.

ST MARY'S BRIDGE, rebuilt 1788. For the Chapel of St Mary *see* above.

DERWENT BRIDGE, 1929, by *C. H. Aslin.*

PERAMBULATION

The MARKET PLACE is the best centre to start from. For Town Hall and Assembly Rooms *see* Public Buildings above. Otherwise a few minor C18 houses, especially Nos 2–3 and 18–19. On the W side the former Bank of Samuel Smith & Co., a good dignified classical structure. E and then N of the Market Place FULL STREET, much interfered with by the recent improvements near the Derwent Bridge. No. 4 is a three-storeyed C18 brick house of five-bay width. It has the rusticated stone lintels typical of much Georgian architecture at Derby. Nos 45–46 is a C17 house with two gables to the street. Behind the Power Station, whose ignoble role in the visual aspect of Derby has already been mentioned, lay John Lombe's Silk Mill of 1717, the first to be established in England. It was a tall broad structure essentially like factories of a hundred years later (*see* an engraving of Derby dated 1728). About 1775 it employed 200 hands. It made use of the power of the river.

N of the Market Place IRONGATE starts. At the corner of SADLER GATE Lloyds Bank, early C18, brick with decorated keystones to the windows. In Sadler Gate two interesting houses: One in No. 53, the Old Bell Hotel, a very restored timber-framed building with brick infillings; four gables at the top; rainwater-heads 1717. The other is No. 48a, later C17, with a heavy doorcase with a segmental pediment displaying the date 1675, first floor with Georgian windows, but the second floor windows evidently C17 (mullion-and-transome-crosses). The gable is at right angles to the street and still of the early C17 shaped kind. – In IRONGATE the best building is No. 27, C18, brick, four-storeyed, with decorated keystones. – Off by the Cathedral to the W into ST MARY'S GATE meeting the W tower of the cathedral axially. Here again three remaining groups of Georgian brick houses. The group at the corner of Irongate, with Nos 40–42 especially successful in a modest way. At the corner of Jury Street the COUNTY LIBRARY, an Early Georgian inn with rusticated lintels and keystones. On the first floor Royal Arms. – Just S of the W end of St Mary's Gate in BOLD LANE the former THEATRE of 1773, an unobtrusive stuccoed front of three bays, the interior entirely remodelled.

Irongate is continued to the N in QUEEN STREET. Here the DOLPHIN INN, timber-framed gabled C16 house, much restored. Off Queen Street in ST MICHAEL'S LANE on the N side the former METHODIST CHAPEL, the first of Derby; in it Wesley preached in 1765. It is a brick rectangle, very plain, with arched windows. The N continuation of Queen Street is KING STREET, where No. 97 is the SEVEN STARS INN, a small but interesting house. It is dated 1680 and has a narrow gabled front.

The front is divided by four string courses, a broad one above the low ground floor, a second at eaves level, and two more in the gable. It is this demonstrative emphasis on horizontals alone that indicates the date of the house. The few original windows still low and mullioned.

From King Street to the E BRIDGE GATE leads towards the bridge. Several Georgian brick houses. More worth inspecting No. 86, a picturesque gabled later C17 brick house. Behind St Alkmund's Church ST ALKMUND'S CHURCHYARD, as a revival of C18 Derby unmatched, a quiet oasis although close to the traffic of the town centre. No houses are specially noteworthy, but the ensemble is very satisfying. From the Market Place S CORNMARKET (Nos 29–30 and Nos 31–36 good examples of how stately the brick buildings of C18 Derby were, one five-bay, one nine-bay front, both pedimented) and farther S St Peter's Street, and then at the N end of LONDON ROAD the COLISEUM Cinema, originally a Congregational Chapel, built in 1842, stuccoed with four-column detached portico and arched windows.

From the S end of Cornmarket W VICTORIA STREET. At the corner the fine group of the ROYAL HOTEL of 1839 (by *R. Wallace*), divided into two parts, the one at the corner rounded and stone-faced with giant Ionic demi-columns, the other long, stuccoed and with a minimum of Grecian detail. Originally the group was Hotel and Athenaeum. Inside, on the first floor, the fine, large, well-preserved Dining Room. On into WARDWICK where the JACOBEAN CAFÉ is a tall two-gabled building, dated 1677 (rather than 1611). Brick and stone dressings, mullioned windows.

The continuation of Wardwick is FRIARGATE, the best 60a street of Derby, although halfway down crossed by a railway bridge (with the most fanciful lacey cast-iron balustrade and spandrels). Many of the houses deserve attention. Most of them are mid Georgian. It is sufficient to single out on the N side: Nos 16–17 (eight bays, four gables, C17 with early C18 glazing-bars to the windows), No. 27 (five-bay, C18, red brick, Tuscan doorcase, centre window on the first floor pedimented), Nos 29–32, No. 41 (five-bay, with three-bay pediment, C18, red brick, Roman doorcase with pediment), No. 42 (five-bay red brick, with one-bay projected centre), Nos 43–44 (three-bay, brick, ground floor with two Venetian windows l. and r.), Nos 47–51 (eleven bays, ashlar faced, with two double porches l. and r. and three-bay pediment in the middle, Late Georgian), No. 56 (five-bay, brick), No. 57 (five-bay brick), etc. to No. 65 (eight-bay brick), Chestnut House (ashlar-faced with Greek-Doric porch, i.e. *c.* 1825) and Georgian House (three-bay, three-storey, brick, with tripartite windows, the top ones semi-circular. On the S side, also from E to W, Nos 116–117 (Georgian brick), Nos 114–115 (C17, two-gabled), No. 111 (C16–17, gabled with overhang), Savings Bank (good symmetrical stone-faced building in the Neo-Greek taste, 1839–40 by *Stevens*), Friary Hotel (fine detached seven-bay mansion of three storeys; elaborate window frames, giant angle pilasters, top parapet; a lower wing on the l.; good panelled room inside, also some stucco-work); No. 103 (corner house with rusticated window lintels), No. 100 (also with rusticated lintels), No. 99 (five bays, three storeys, Tuscan doorcase). Off Friargate at the S end of VERNON STREET with its nice ensemble of modest early C19 terraces, the one-storeyed, plastered, broad, long and forbidding Greek-Doric front of the former GAOL by *Goodwin.* Friargate continues in ASHBOURNE ROAD with a few more notable houses, mostly early C19, stuccoed. Especially stately No. 34 with one-storeyed stone porch on Tuscan columns. No. 35 opposite is mid C18, brick, of five bays with pedimented doorway.

DERWENT WOODLANDS *see* LADYBOWER

DETHICK

ST JOHN THE BAPTIST. In a fine position on a hill close to the buildings replacing the manor house of the Babingtons and the surviving big stone-built C16 BARN. The view to the S across the valley is splendid. The church possesses, thanks to Sir Anthony Babington, a lavishly built W tower, dated 1539. It has diagonal buttresses and the unusual feature of a tall polygonal SE stair-turret. The windows are Late Perp, and a frieze with a proud display of the shields of Sir Anthony and his kinsmen runs below the bell-openings. Eight short pinnacles on the battlements. The tower arch towards the nave is surprisingly narrow for its height. The church itself is insignificant after this monumental tower, aisleless and without visible division between nave and chancel. Two lancet windows show that it is C13, and the difference in material shows that the clerestory was later. No furnishings of interest.

CHRIST CHURCH, 1901–3, by *P. H. Currey*. With big crossing tower and freely Perp details. The position is as fine as that of the old church.

LEAHURST, ½ m. S. C17 gabled house with low mullioned windows, much enlarged in 1825.

LEA WOOD, W of Leahurst. By *Nesfield*, 1870–6, in the typical style of this architect and his partnership with young Norman Shaw. Many materials freely mixed: stone, fancy tiling, tall brick chimney-stacks, half-timbered gables, and plaster infillings with incised floral patterns. Not at all connected with local traditions.

LEA HALL, 1 m. NE. Early Georgian stone building of five bays, the centre bay distinguished by Roman Doric giant pilasters. Door with pediment and Gibbs-surround. Short brick side bays.

DOLL TOR STONE CIRCLE *see* STANTON MOOR

DOVERIDGE

ST CUTHBERT. The church was in the grounds of Doveridge Hall. Now that the Hall has been pulled down, it lies in a happy green solitude close to the river Dove. Lately, however, Uttoxeter housing has begun to creep towards it. To its E a very old yew tree and a yew canopy. The building itself is distinguished by its broad and wide C13 chancel with fine long lancet windows and a S doorway with one filleted order, and a W tower in its lower parts Norman (recently discovered corbel-table and arch into the nave), but remodelled in the C13. The tower windows are lancets and above coupled lancets with dog-tooth decoration. The upper parts of the tower and the spire recessed behind the broad battlements are later. The aisles have Dec windows with flowing (S, renewed?) and reticulated tracery (N). The nave is very wide too and the absence of a chancel arch (and of stained glass) emphasizes the airiness of the interior. The N arcade is of three bays, the S arcade of four smaller ones. Both sides have octagonal piers and double-chamfered arches. The C13 W tower arch is very low and narrow; the clerestory is C15. – STAINED GLASS. Jumbled fragments of medieval glass in the SW window. – MONUMENT. Big epitaph to William Davenport † 1640 and his wife † 1639. Of her the inscription says:

Wearied with lingering motion drop erewhile
A star to rest under this quiet pile
Whose unstain'd lustre more adorned her sphere
Than all the glorious beauties sparkled there.

DRONFIELD

ST JOHN THE BAPTIST. A dark grey church with a Perp W tower with spire, and a tall chancel, more ambitious than the rest of the church. Its high and wide N and S windows have (renewed) early C14 tracery, intersected; but at the top the intersections are interrupted and replaced by a cusped quatrefoil. The E window is very odd indeed, of seven lights and only divided by mullions and transomes: no curve, no diagonal. Is it C17? To the N of the chancel is a two-storeyed vestry. The S aisle has intersected E and W windows, also with the top intersections replaced by quatrefoils, but here within circles. The S doorway goes with that date. Inside, the tower-arch tells of a date earlier than the exterior reveals. The imposts on the nave arcades look early C14. In the chancel an ugly modern roof, an ogee-headed doorway into the vestry and Sedilia with thin filleted shafts and thickly crocketed ogees and gables. The arches are double-cusped with small figures in the cusps. The Piscina, against the custom quite away from the Sedilia, is of two lights with ogee tracery. – STALLS. Some old parts, also poppy-heads. – PULPIT. Jacobean, of very good quality, similar to that at Chesterfield. The columns are studded with small knobs all over. – PLATE. Paten of c. 1530. – MONUMENTS. Plate with brasses of two Priests, Thomas and Richard Gomfrey, 1399, the figures c. 33 in. long. – Sir Richard Barley, alabaster effigy of mid C15 date on tomb-chest with angels holding shields. – Brass to John Fanshawe † 1580, wife and children.

THE TOWN. Dronfield must have been especially prosperous in the C18. The town and the outskirts have a remarkable number of sizeable mansions. At the far end of the High Street the MANOR HOUSE (Council Offices), probably early C18, with upright windows of one mullion and one transome, hipped roof and Tuscan pilasters to the l. and r. of an arched doorway. In front of it the highly Gothic TOWN CROSS, erected in 1848 to commemorate the repeal of the Corn Laws. The UNITED METHODIST CHURCH, though dated 1863, is still Late Georgian in style with arched door, arched windows and pediment. Opposite the church the former Grammar School HEADMASTER'S HOUSE, dated 1731. This is of brick with quoins, as is the neighbouring and contemporary OLD VICARAGE with two canted bay-windows.

The other houses are farther away. CHIVERSTON HOUSE to the W, across the railway, just above the A Road, is dated 1712. It has a symmetrical front with the same windows as the manor house but still a middle gable. The doorhead is depressed segmental and rusticated. Next to it ROSE HILL in spite of its date, 1719, still with low mullioned windows and a thin semicircular doorhead (like the Peacock at Rowsley, 1652). It combines two symmetrical outer gables with a balustrade between, i.e., the old and the new roof motifs (cf. Bagshaw Hall Bakewell, 1684). HALLOWES GOLF CLUB HOUSE lies on the hill to the SE. This, of H-shape, with gables on the wings, has a date stone 1657 over the door and on the other side an C18 segmental pediment over the other door. The windows are low and mullioned, but their arrangement is symmetrical and they are tied to a long uninterrupted string course.

DUFFIELD

ST ALKMUND. Outside the village, to the SE. W tower with angle buttresses connected on top by a horizontal band below the battlements; recessed spire. Tower arch to the nave treble-stepped. All this looks C14, and probably early. The church is much restored, and it is not certain how much of the detail is reliable. N aisle, E window, and N transept E window of three stepped lancet lights, i.e. *c.* 1300 or earlier. Chancel E window Perp of five lights with panel tracery. The other windows straightheaded (S aisle windows C19). The interior has three-bay arcades on both sides with octagonal piers and double-chamfered arches. The N chamfering seems earlier. The date is controversial. Dr Cox called the N arcade C17, Mr Ward thinks of a Norman core much remodelled. In the chancel N wall a broad low ogee-arched recess. – MONUMENTS. Sir Roger Mynors † 1536 and wife, alabaster effigies on a tomb-chest with saints in round-arched cusped panels. – Anthony Bradshaw † 1614; a remarkably original standing wall-monument set up in 1600. No effigies; instead a frieze dividing the substructure with rusticated pillars and inscription tablets from the superstructure also with rusticated pillars. On top are inscription plate and obelisks and achievement. On the frieze incised demifigures of husband in the middle, two wives at the outer corners and twenty children between, four sons on the left of the father, sixteen daughters in two tiers to the right of the father. All figures have their initials to the l. and r. of their heads. Acrostic at the foot of the inscription below the figures.

DUFFIELD CASTLE, one of the most formidable Norman fortresses in England, was erected by the Ferrers, a leading family in the county. It had a keep of 95 by 93 ft with walls *c.* 15 ft thick. The size of the keep was thus only matched by the White Tower in London and by Colchester. Nothing of it remains above ground. The mound is at the bottom end of Castle Hill.

DUFFIELD HALL (St Ronan's School for Girls). The main block is Elizabethan or a little later, with two bay-windows of 1870. A large W addition also of 1870 and a smaller on the r. of the main (E) front. Farther W on the N side a rectangular outbuilding older than the rest.

The village street S of the Castle is unusually rich in Georgian houses. Note especially by the N end a three-bay brick house with tripartite windows and with Adamish trim, then THE FERNS (brick, three bays, one-bay pediment, quoins at the angles and flanking the centre bay), THE MEADOWS with its stables, Later Georgian (also brick), and the delightful BAPTIST CHAPEL of 1830 with brick front facing the little triangular churchyard to the S. A dwelling house is attached to the chapel.

EASTWOOD HALL *see* ASHOVER

ECKINGTON

SS PETER AND PAUL. A church of exceptional architectural interest for its contribution to the C12 and C13 styles in Derbyshire. The tower is the most impressive piece, big and square, with broad, flat buttresses, an ambitious picturesquely decayed W doorway of three orders with E.E. detail but a round arch, two large lancets on the stage above, then one small lancet, and then the bell stage with three lancets towards each side. All this can hardly be later than the first years of the C13. The spire (with one tier of dormer windows) is recessed behind a parapet (no battlements). It is relatively broad and may be early C14. The tower arch towards the nave rests on imposts with keeled demi-shafts; the arch is double-chamfered. There were originally lower double-chamfered arches on double-chamfered imposts to the N and S as well to connect the tower with former aisles projecting that far W. The uncommonly tall nave arcades link up with this story in an instructive way. They are of five bays, and the two E piers are evidently a little earlier than the rest. The E responds are keeled, the capitals waterleaf on the N side and some sort of crocket type on the S, i.e. late C12 rather than early C13. The piers are circular, the capitals moulded, the arches round and double-stepped. The two pairs of W piers are octagonal, the arches as before. So these bays are presumably of the time of the tower. The chancel arch goes with the E responds, but is near enough in style to the tower arch to show that building proceeded fast. The exterior of the church tells nothing of this interior story. The N aisle shows that the E parts are early C14 (*see* the E window, only visible inside), its W parts C15; the castellated clerestory is Perp too, and the S aisle and S porch were completely remodelled in the C18, in a not at all provincial style. The porch is heavily rusticated, the aisle windows are arched. The chancel was treated similarly, but re-Gothicized in the C19. An unusually elaborate squint connects N aisle and chancel. – COMMUNION RAIL. Handsome early C18 with foliated balusters. – ALTAR PAINTING. Said to be by one of the *Carracci*; bought in Spain by Sitwell Sitwell. – MONUMENTS. George † 1667 and Margaret Sitwell † 1658, epitaph with two wildly gesticulating demi-figures. – Sir Sitwell Sitwell † 1811, tall Corinthian column embedded in the wall; it carries a small urn. Several more Sitwell epitaphs.

MOSBOROUGH HALL. Elizabethan or Jacobean house with two projecting wings and a recessed centre. Of the original date the only witnesses are some mullioned windows, now partly hidden inside the house, and some moulded beams and plaster work. The entrance side was remodelled in the C18 and the centre between the wings filled in; *see* the doorway, the arched central window, and the characteristic oval window of the entrance side, and the broken pediment of the doorway in the centre of the main front.

Scenery: Dovedale

(a) *Scenery:* Winnats Pass in the High Peak

(b) *Scenery:* High Tor, a limestone crag in Matlock Dale

Scenery: Hopton Wood quarries near Middleton

Anglo-Saxon Sculpture: Wirksworth, Stories of Christ, *c.* 800

(b) *Anglo-Saxon Architecture:* Repton, Crypt, probably tenth century with eleventh-century columns

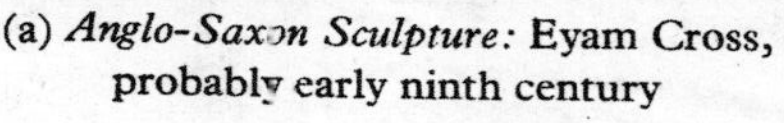

(a) *Anglo-Saxon Sculpture:* Eyam Cross, probably early ninth century

Norman Church Interiors: Melbourne

Norman Church Interiors: Steetley, Apse

STOKE-ON-TRENT PUBLIC LIBRARIES

(a) *Norman Decoration:* Ault Hucknall, Tympanum

(b) *Early English Decoration:* South Normanton, Vestry doorway

Early English Church Exteriors: Bakewell; the spire is rebuilt fourteenth-century work

(a) *Early English Church Exteriors:* Breadsall, thirteenth-century tower with early fourteenth-century spire

(b) *Early English Church Exteriors:* Dale Abbey, East end, late thirteenth century

Early English Church Exteriors: Ashbourne, Chancel

Late Thirteenth-Century Sculpture: Bolsover, Nativity

Early Fourteenth-Century Church Decoration: Ashbourne, Capital in the nave

(a) *Fourteenth-Century Church Exterior:* Tideswell

(b) *Fourteenth-Century Church Exterior:* Norbury, Chancel, *c.* 1355–70

Early Sixteenth-Century Church Exterior: Derby Cathedral, Tower

(a) *Fourteenth-Century Church Interior:* Chesterfield, *c.* 1325–50

(b) *Georgian Churches:* Derby Cathedral, by James Gibbs, 1723–5

(a) *Church Furnishings:* Youlgreave, Font, twelfth century

(b) *Church Furnishings:* Ashover, Font, lead, late twelfth century

Church Furnishings: Fenny Bentley, Screen, wood, early sixteenth century

(a) *Church Furnishings:* Ilkeston, Screen, stone, early fourteenth century

(b) *Church Furnishings:* Derby Cathedral, Screen by Robert Bakewell, *c.* 1730

Church Furnishings: Darley Dale, Gillum window, probably by Ford Madox Brown and others, *c.* 1861

Church Painting: Haddon Hall, Chapel, St Christopher, early fifteenth century
(*Copyright Country Life*)

Church Monuments: Bakewell, Sir Geoffrey Foljambe, 1377

(a) *Church Monuments:* Hathersage, Robert Eyre, 1459, and the younger Robert Eyre and family, kneeling, *c.* 1500

(b) *Church Monuments:* Norbury, Sir Ralph Fitzherbert, 1483

Church Monuments: Norbury, Sir Ralph Fitzherbert, 1483, mourners

(a) *Church Monuments:* Youlgreave, Robert Gylbert, 1492

(b) *Church Monuments:* Morley, Katherine Babington, 1543

Church Monuments: Wirksworth, Anthony Lowe, 1555

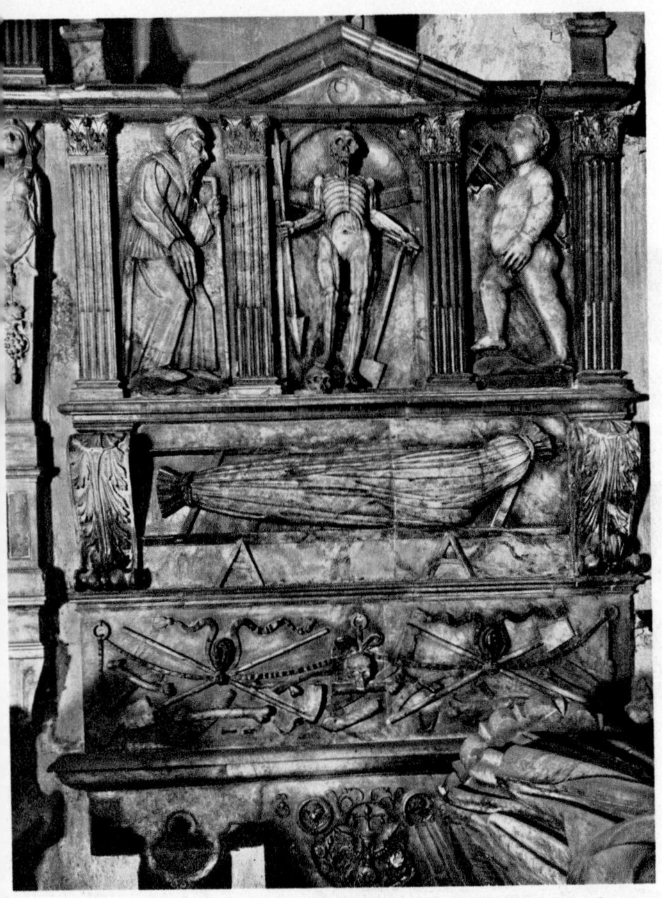

Church Monuments: Chesterfield, a Foljambe monument, *c.* 1580–90

Church Monuments: Chesterfield, Godfrey Foljambe, 1598

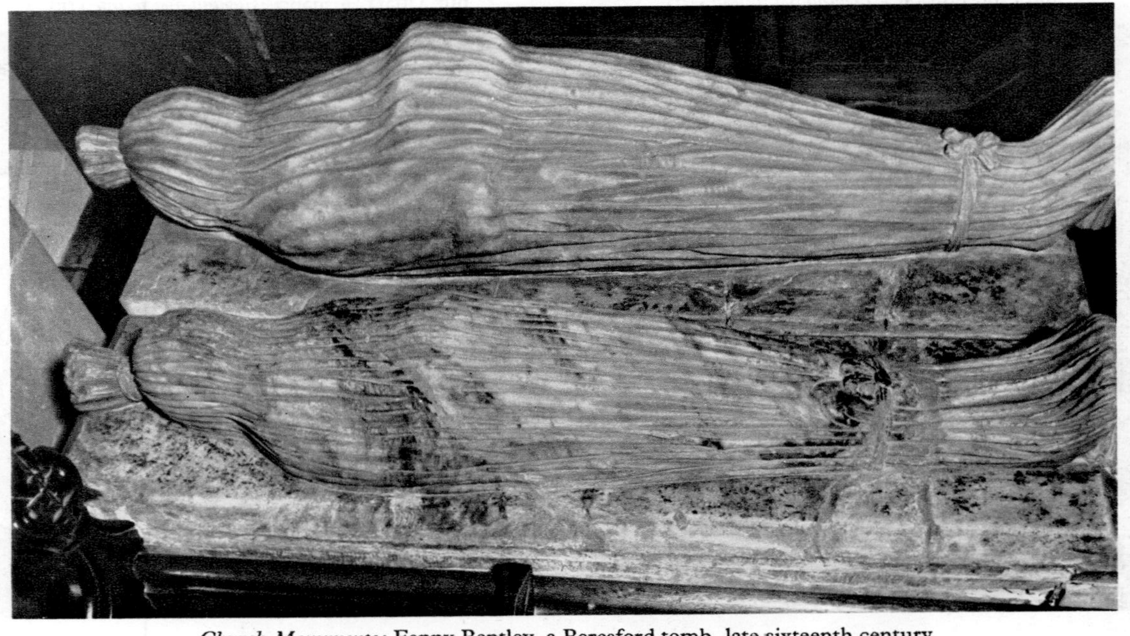

Church Monuments: Fenny Bentley, a Beresford tomb, late sixteenth century

(a) *Church Monuments:* Edensor, Henry and William Cavendish, died 1616 and 1625

(b) *Church Monuments:* Weston-on-Trent, Richard Sale, 1615

Church Monuments: Ault Hucknall, figures on the monument to Anne Keighley, 1627

STOKE-ON-TRENT
PUBLIC
LIBRARIES

(a) *Church Monuments:* Radburne, German Pole, 1684

(b) *Church Monuments:* Alfreton, George Morewood, 1742

Church Monuments: Ashbourne, Penelope Boothby, 1791, by Thomas Banks

(a) *Castles:* Peveril Castle, *c.* 1176

(b) *Manor Houses:* Haddon Hall (*Copyright Country Life*)

Manor Houses: South Wingfield Hall, begun in 1440

Manor Houses: Haddon Hall, Hall, *c.* 1370 (*Copyright Country Life*)

(a) *Manor Houses:* Haddon Hall, Parlour, *c.* 1500
(*Copyright Country Life*)

(b) *Manor Houses:* Hazlebadge, 1549

(a) *Manor Houses:* Somersal Hall, perhaps 1564

(b) *Manor Houses:* Snitterton, *c.* 1570

Country Houses: Hardwick, Old Hall, 1580s

Country Houses: Barlborough Hall, 1584

Country Houses: Hardwick Hall, 1590–7

(a) *Country Houses:* Hardwick Hall, Presence Chamber

(b) *Country Houses:* Haddon Hall, Long Gallery, early seventeenth century (*Copyright Country Life*)

(a) *Country Houses:* Haddon Hall, Long Gallery, exterior
(*Copyright Country Life*)

(b) *Country Houses:* Hardwick Hall, relief of the Nine Muses
(*Copyright Country Life*)

(a) *Country Houses:* North Lees near Hathersage, sixteenth and seventeenth centuries

(b) *Country Houses:* Bolsover Castle, the Keep, 1613

Country Houses: Bolsover Castle, Gallery, *c.* 1625–30

(a) *Country Houses:* Bolsover Castle, Gallery, doorway

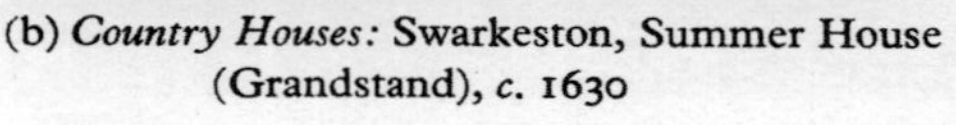

(b) *Country Houses:* Swarkeston, Summer House (Grandstand), *c.* 1630

Country Houses: Eyam Hall 1676

(a) *Country Houses:* Sudbury Hall, *c.* 1613 and 1670–95

(b) *Country Houses:* Sudbury Hall, Long Gallery, *c.* 1675

(a) *Country Houses:* Chatsworth, 1687–1707, the Right wing 1820 etc.

(b) *Country Houses:* Chatsworth, West front, 1700–3

Country Houses: Chatsworth, Chapel, completed 1694

Country Houses: Chatsworth, Aqueduct, *c.* 1694

Country Houses: Melbourne Hall, the Arbour, probably by Robert Bakewell, *c.* 1740

(a) *Country Houses:* Sutton Scarsdale, 1724, by Smith of Warwick

(b) *Country Houses:* Foremark Hall, *c.* 1760, by David Hiorns
(*Copyright Country Life*)

(a) *Country Houses:* Kedleston, North front, 1761, by James Paine

(b) *Country Houses:* Kedleston, South front, 1761–70, by Robert Adam (*Copyright Country Life*)

Country Houses: Kedleston, Great Hall, *c.* 1770, by Robert Adam
(*Copyright Country Life*)

Country Houses: Tissington Hall, Gothick fireplace, *c.* 1750
(*Copyright Country Life*)

(a) *Country Houses:* Willersley Castle, Cromford, 1782–8, by William Thomas

(b) *Country Houses:* Renishaw Hall, 1793–1808, the core Jacobean

Country Houses: Bretby Park, 1812–13, by Sir Jeffry Wyatville

(a) *Town Buildings:* Ashbourne, Grammar School, 1586

(b) *Town Buildings:* Derby, County Hall, 1660

(a) *Town Buildings:* Derby, Friargate, a Georgian street

(b) *Town Buildings:* Derby, Assembly Rooms, 1763–4

(a) *Town Buildings:* Buxton, The Crescent, *c.* 1780, by John Carr

(b) *Village Buildings:* Etwall Hospital, 1681

(a) *Village Buildings:* Edensor, *c.* 1839, by John Robertson

Early Industry: Curbar, Calver Mill, 1785

Early Industry: Cromford, Masson Mill, 1783

Early Industry: Morley Park Farm, Furnace

RECTORY. Handsome Late Georgian stone front, five centre bays and two broad pedimented angle bays with Venetian windows and tripartite semi-circular windows above. The present appearance of the house is due to the *Rev. Christopher Alderson*, who also improved the grounds. *The Gentleman's Magazine* of 1795 says that he was so renowned as a garden improver that he was employed at Windsor as well.*

HAGGE FARM, 2¼ m. SW. Small, very tall symmetrical house with square porch projection between two gabled bays, Built according to White in 1630.

EDELSTOW

2¼ m. NE of Matlock Bank

The barn behind the house has two fireplaces, probably older than the house which, with the few surviving mullioned windows at the back and the gabled two-storeyed porch, appears Elizabethan or Jacobean.

EDENSOR

The village of Edensor was removed from its original to its present site about 1839. It was the wish of the sixth Duke of Devonshire to have it out of sight of Chatsworth, and the planning of the new site and perhaps more lay in the hands of his gardener *Paxton*. The houses of the new village were designed by one *John Robertson*, said to have been a Derby architect.‡ The church came a good deal later, though it now dominates the picture. Its spire spoils the scale of the village.

ST PETER. 1867, by *Sir George Gilbert Scott*, with tall E.E. tower and spire, E.E. interior with two aisles, circular and octagonal piers, clerestory and chancel (typical, competent Scott). In the chancel Sedilia in the best crocketed ogee style. In the S porch a few Norman fragments from the old church and a foliated CROSS SLAB. At the E end of the N aisle the vast MONUMENT to Henry and William

* Information kindly given by Sir Osbert Sitwell.

‡ But his name is not in Bagshaw's Derby directory of 1840.

30a Cavendish † 1616 and 1625. The two bodies under a low fourposter with black columns and black covering slab. Henry appears as a skeleton on a straw mat, William in his shroud with his face exposed. Extremely grand back architecture with two martial flanking figures, then arches with on the left armour, on the right purple, crown and sword hung up, and in the middle an angel holding the black inscription tablet and blowing a trumpet. The whole is surmounted by a big broken pediment. Mrs Esdaile attributes the monument to *Colt*. – STAINED GLASS. S aisle E window 1882 by *Hardman*.

At the foot of the church a Green with the older Coach-houses on one side, close to it the castellated entrance lodge to the Village and a beginning of the typical architecture of Edensor. This is an attempt at making the Blaise Castle type of picturesque and fanciful artificial village respectable by good solid stone masonry and a display of more serious architectural styles, a Norman fountain by the side of the Green, next to it a house with a Swiss *châlet* roof and a Georgian segmental pediment 62a to the door and so on. Higher up the village street one can see the hideously elongated debased Italianate windows which Loudon liked so much in his *Encyclopaedia of Villa Architecture*, side by side with Jacobean gables, bargeboarding, Norman window surrounds, and Tudor chimneys. The best part of the design is the general loose and leafy layout, for instance, the way in which the village street ends on top with an octagonal house and looks down from there across the valley to the Hunting Tower of Chatsworth. 'Everything', says Bagshaw's Gazetteer of 1840, 'tends to show his Grace's taste, good feeling, and liberal disposition towards those in humble circumstances.'

Outside the Edensor village gate and through the Buxton Lodge on the N a further, typically Loudonesque villa is preserved. – The BUXTON LODGE itself is a design of *Wyatville*, a by-product of his vast work at Chatsworth (in a far more playful romantic spirit than Edensor village) half-timbered with brick infillings, and fancy bargeboards. Opposite the EDENSOR INN, a fine brick building of *c.* 1775: five bays with projecting lower wings with Venetian windows. The big porch looks later. It was built to serve the needs of well-to-do travellers along the fourth Duke's new NS road through the park.

Farther N on the way to Baslow on the W side an Italianate Villa of 1844, the original purpose of which is a mystery, and then on the E side BARBROOK HOUSE, *Paxton's* house, designed by him in the same style and built at about the same time.

EDLASTON

ST JAMES. Small and low. The distinguishing feature the extremely pretty bellcote of 1900, with two bells hanging exposed and all the details typical of the date. Who was the architect? Chancel of the C14 with C19 E window. The chancel arch also C14. The nave S side has a picturesque haphazard grouping of straightheaded windows.

EGGINTON

ST WILFRID. A small church mostly of *c.* 1300, *see* the W tower bell-openings (but the W window Perp), the N aisle windows, and the chancel windows, and inside both arcades. That on the S side has short quatrefoil piers, that on the N circular piers. Double-chamfered arches on both sides. In the chancel Sedilia and Piscina trefoil-headed. The S aisle windows from outside form a nice muddled group with a later Tudor window in the middle. Inside in the S aisle S wall an equally muddled series of recesses. – STAINED GLASS. Good fragments of Crucifixus, Virgin, St John, other figures, all small, dark colours, *c.*1400. – MONUMENTS. Civilian, holding his heart in his hands, very damaged. – Francis Every † 1690, black medallion with white frontal bust, cheek propped up on the hand, badly done.

MONKS' BRIDGE. Medieval but widened in 1775. Four segmental arches, three with chamfered ribs.

EGGINTON HALL. Attributed to *James Wyatt* and a date

c. 1780. The finely detailed porch leads into a circular room projecting as a bow in the middle of a nine-bay front. The other main front with two bows and a tripartite window between. All plain, of brick, two-storeyed with top balustrade.

ELMTON

ST PETER. Rebuilt completely in 1773. The W tower was left incomplete. Nave and lower apsed chancel. The windows are arched. On the N side no windows at all. – PULPIT, with Tester: nice contemporary work.

ELTON

ALL SAINTS. Unbuttressed W tower with arched windows and battlements: 1812. The nave has lancet windows of two lancet lights with pierced spandrels and the chancel an E window with intersected tracery. Or are these windows slightly later alterations? Two N windows in the nave are simply arched.

In the village a number of worthwhile houses, especially one with a big semicircular pediment above the door, dated 1668, and one still with two-light low mullioned windows, dated 1717.

ELVASTON

ST BARTHOLOMEW, In the grounds, close to the mansion. The W tower of unusual design, tall, three-storeyed, with angle buttresses and on each side two tall two-light bell openings placed under one ogee arch. Top with eight pinnacles. Nave and S aisle. The latter has a lancet W window and S windows with intersected tracery, i.e. late C13. The arcade piers (three bays) are octagonal and carry double-chamfered arches. The N nave windows with straightsided arches. This and the clerestory Perp. The lower chancel extended by *Bodley* in 1905 (GR). It has Bodley's characteristic stencilled wall decoration and pretty roof. – SCREENS to chancel and E bay of S aisle. Both have ogee-headed one-light sections with panel tracery above; the rood screen with richer crocketing than the parclose screen. Behind the latter a Jacobean FAMILY PEW. – PAINTING. Virgin and Child by *Pasinelli*, 1693. – PLATE: Slender Chalice and plain Paten; early C17. – MONUMENTS. Sir John Stanhope † 1610, standing wall monument with alabaster effigies between coupled columns under deep coffered arch. – Memorial to William Piggin, plasterer, 1621, handsome simple epitaph with brass inscription. – Sir John Stanhope † 1638, the fragments reassembled in 1731; in a transeptal extension with a tall mullioned and transomed side-window, under a fine classical ceiling, typical of *c.* 1730–5. – Third Earl of Harrington † 1829, large epitaph with musing allegorical figure, by an urn on a tall pedestal against which leans a shield with the head of Medusa; by *Canova*. – Algernon Russell Gayleard Stanhope † 1847, recumbent boy lying on a straw mat. Unsigned. – Fifth Earl of Harrington † 1862, recumbent effigy on tomb-chest, unsigned. The inscription says that the Earl 'was with Lord Byron in Greece' and there erected the first school and the first printing press, entirely at his own expense.

ELVASTON CASTLE. The grounds are more famous than the house. They can boast long straight avenues as well as fine landscaping, a large serpentine lake (made only about 1855–60 by Mr Barron) and also plenty of topiary. The house was remodelled to the designs of *James Wyatt* and executed after his death in 1817 by *Mr Walker*. It has a symmetrical entrance front with a one-storeyed porch and two slightly projecting ends flanked by turrets. The r. one is the one remaining part of the original house, brick with a canted bay with mullioned and transomed windows. It carries the date 1633. A cistern is dated 1705, and from that date survives the drawing room inside. The C19 work is ashlar-faced, has also a symmetrical side front, and a stuccoed side to the stables, with a picturesque tower. The Entrance Hall, black and gold with an elaborate tierceron vault with pendants and with niches for coats of armour, is the best early C19 interior. Apart from this the finest rooms are late C18, especially the spacious Staircase and some fireplaces, etc., in other rooms. In the grounds the MOORISH TEMPLE, with a roof with convex slopes and odd fancy-shaped windows, no doubt of *c.* 1855–60.

END LOW *see* YOULGREAVE

ETWALL

ST HELEN. Nicely placed between the village street and the Almshouses. Short W tower with diagonal buttresses and low unembattled body. The windows all Perp. or later. On the S side they are of an unusual design, perhaps late C17 or C18. The only external feature telling of a greater age is the S doorway, roundheaded, C13. But inside the N arcade of three bays is Norman. The piers are circular, the capitals scalloped, and the arches unmoulded and unchamfered. The fourth arch taller, wider, pointed and double-chamfered. – SEATING. N chancel chapel: Elizabethan. – S DOOR. C17, handsome. – LECTERN. Stone, built into the N chancel wall (cf. Spondon, Crich), probably C13, i.e. a proof that the chancel wall is as old as that. – MONUMENTS. Incised alabaster slab of civilian † 1500, wife and children, badly preserved. – Brass to Henry Port † 1512 and wife and children; his brass lost. – Top of tomb-chest with civilian and two wives, the heads broken off. Probably Sir John Port † 1541. The figures in sunk relief so that a broad band can run across their bodies at the level of the border of the slab. The canopy may belong to the early C19 restoration. – Sir John Port † 1557. Brasses of husband, wife and children kneeling, against the back wall of a finely carved straight-topped recess in the chancel S wall.

ETWALL HALL, early C18. Stone fronted, the stone said to come from Tutbury Castle. The S front of five bays and two storeys with top balustrade, well proportioned sash-windows and a centre doorway with segmental pediment on Tuscan pilasters; in addition on the l. and r. two and a half storeyed projections with top-balustrades. Gates of wrought iron by *Robert Bakewell*.

ETWALL HOSPITAL. Almshouses founded by Sir John 61b Port who also founded Repton School. Rebuilt in 1681. Of this date only the central frontispiece gives evidence by its scrolly pediment. The rest of the large composition might well be considered much older. It is a structure on three sides of a courtyard, the ground floor with four-centred doorway and two windows for each little house, all these features stone-framed so that the ground floor appears all stone, whereas the plain gables expose their brickwork.

Several nice houses in the village, notably an early C18 one facing the Longford road (five bays, two and a half storeys) and its Late Georgian neighbour, and the Post Office (front with three Neo-Jacobean shaped gables, probably Early Victorian, though the house itself is older).

EYAM

ST LAWRENCE. C13 chancel with lancet windows, C13 N arcade of three bays with one circular pier and one quatrefoil pier keeled. The arches are double-chamfered, but one of the two chamfers is slight. The S arcade has octagonal piers and seems to be C15. The clerestory and nave roof probably of the same time. The W tower also appears Perp, though it has a tower arch to the nave which seems C14 and a date-stone saying 1615. The N aisle was widened in 1868 (by *Street*) the S aisle in 1882. – FONT. Norman, circular, with blank arches on columns (cf. Hognaston; found in a garden at Hathersage). – PULPIT. Plain C18. – SCREENS to chancel and tower, made of parts of the former Stafford Pew, Elizabethan or a little later. – MOMPESSON CHAIR. A chair was given to the church by a former Rector which has on its back a very crude representation of the Virgin and above it the inscription MON 1665 EYAM. It records William Mompesson, the quiet hero of Eyam who shut the village off from the outer world in 1666 when the plague had been brought in from London, and went on ministering

amongst the dying and holding services in the open. His wife was amongst the victims and is buried in the church-
5a yard. – In the churchyard also SAXON CROSS, notable for the survival of the cross-head. Defaced figures in the head, coarse vine scrolls (of Northumbrian derivation) and interlace on the shaft, of which unfortunately the top two feet or so are missing. The date is probably early C9.

Nice houses around the churchyard, especially the RECTORY, mid Georgian, with canted bay windows and above them semicircular tripartite windows.

47 EYAM HALL. Dated 1676 on a rain-water head. The date goes with the front towards the formal trimmed garden and its central gateway to the street. That is, it would be very late in counties of the S, but corresponds to other later C17 houses of Derbyshire. The front is a half H with the sides projecting far. It is three storeys high with string-courses sharply dividing the storeys from each other and a straight top interrupted by three small gables above the centres of the wings and the centre of the recessed part. The windows are low and mullioned of three and four lights, symmetrically arranged, and touch with their tops the string-courses. This latter feature as well as the comparatively classical door-surround tally with the date 1676. The E front is different, with three gables and windows with individual hood-moulds not quite symmetrically arranged. At the back two projecting parts show earlier masonry. In one of them the staircase, said to have come from Bradshaw Hall, but appearing in its right place and of a date, probably Late Elizabethan or Jacobean, which might well be that of the masonry. The Hall could also be Elizabethan in position, but the central entrance from the S which makes it into an entrance hall instead of a hall in the medieval and Tudor sense must be a contribution of 1676. Older parts to the W.

BRADSHAW HALL. The manor house before Eyam Hall. Of this only one smallish building remains, now a barn. Its front windows are not older than the C17, the others may be, but there is no easily visible pre-Reformation evidence.

WET-WITHENS MOOR, 1¾ m. ENE Eyam. Stone circle, of Bronze Age date, consisting of 16 stones standing on the inner edge of a circular bank of earth. The circle measures about 100 ft across.

FAIRFIELD NR BUXTON

ST PETER. 1839. W tower with quoins, battlements and pinnacles. Windows of a characteristic pre-archeological shape: Late Perp arches, but late C13 tracery. No aisles; W gallery on cast-iron columns. Transepts and chancel 1902.

THE FRONT, i.e. the houses alongside the Green or Common. Among them OLD HALL COTTAGES, dated 1687, but still with gable and low, hood-moulded, mullioned windows, and GOLF COTTAGE, earlier C17.

FANSHAWEGATE HALL FARM *see* HOLMESFIELD

FENNY BENTLEY

ST EDWARD. W tower renewed in 1850. N aisle 1850, S side of the nave with one intersected and one coarse Dec window, the latter probably C19. The chancel E window of five lights, an odd design, but possible *c.* 1300. Nothing remarkable in the interior architecture. – SCREEN, with two-light openings with very cusped ogee tops and no panel tracery. The groining is preserved. Probably from the former Beresford Chantry, founded in 1511. – PARCLOSE SCREEN, with single-light openings and very Flamboyant tracery. Said to date from 1519. – CHEST, with elementary ironwork (C13?). – STAINED GLASS. E window 1877, five big figures, good work, by whom? – MONUMENT. A member of the Beresford family and his wife; Elizabethan. The two effigies shrouded and completely bundled up (cf. Chesterfield). Against the tomb-chest the children upright and equally bundled up: a weird, grotesque idea.

18

29

BENTLEY HALL. Square medieval tower with small openings except for one large partly blocked low seven-light window with one transome, and attached to the tower a gabled house, also with mullioned and mullioned and transomed windows.

FIN COP *see* ASHFORD-IN-THE-WATER

FINDERN

ALL SAINTS. 1863. From the previous Norman church one tympanum survives, very raw, with two small figures standing l. and r., and, in the centre, two rows of saltire crosses and above a large cross with chequer-board patterns l. and r. – FONT. The characteristic type of 1662; small (*see* Weston-on-Trent, Southwell Notts., etc.). – PLATE. Chalice with a band of engraved strap-work decoration and Paten of 1565.

FIVE WELLS TUMULUS *see* TADDINGTON

FOOLOW

MANOR HOUSE. Small, C17; in the centre of the front a canted bay window with transomed windows.

CHAPEL. 1836, yet still with a heavy Tuscan porch and thin lancet side windows, as if the date were thirty years earlier.

FORD HALL

1¼ m. NE of Chapel-en-le-Frith

A *Mixtum Compositum* of one remaining gabled bay of early C17 date with mullioned window, a C20 Neo-Georgian bit in replacement of the remainder of the Jacobean house, a genuine Georgian front of *c.* 1727 (five bays, central pedimented ground floor windows) and mid C19 additions. Outside the grounds the STABLES (? SLACK HALL) dated 1727, still with low two light windows, although these are now symmetrically arranged and 'hanging' from a string course. Two gables, and in the middle between them a giant recess connected no doubt with the original function of the building.

FOREMARK

ST SAVIOUR. An uncommonly interesting building, in so far as it was built completely in 1662 (by Sir Francis Burdett) and has kept most of its original furnishings intact. The style of the exterior is still entirely Gothic: embattled W tower and embattled nave without aisles; Perp windows (five cusped lancet lights under a depressed arch). Where the real date comes out is in the following features. First of all the nave has a central buttress and the two windows are placed symmetrically to its l. and r. with stretches of bare wall further out. So the wall is a completely symmetrical composition. Also the windows have hoodmoulds on the typical square stops of the C17. Finally above the E window is some strapwork decoration with two small figures. The interior has a rich rood screen, still wholly Jacobean in character, except that the steep big central pediment is characteristic of the mid C17. The wooden frames of the stone altar-mensa and the box-pews are also original. The W gallery was put in in 1819. Three-decker pulpit. The communion rails are of iron, Early Georgian, probably by *Bakewell* of Derby. Also probably by him the Gate to the avenue which leads from the E end of the church to the mansion.

FOREMARK HALL, built *c.* 1760 by Sir Robert Burdett. 53b The architect was *David Hiorns* of Warwick. The style is the correct Palladian of the period, seven bays width plus broad canted bays at the angles. These have cupolas like Kent's Houghton. The garden front (S) has as its centre a giant detached portico with pediment, the side towards the original drive (N) a simple doorway. Large outer staircases lead up to this and the portico. The elevation of the house is of basement plus 1½ storeys. The only criticism of the composition is that the cupolas come rather near the pediment so that the effect is somewhat tight and compact. There are curved screens on both sides connecting them with tiny inaccessible pavilions—a miniature version of a favourite Palladian motif ('Venetian vanities', wrote Torrington, in 1790. He found the house 'of vile architecture'). Inside, the entrance hall goes across and has a handsome staircase to its one side and a large saloon beyond, filling the W side entirely. North lodge with excellent Iron Gate, also presumably by *Bakewell*.

ANCHOR CHURCH, N of Foremark. This is not a church but caves in the cliff of the escarpment S of the river Trent traditionally connected with an anchorite.

HEATH WOOD, INGLEBY, 1 m. NE. Sixty burial mounds have been found. The site slopes gently downhill to the river Trent. The mounds were erected by pagan Danish settlers soon after A.D. 877. They measure between 20 and 45 ft in diameter, and are between 18 in. and 5 ft high.

GANTRIES HILL *see* CHAPEL-EN-LE-FRITH

GIB HILL *see* YOULGREAVE

GLEADLESS

CHARNOCK HALL JUNIOR SCHOOL. 1949–51. One of the recent standard steel and brick schools set up by the County Education Department (*see* Introduction, p. 33).

GLOSSOP

ALL SAINTS. The parish church of Old Glossop. Of the medieval church no more remains than one arch (N aisle E end) on two head corbels not originally part of it. The W tower is of 1853, the new of 1914–15 (by *Charles Hadfield*), the chancel of 1923 (also by *Hadfield*).

Behind the church an exceptionally well and completely preserved group of C17 cottages with low mullioned windows and gables. One of them is dated 1638.

Also close to the church GLOSSOP HALL, a mansion of 1850, once the Duke of Norfolk's, now a school. From the Howard time dates the church of

ALL SAINTS. Church Terrace. 1836 by *Wightman & Hadfield*, severely Neo-Greek, or rather Neo-Etruscan (cf. Hassop). Heavy front of Tuscan pilasters with pediment. Coved ceiling and shallow apse inside.

The centre of New Glossop (or Howard Town) is the SQUARE with the TOWN HALL of 1838, by *Weightman & Hadfield*, an unusually well and quietly designed building with central lantern and slender arched windows. On the E side of the square the LIBERAL CLUB of 1914, by *Paul Ogden*, tall and fanciful, in a kind of free Neo-Tudor.

Of early industrial architecture in and around Glossop, (LOGWOOD MILL of 1804) and WREN NEST MILLS of *c.* 1800–10 plus small extension of *c.* 1815 plus extension with polygonal tower of 1818(?) plus newer additions deserve notice.

MELANDRA CASTLE, *see* p. 180.

GRANVILLE PITHEAD BATHS *see* SWADLINCOTE

GREAT LONGSTONE *see* LONGSTONE

GREY DITCH *see* CASTLETON

GRIND LOW *see* BAKEWELL

HADDON HALL

Haddon Hall is the English castle *par excellence*, not the forbidding fortress on an unassailable crag, but the large, rambling, safe, grey, lovable house of knights and their ladies, the unreasonable dream-castle of those who think of the Middle Ages as a time of chivalry and valour and noble feelings. None other in England is so complete and convincing. It is set in gentle green surroundings, with woods above and lush fields and the meandering river below. The river in its winding course enhances the charms of the W as well as the S side. The slope up to the house on the W is steep but not high, and grassy not rocky. The towers and turrets and crenellations look exactly as if they were taken out of the background of some C15 illuminated manuscript. There is any amount of variety and no architectural system whatsoever. The architectural critic and historian would indeed be hard put to it if he were asked to define what in the sensations

34b

of a first visit to Haddon Hall is due to aesthetic and what to extraneous values.

There is first of all the approach, across the broad bridge of 1663 to the C16 stables (with their odd decoration by a sheila-na-gig) and to the NW Gate Tower, the highest element in the whole agglomeration of parts, and placed in the lowest position. This, however, became the main access to the Hall only in early C16, and it is usable only on foot, having steps to connect it with the courtyard. So its use demands the stables below and testifies to a time when fortification did not much matter any longer.

Access in the earlier Middle Ages was at the highest level of the site by Peveril's Tower close to the NE corner. The other sides were defended by nature. Here masonry of the C12 is most clearly discernible. There is a document of 1195 allowing Richard de Vernon to fortify 'domum suum de Heddon muro exalto XII pedibus sine kernello'. The tower, it is true, has crenellations, but they are of the C14. The Vernons had come into Haddon by marriage about 1170 and kept and developed it, until, again by marriage, it passed to the Manners family in 1567, the marriage this time being that of Dorothy Vernon to John Manners after their celebrated (but historically unproven) elopement in 1558. The Manners family has held it ever since. It ceased to be inhabited about 1700, and was left alone for two hundred years.

But while, as the Torrington Diary says, the house had an 'awful and melancholy look', walls and roofs remained sound, and when restoration started in 1912 and was carried on slowly and carefully for some twenty years, nothing drastic had to be done. The house is in its whole extent in remarkably genuine and good condition. Its whole extent is about 220 by 110 ft; and that area must already have been covered one way or another by the Norman stronghold. For there is masonry attributed to the C12 not only in Peveril's Tower, the lower bastions flanking it (and originally connected on the E side by a passage-way on corbels which are still visible), and the wall to the S of that group, but also all along the S wall, the centre of the W wall, and in the Chapel W and S walls (in the latter with small lancet windows of deep inner reveals). There is no evidence, however, for a cross-wing nor for a keep.

This cross-wing, which divides a Lower from an Upper Courtyard, was the creation of Sir Richard Vernon IV about 1370 and is the architecturally most important part. It contains the Hall, Parlour, Kitchen, and Offices in their familiar arrangement, very similar in many ways to Penshurst in Kent begun about twenty years earlier. At about the same time the chapel S aisle was widened and a N aisle created. The lower parts of the Long Gallery range (Upper Courtyard S range) also belong to this period.

During the fifteenth and earlier sixteenth centuries the Lower Courtyard assumed its present form. The NW Gate Tower dates from *c.* 1530, the apartments to its E from the same time, those to its S towards the chapel from a few years before.* The chapel received its new chancel in 1427, the Hall its porch, chimney, and battlements about 1450. Contemporary internal alterations will be mentioned later.

As to the exterior, Elizabethan and Jacobean improvements show themselves towards the courtyards only in windows, bay windows, and such like additions (especially the staircase cube to the SE of the Hall and the canted bay window to the S of Peveril's Tower), but towards the outside the whole S front was radically modernized about 1600, when John Manners built his Long Gallery with its three broad well-spaced bay windows, stimulated no doubt by Hardwick, completed in 1597. He also added oriel windows of similar type but smaller size to the W, to what had been the Long Gallery before his time. 43a

Before entering these various rooms, Architectural Details

* This difference in time and the fact that the W range stands on Norman walls account for the odd and ingenious way in which the new gateway could find an entry into the courtyard without running against the E wall of the W range. The wall was canted back, and complicated squinches above bring it back to the line along which the rest of the wall runs.

may be examined, first the late C12 lancets of the Chapel S wall, already mentioned, and then the characteristic Hall windows of *c.* 1370, almost identical with those at Penshurst (tall, of two lights, with steep two-centred arches, one transome, and tracery consisting of the cusping of the two lights and an ogee quatrefoil in the spandrel). The E doorway is contemporary. A porch was apparently not yet regarded as necessary. The buttery N of the porch is again of the C14, as is proved by its excellent gargoyles (gargoyles also on the E side of the Hall range). Of the early C15 are the big five-light Chapel E window with its conventional Perp panel tracery, and the Chapel S and N windows, straightheaded of three and two lights with arched cusped heads to the individual lights. These windows date from 1427, the picturesque octagonal chapel turret from *c.* 1450. The window shapes of the sides of the chapel remained in fashion for another century. They are the same in the broad W window of Sir Henry's Parlour of *c.* 1500 (ogee-headed lights), the W range of the Lower Courtyard (depressed heads), and in the three upper storeys of Sir George's NW Gate Tower of *c.* 1530 (depressed heads). Here, however, they have those hood-moulds to which minor Derbyshire manor houses were to stick for another 150 years. The earliest example at Haddon of the 'Elizabethan' mullioned window with straightheaded lights seems to be the S bay window of the Parlour. There is no accurate date for it, but it is clearly later than the room itself (*c.* 1500) and earlier than the Elizabethan Age. The panelling inside (cf. below) is indeed dated 1545. Elizabethan and Jacobean detail is plentiful, and no one would not recognize the twice-transomed windows of the Long Gallery, the Staircase from the Hall to the Great Chamber (facing E), and the Great Chamber itself (facing W).

It is now time to examine the Interior of Haddon Hall so far as it is open to the public. The public entrance is by the NW tower.

The CHAPEL is the first room shown, and rightly so; for it affords, small as it is, a cross-section through all the building periods of the house. Nave of two bays with circular pier on the S, octagonal pier on the (later) N side, double-chamfered pointed arches. The clerestory belongs in date to the more spacious chancel of 1427. – FONT. Plain, circular, Norman, with Jacobean cover of double-curved scrolls meeting below a central knob. – WOODWORK remarkably well preserved, of the same date as the roof-beams which bear an inscription *G.M.* 1624. – SCREEN still with a broad band of Flamboyant Gothic tracery as the dado; above widely set slim balusters; straight cornice. – Three-decker PULPIT, PEWS. – PAINTING. The grisaille or almost grisaille wall decoration of the Chapel has come out wonderfully in the C20 restorations. Nave clerestory: large figure of St Christopher with scrolly waves, and plenty of fishes and plants, and to the l. and r. extensive areas of verdure; late C15. Nave W wall: The Three Quick and the Three Dead. Chancel: Lives of St Nicholas and St Anne, and a simple extremely pretty all-over pattern. – SCULPTURES. Reredos of Nottingham alabaster, bought in the C20, with the familiar scenes in the familiar renderings. – STAINED GLASS. E window (Christ Crucified, Mary, St John, and smaller figures, e.g. the Annunciation, in the tracery), and, in very good preservation, N window (St Michael, St Anne and the Virgin, St George). The inscription which runs across the whole E window dates the glass and the chancel: Orate pro animabus Riccardi Vernon et Benedicte uxoris eius qui fecerunt anno dni 1427.

21

HALL. The roof was renewed in 1923–5; otherwise there is nothing here less than 350 years old. On the other hand, none of the furnishings are of the date of the structure, i.e. *c.* 1370, except perhaps the stone flooring. Part of the structure are the E doorway and the three doorways behind the screen to buttery, kitchen, and pantry. – SCREEN, *c.* 1450, and one of the best early hall screens in the country. Note the shapes and mouldings of the panels and the blank tracery identical with what one finds in church screens. – PANELLING, *c.* 1600. – E GALLERY, *c.* 1600, incongruous and picturesque; inserted to make

36

communication from W to S less cumbersome. The meaning of domestic comfort had dawned upon the English in the time of Queen Elizabeth. – TABLE, Elizabethan. – The exquisite armorial millefleurs TAPESTRY behind the table is of the C15 and may well form part of the remodelling of the Hall under Sir William.

KITCHEN. The Kitchen belongs to the same building phase as the Hall. It was originally higher and may have had a louvred roof. The low ceiling was put in in the C16. The surviving fitments are unique in number and variety, grates and baking ovens, entrance door with serving-shelf, log-box, wooden salting bath, carving table, and stone troughs for water storage.

37a PARLOUR AND SOLAR. S of the Hall on the ground floor is the Parlour (now called Dining Room), altered *c.* 1500. It has its original W window and, *mirabile dictu*, its original painted ceiling decoration (restored by *Professor Tristram*). This consists of diapers half white and half red and heraldic shields. The moulded beams are also painted. The panelling, covering the whole walls, with its ornamental top frieze, has a date 1545, and this probably refers to alterations which comprised the addition of the exceedingly pretty S bay window. As an example of dated panelling prior to 1550, it is of great historical importance. Above the Parlour is the Solar or GREAT CHAMBER reached from the Hall by a staircase which is in exactly the same position as the C14 staircase at Penshurst, but in its present form Elizabethan or Jacobean. The roof of the Solar is a splendid example of domestic joinery of *c.* 1500. The blocked window in the S wall belongs probably to the same date. Above the bay window of the Parlour is an identical one in the Solar, though its mullions have been removed at a later date. The plasterwork inside the bay, and the quadruple frieze all along the wall of the chamber, are Elizabethan; earlier, that is, than the panelling which goes with the renewal of the W window and is probably early C17.

THE EARL'S APARTMENTS. A door from the Solar leads to this room which receives its name from a time in the

C17 when it was subdivided into three chambers. It was made, it seems, about 1500 out of earlier medieval masonry and some also slightly earlier timber-framing. So presumably there were here no rooms for family use, before Sir Henry created his 'Long Gallery'. The ceiling is good and sturdy and very similar to that in the Solar. A door from its W end led to an outer staircase, the easiest access to the Chapel.

LONG GALLERY. Undated, but no doubt earliest C.17. The room lies to the E of the Solar and rests partly on Norman masonry. It is 110 ft long and only 15 ft high; that is, much shorter and lower than the Gallery at Hardwick. But from Hardwick Sir John Manners probably caught the ambition of having such a gallery at Haddon and the idea of enriching it by three bay windows. Their beautiful spacing and proportions, however, are his, and the atmosphere of the Haddon Gallery is indeed as different from Bess of Hardwick's as was her character from Sir John's. The Haddon Gallery has none of the demonstrative grandeur of Hardwick. It is intimate and warm, with the sunlight reflected on its exquisite panelling. Its panelling is indeed its finest feature; for the plaster ceiling is modest, though graceful. High dado, pilasters with scale pattern carrying arches. A specially attractive touch is the introduction of two N windows throwing light on those parts of the S wall between the bay windows, which would otherwise appear to the eye as expanses of darkness. 42b

Close to the E end of the Gallery a door and an outer staircase of about a dozen steps lead into the terraced S GARDEN. This is also one of the glories of Haddon. It was made early in the C17, although gardens no doubt had existed before. In fact the narrow doorway just W of the early C16 gate tower, which is of the same date and decorated with a coat of arms and a quatrefoil frieze, leads one to believe that here was one of the ways of access to it. But as the gardens are at present, they are C17 with their typical top balustrade and lower down their formidable looking substructures with a strong batter. A long staircase leads down from the S side of the Chapel to the river which is here crossed by a PACKHORSE BRIDGE (Dorothy Vernon's way of escape, we are told, and ready to believe).

HADFIELD

OLD HALL, Old Hall Square. L-shaped with two- to five-light mullioned windows under hood-moulds on heavy square stops. The date is 1646.

HAGGE FARM *see* ECKINGTON

HALTER DEVIL CHAPEL *see* MUGGINTON

HARDWICK HALL

41 Bess of Hardwick was born at Hardwick Hall in 1520. Her father, John Hardwick, Esq., owned the manor, a minor manor, and lived in a minor manor house. Here she grew up, ready at the age of 13 to marry Robert Barlow, Esq., of Barlow. He died almost immediately, and at the age of 27 she became the third wife of Sir William Cavendish, Treasurer of the Chamber to the King. He was not a Derbyshire man, but she induced him to sell his Suffolk properties and buy the Chatsworth estate to settle down in her county. Here Bess could for the first time indulge in what was to become her master passion, a building mania, nobler no doubt than her other passions. For she appears from her actions and from contemporary records and accounts as a grasping and intriguing, if undeniably able, woman. The new Chatsworth was begun in 1557. Five years later Sir William Cavendish died, leaving Bess a woman of considerable wealth. She was only 37 and, although not physically attractive, it appears, she found a third husband at once, Sir William St Loe. He, however, after less than ten years, also died. Bess was now in her mid forties, but instead of resigning herself to a comfortable widowed retirement, she set out to find yet another husband. She was successful, and it turned out to be the great *coup* of her life. Her second and third husbands had been rich, and their wealth had been conducted by her into her hands. The fourth was richer and more powerful than either: George Talbot, sixth Earl of

Shrewsbury. Their marriage took place in 1568, and in the same year (a characteristic touch) she made her position trebly sure by arranging for two of the Cavendish children to marry two of his. Building soon started on some of the Talbot estates, especially at Worksop. The story of the Earl's guardianship of Mary Queen of Scots, of her intrigues, of Queen Elizabeth's intrigues, of Bess's intrigues, does not concern us here. The Earl died in 1590, seven years after he had separated from Bess. In

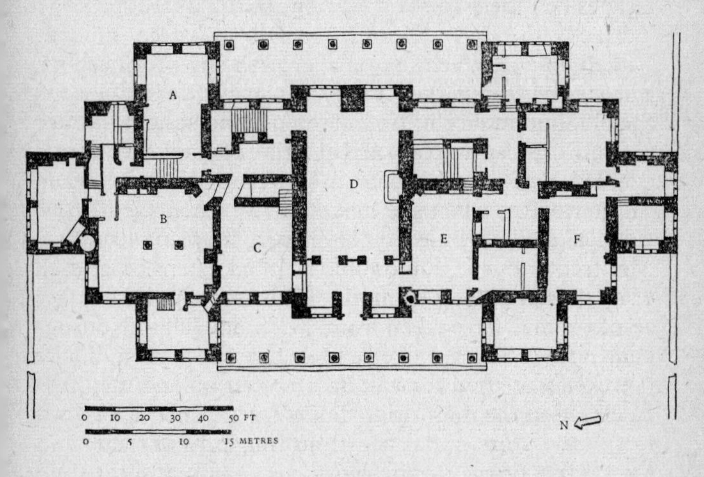

A. Chapel B. Kitchen C. Buttery D. Hall E. Pantry F. Nursery

that year she had deliberately created a rumour of a liaison between him and Mary. That she had also called him 'knave, fool, and beast to his face' was a minor point. During those last years of the Earl's life, Bess had begun converting the old manor house into a large mansion, the mansion now known as HARDWICK OLD HALL and in 39 ruins. The ruins do not tell their architectural story, and special research has not yet been done. The house was large, nearly 200 ft long, and tall, with the State Rooms apparently on the highest floors. There at least are the largest windows, windows very similar to those of the new Hall (with two and even three transomes), and there are remains of plasterwork, especially a frieze, so similar to that in the Presence Chamber of the new Hall that it must be the work of the same craftsmen. But the job at the Old Hall was in spite of all the lavishness bestowed on it only an adding and adjusting job. Regularity might be achieved in the new outer garden wall with its two summerhouses and its gateway in axis with the new broad central porch, but in the main planning of rooms and façades (*see* the S front) it was out of the question.

So, directly the Earl had died and Bess was free, she embarked on a new venture, crazier than any previous one. She started to build a NEW HALL at Hardwick, close to the old, but on virgin ground, on a grand scale, to a new entirely up-to-date plan, and at a rate of employment that enabled her to finish the job in six years. She was 71 when she started, 77 when she moved in, 87 when she died.

Hardwick Hall is basically H-shaped in plan, like, say, Montacute, but with a double-stepped extension at each of its shorter ends. The motif of this stepping Bess or her architect may have taken from Wollaton Hall in Nottinghamshire, completed five years before she started. There however it is used for a square not an oblong mansion. In elevation the most original feature at Hardwick is that it is of two storeys, but the projecting arms of the H and the centres of the stepped-forward additions are carried up to form three-storeyed pavilions, or square towers. That motif comes without doubt from Barlborough, built in 1584. But whereas Barlborough has only four towers and they are polygonal and relatively slender so that their effect is rather like that of the raised turrets of Tudor gate houses, the six towers at Hardwick are four-square and massive. Four-square is indeed the whole house. There are no curves anywhere, save in the rather niggly strapwork frills of the tower balustrades which frame Bess's proud and ostentatious initials, E.S., E.S., E.S., E.S., four times along each of the long fronts, and three times along the short ones. The stepping on the l. and r. moves in hard r. angles, a colonnade with straight entablature runs along the ground floor between the towers of the main façades,* a balustrade finishes the composition at the top, the roof is flat, the central bay window only slightly canted on the second upper floor, and all the windows are mullioned as well as transomed. 'Hardwick Hall more window than wall'; it is indeed the size and the rhythm of the windows that distinguishes Hardwick from all other Late Elizabethan houses. The close grid of the mullions and transomes sets the pace, and no obstacle gets into its way. One transome on the ground floor which is treated as a basement, two transomes on the first, three on the second and third.‡ It is of a consistency and hardness which must have suited the old woman entirely. And as the house stands on the flattened top of the hill, there is nothing of surrounding nature either that could compete with its uncompromising unnatural, graceless, and indomitable self-assertiveness. It is an admirable piece of design and architectural expression: no fussing, no fumbling, nor indeed any flights of fancy.

That is different inside. Here a show of luxury was aimed at, and at once the style becomes coarse, as it does so often in the art of decoration in Elizabethan England. We shall take the rooms in the order in which visitors will see them.§ The ENTRANCE HALL is, from the planning if not from the decorating point of view, the most remarkable room in the house. The Hall of Elizabethan houses is still in the position in which it had been ever since the Middle Ages: in the middle. But while in the Middle Ages it extended asymetrically along part of the front and was approached at one end by a door leading into the Screens Passage, now at Hardwick the entrance is central and the Hall is central and has its large axis not parallel

* It was originally meant to run all round the building, but the idea was given up during building.

‡ The heightening from three to four tiers of panes was an afterthought. It was resolved on in 1593.

§ It must be remembered that *The Buildings of England* do not discuss movable furnishings in houses. Hence neither the magnificent old oak nor even the needlework and tapestries will here be mentioned.

with the front but at r. angles to it, going right across the middle of the house. There is no known example earlier than Hardwick of this arrangement which was repeated only occasionally in the early C17, but there were similar experiments with the same purpose of getting away from the traditional, asymmetrical, and therefore no longer satisfactory placing of the Hall. The chief examples are the same again which had to be mentioned in comparison with the Hatfield elevations. Barlborough has no proper Hall at all, and Wollaton has a Hall right in the centre of the square block and rising higher than the rest. Hardwick is in line with these developments of the eighties and makes its own original contribution.

Here lies the principal reason why one is inclined to attribute the design of Hardwick to *Robert Smythson*, architect of Wollaton. The Smythson family worked for the Cavendishes at Welbeck and at Bolsover. Also Wollaton has the same ringed columns as in the ground floor colonnade at Hardwick and medallions with busts similar to Barlborough. Moreover, one of Bess's chief sculptors, *Thomas Accres*, came to Hardwick from Wollaton. The building accounts of Hardwick mention no designer or master of the works.

The ENTRANCE HALL has a Screen, as earlier Halls had, but it now runs across as a kind of lobby separating an area of moderate size by the chief entrance from the rest of the Hall. A dais and High Table can never have existed. The Screen has remarkably correct Roman Doric columns, and supports a gallery on the first floor, the only connexion between the rooms of the N and S halves. The fireplace is adorned with rather flat strapwork, but the overmantel introduces us to the bold and always rather gargantuan displays of *Abraham Smith*, Bess's chief plasterer, coarse but jolly work. From the Screens Passage or Lobby the Pantry was reached on the S, the Buttery and Kitchen on the N. Doors in corresponding positions near the E end of the Hall led to the main stairs on the S, the secondary stairs, and the so-called Lower Chapel on the N. These rooms, however, were altered later. In the case of the Chapel we know that it went originally through two floors (as in medieval episcopal chapels and, for instance, at Versailles), the ground floor for the servants, and the upper floor gallery (at first floor level) for the mistress and her family and guests. What has happened to the staircases we do not know. They are remarkably dramatic, it is true, but I cannot believe them to be Elizabethan. The sixth *Duke of Devonshire* between 1820 and 1858 did so much ingenious adjusting and heightening of effects at Chatsworth and did it often to his own ideas that I consider him the most likely designer of the two staircases as we now see them.

The chief rooms on the FIRST FLOOR are the Dining Room (originally the Low Presence Chamber) and the Drawing Room (originally Withdrawing Room), lying to the N and the S of the upper area of the Entrance Hall and connected by the gallery or balcony above the Screen, and the Chapel N of the second stair in the NE tower. The Drawing Room has an overmantel similar to that of the Entrance Hall though more modest, the Dining Room an overmantel with unimaginative strapwork and two stiff, elongated, female nudes. The inscription says: 'The conclusion of all things is to fear God and keep his commandments.' Bess might well have felt uneasy about the ninth. In the Chapel the most interesting feature is the wooden screen which originally separated the Countess's Gallery from the open area. It is very simple, as if the panels were taken out of an Elizabethan wall panelling. There are no Gothic reminiscences at all. Next to the Chapel is the former Little Dining Chamber, now Paved Bedroom with an overmantel relief of Ceres, made by *Smith*, no doubt from a Flemish engraving. The figure is like on late C16 monuments, the execution far from elegant. Next to the Drawing Room follows the Green Bedroom with a fireplace more architectural than the others and a figure of Charity sculpturally far more competent. It belongs in style closely to the Gallery fireplaces (cf. below).

The principal rooms on the SECOND FLOOR are the Long

Gallery and the High Great Presence Chamber, the one running all along the E front to a length of a full 166 ft, the other placed in the middle of the W front so that the canted bay window in its centre and the two adjoining windows on each side belong to it. The PRESENCE CHAMBER is one of the most impressive and most characteristic rooms of its date in England, large, light, and broad in treatment. Broad indeed is *Abraham Smith's* coloured plaster frieze, forest scenes with plenty of animals and figures of divers size. It must be a monstrous show in the eyes of a visitor from Fontainebleau or Florence, barbaric in the extreme. The same comment would have been made of Elizabethan furniture such as filled and still fills Hardwick. The bay window walls are panelled to the top cornice and on the panelling coloured engravings are stuck and varnished over. The fireplace is of alabaster, Derbyshire marble, and touch. The great sensation of the GALLERY is its three bay windows, each the size of a C20 council house. On a sunny day the Gallery is as light as a factory in the modern style. Let nobody say that C20 fenestration is alien to this island. Along the back wall facing the windows between the bays are two large fireplaces, again, like that in the Green Bedroom on the first floor, clearly more architectural than *Abraham Smith's*. They both have coupled banded pilasters below and coupled black columns above, and in the middle, surrounded by strapwork of far more vigour and tension than *Smith's*, small figures of Justice and Misericord in oval frames. The figures are obviously by the same hand as the Charity in the Green Bedroom. Could the hand be that of *Maximilian Colt* (cf. his work at Hatfield)? The tapestries of the Gallery must at least have one word; for they are here part of the original furnishing scheme. Bess bought them in 1592 from the heirs of Sir Christopher Hatton, Queen Elizabeth's Lord Chancellor. She paid £326 15*s*. 9*d*. for them, an enormous sum, as will be realized if one compares it with the £600 which Sir William Cavendish had paid for the whole Chatsworth estate. N of the PRESENCE CHAMBER are a number of

42a

bedrooms, lower so that another set could be housed on top of them, the two tiers behind one set of three-transomed windows. The chief thing to mention in these bedrooms is again their mantelpieces. In the State Bedroom adjoining the Presence Chamber is the best piece of sculpture at Hardwick, a large alabaster relief of Apollo and the Muses by an unknown sculptor who without doubt was neither English nor Flemish. It does not belong to the house but was brought over from Chatsworth where nothing is known about it either. In Bess of Hardwick's Bedroom is a fireplace with caryatids and a big handsome three-dimensional strapwork cartouche. 43b

Bess of Hardwick's gardens have disappeared, but the madly crenellated garden wall and the gateway, triangular lodges, and triangular bastion-like summer pavilions with their crazy headgear are all miraculously well preserved.

HARTHILL *see* STANTON MOOR

HARTHILL HALL FARM *see* ALPORT

HARTHILL MOOR *see* ALPORT

HARTINGTON

ST GILES. High up above the little town. Perp W tower of red ashlar sandstone with set-back buttresses, gargoyles, battlements, and pinnacles. The body of the church is distinguished by the presence of transepts (cf. Ashbourne, Wirksworth), that on the S side with a W aisle. This plan dates back to the late C13 or a little later: *see* the arcades between nave and aisles exactly as at Wirksworth (quatrefoil piers with fillets and the E responds slimmer with shaft-rings), the lancet windows in the chancel N wall and N transept W wall, the two S windows of the S transept, especially the large one which is worth some study (a five-light window of intersected tracery cusped but with the very top quite illogically interrupted to leave space for a quatrefoil with a pointed, elongated lower lobe), the S

STOKE-ON-TRENT PUBLIC LIBRARIES

transept E window, the chancel E window (five-light intersected), the N transept windows, the S doorway, the Piscinas in the two transepts, and the low finely moulded arch of a tomb recess in the S transept. The two-storeyed porch is a picturesque and felicitous addition of the late Middle Ages with its W wall in line with the S aisle W wall, broadening the aisle for the eye, and with its embattled parapet sloping up towards the transept. One feature at Hartington differs from Wirksworth. The S transept has a W aisle (octagonal piers, C14 capitals). – FONT. Perp, octagonal, with divers tracery panels (similar to Darley Dale). – GAUNTLET, of unknown provenance, inside the tower arch. – MONUMENTS. Several top parts of lids with foliated crosses, *c.* C13. – Effigy of a lady under trefoiled arch. She is only visible to the height of her folded hands; the rest is hidden by the slab as if she were tucked in under a blanket. C13.

HARTINGTON HALL. Above the church to the SE. 1611, with three gables, two of them on l. and r. symmetrical projections. Three- to five-light mullioned windows with hood-moulds. Minor plaster ceilings.

In the town Market Place with cottages of C18 and C19 dates (1777, 1828) and a classical TOWN HALL of 1836 with a ground floor of three rusticated depressed arches.

HARTSHORNE

ST PETER. 1835, with Perp tracery of cast iron in the lancets, and a W gallery on cast iron columns, medieval (C15) only the W tower with spire recessed behind battlements. – FONT. Octagonal, tapering, plain, probably C14. – PLATE. Paten of *c.* 1480 with a face of Christ, one of the oldest pieces of plate in Derbyshire. – Chalice of 1612. – Pewter Flagon dated 1638. – MONUMENT. Humphrey Dethick † 1599 and wife, recumbent alabaster effigies; on the tomb-chest the six children, standing up, in two panels, each with a triple arch.

HASLAND HALL *see* CHESTERFIELD

HASSOP

ALL SAINTS, *c.* 1816, by *Ireland* (GR). Roman Catholic, built by the Eyre family, a family with distinguished Catholic traditions. The design in the severest Classical Revival style: a correct Etruscan temple front, tetrastyle, prostyle. Five Grecian side windows and Tuscan pilasters at the back. The interior has a coved coffered ceiling. – PAINTING. Large Crucifixion with the Virgin and St John said to be by *Lodovico Carracci*. – MONUMENT. Thomas Eyre † 1833, epitaph with figure of Faith and portrait medallion on a pedestal, by *H. Carew* of Brighton.

Near the church a plain, quite big, late C17 house with three gables and two non-intermittent stringcourses to which the (altered) windows are tied.

HATHERSAGE

ST MICHAEL. High up at the end of the little town; a typical Derbyshire sight with its castellated aisles, porch, and clerestory, its gargoyles and its spire. Good Perp W tower with diagonal buttresses, and traceried W window. The spire is recessed behind the battlements and crocketed. The tower arch to the nave is tall and has the unusual feature as part of its capitals of a broad band of big leaves, embattled. The arcades are of four bays, that on the N side with very odd capitals on its octagonal piers. They are mostly renewed (restoration by *Butterfield*, 1852), but what is old seems to have a kind of upright leaf of *c.* 1200. The church is supposed to have been built in 1381. The S arcade might correspond to that date and the chancel; *see* the Sedilia and the N window, cut into by the Eyre monument (cf. below). The E window, however, was put in only in 1949. It comes from Derwent church and was transferred, when that church was submerged in the new lake. Of the C15, besides the tower, the clerestory and the N chancel chapel. This was added as an Eyre chantry in 1463. – STAINED GLASS. Of the time of the restoration and specially praised in Murray's *Handbook* of 1874. W window 1856, S aisle windows probably *c.* 1852. – 23a MONUMENTS. Remarkable set of Eyre brasses. Tomb-chest with foiled panels and on it the excellent brasses of Robert Eyre † 1459 in armour and his wife and, below, their children. The chest stands between chancel and chancel chapel and has above a big heavy ogee-headed recess with very curious tracery below. Is it contemporary or was it tampered with when the Countess of Narborough restored it in 1832? – Robert Eyre, *c.*1500, wife and children, kneeling figures, placed against the back wall of the recess just mentioned. – Ralph Eyre † 1493 and wife, standing figures. A fragment of two daughters above. – Sir Arthur Eyre *c.*1560, kneeling, with wife.

ST MICHAEL, R.C., 1806. Plain parallelogram with altered interior. The outside surprisingly heavily detailed, with big quoins, a broad doorway on big corbels, and arched windows with thick frames.

Two early C19 MILLS, one by the Derwent Bridge, the other at the head of the town (which incidentally is the Morton of *Jane Eyre*). With the latter mill ROCK HOUSE seems to be connected, a neurotic attempt to use the extremely heavy rustication of *Paine's* Chatsworth stables for modest domestic purposes. All windows and the door of the two-storeyed house of five bays have colossal rock-faced frames as if they were at Mantua and by Giulio Romano.

HATHERSAGE HALL. Two-storeyed front of *c.* 1820 and three-storeyed back with remains of the late C16 or C17.

HIGHLOW HALL, *see* p. 160.

HAZELFORD, *see* p. 169.

STANAGE EDGE, 2¼ m. N. Remains of a Roman road.

HAYFIELD

ST MATTHEW. 1818, by *Bradbury & Rangeley* (GR), characteristic of its date, with its arched windows and windows with intersected tracery. The chancel was added in 1894. Inside, galleries on three sides on thin iron columns. –

BOX PEWS. – MONUMENT. Epitaph of Joseph Hayne † 1786 (from Glossop church). Inscription tablet with a fluted superstructure diminishing in size and ending in a big full-round bust.

PARK HALL, 1 m. N. 1811. Two-storeyed, seven-bay house with one-storeyed Ionic entrance colonnade. Fine semicircular stables with end pediments.

HAZELFORD

1 m. S of Hathersage

C17 house with porch, gables with ball finials, and four- and five-light mullioned windows.

HAZLEBADGE HALL

¾ m. S of Bradwell

The coat of arms of the Vernon and Swynnerton families 37b and the date 1549 appear in the W gable of a rectangular building whose windows are on the side with the date still six-light and five-light mullioned with depressed pointed arches to each light. On the S side they are normal, straightheaded, and mullioned. The SW room has moulded ceiling beams.

COP LOW, ½ m. SSW, round barrow.

HAZLEWOOD

ST JOHN, 1840, by *Stevens* (restored after fire in 1903 : GR). Stone nave and chancel, bellcote, lancet windows.

HEAGE

ST LUKE. The church has a T-plan owing to an addition of 1836 to a medieval building. The plan turned out (by chance probably) to be one of those specially recommended for Protestant worship from early days. The old part has its E window of three stepped lancet lights cusped, and small straightheaded C16 or C17 side windows. The new part is taller and has the typical early C19 lancets of two lancet lights with pierced spandrels. Over the entrance a polygonal bell-turret (1896?). The date 1752 on the door lintel does not refer to either main building period.

HEANOR

ST LAWRENCE. 1868, except for the dark grey Perp W tower with angle buttresses. It has on each side two large two-light bell-openings with transomes (altered in the C19). In the church EPITAPH to Samuel Watson † 1715, the chief wood-carver at Chatsworth ('Watson is gone, whose skilful Art display'd / To th' very life whatever Nature made / View but his wondrous works at Chatsworth Hall / Which were so gazed at and admired by all').
WESLEYAN CHAPEL, 1839, red brick, three-bay front, still in the Georgian tradition.

HEATH

ALL SAINTS. 1853, by *Stevens* (GR). Rock-faced, with spire.

HEATH WOOD, INGLEBY *see* FOREMARK

HIGHLOW HALL

1½ m. SW of Hathersage

Small manor house, probably C16, the front crenellated with square porch projection. Several of the garden gateways (C17) survive.

HILTON

OLD HALL. Pretty half-timbered house with symmetrical front, gables of equal size l. and r. The timberwork with various ornamental motifs, lozenge in square, oval in square within square, ogee lozenge in square.

HOB HURST'S HOUSE *see* BEELEY

HOGNASTON

ST BARTHOLOMEW. Amazing Norman doorway. The tympanum shows incised pictures of a bishop with a crook, the lamb with cross, two fishes, a hog (?), and several other beasts. What on earth did our forbears mean by such representations? And how can one account for this total absence of a sense of composition and this utterly childish treatment? The doorway has one order of colonnettes with very stylized beakheads, no more than tongue shapes. The label has head stops and a head at the top. The W tower is C13, square and unbuttressed with small lancet windows. The ground floor is of stone different from the first floor (broad low buttresses). The ground floor opens into the nave in a three-stepped arch on the simplest imposts. The first floor, however, has also lancets. The top is Perp, with battlements and C19 pinnacles. A big buttress up the middle of the W side. The rest of the exterior is all C19. Inside, the chancel arch is early C14; *see* the keeled shafts and the moulded capitals (cf. Bradbourne). – FONT. Norman, tub-shape, with short stumpy arcades.

In the village a few good C17 stone houses, e.g. opposite the church.

HOLBROOK

ST MICHAEL. Plain parallelogram with broad angle pilasters; built in 1841. On the N side still long arched windows and a pedimented porch which probably go back to the previous building of 1761. Much altered and enlarged early C20.

HOLBROOK HALL. Five-bay, two-storeyed, stone house with quoins, a segmental pediment above the doorway, another above the middle window going up into the roof. The date is 1681, surprisingly early for such details in Derbyshire.

HOLME *see* BAKEWELL

HOLMESFIELD

ST SWITHIN, 1826. W tower with odd battlements and crocketed pinnacles. Nave with long slim arched windows, with frames of rusticated blocks of alternating size. The chancel was added in 1895.

HOLMESFIELD HALL. Dated 1613 inside. Mullioned windows with straight hoods. The front redone in the C18 with a doorway with open pediment and swagger coat of arms. The windows still mullioned, but unmoulded frames and mullions.

CARTLEDGE HALL. Asymmetrical gabled Elizabethan or Jacobean farmhouse. Inside panelling, plaster ceilings, and a carved fireplace with a relief of the Fall of Man.

FANSHAWEGATE HALL FARM, ½ m. NW. Two pairs of elaborate C17 garden gateposts now lead only to a farmhouse with low mullioned windows, probably an outbuilding of the former Hall which was apparently dismantled in 1636. To its E a pretty dovecote.

WOODTHORPE HALL, ½ m. N. Sizeable L-shaped C17 manor house, much renovated. The materials said to come from Fanshawegate Hall (*see* above). The front with three gables of which that on the r. larger than the others, the side with two gables. Of the two porches one incorporates the original main doorway, the other was bought from Owleston Hall, Sheffield.

HOPE

ST PETER. Early C14 W tower with angle buttresses. Heavy, i.e. early, broach spire on it starting direct from the top of the unembattled tower. All tower and spire windows are Dec (bell-openings C19). The chancel was rebuilt in 1882, but incorporates Piscina and Sedilia of *c.* 1300 or the early C14. N and S aisles, clerestory, and S porch all Perp and unusually complete, obviously a rapid and steady rebuilding job. Battlements everywhere and oversized gargoyles on the S side. The aisle windows of three lights with panel tracery, the arcades of four bays with tall slim octagonal piers and moulded capitals of a section which one does not meet often. The S porch is two-storeyed with a good front with ogee niche between two windows. – STALL BACKS. Made up from parts of the former box pews (cf. Castleton). Dates 1587, 1632, 1658, 1690. – PLATE. Caroline Chalice and Cover; big Flagon, 1715. – MONUMENTS. Two C13 foliated cross slabs to Forest officials (*see* the horns), N aisle W end.

In the churchyard SAXON CROSS SHAFT, with interlace and on the E and W faces pairs of figures, badly preserved, *c.* C9.

Near Hope are the large CEMENT WORKS of Messrs G. & T. Earle. They are sited well away from the village, and for their future development a landscape plan has been worked out by *G. A. Jellicoe* and accepted. According to this the limestone quarries should always have as narrow a mouth as possible and then extend fanwise into the hill. When one quarry is exhausted the waste from the next is to be used to restore the original hillside. All excavations of sand will in the end form a chain of lakes with planted banks.

HOPTON HALL NR CARSINGTON

An Elizabethan house with two gabled projections, redone in the later C18, when the garden front received Venetian windows, the centre between the projections was filled in and crowned by an oversized heavy segmental pediment (cf. Brizlincote), and the entrance side completely Georgianized. In the gardens a brick forcing wall for fruit made into a handsome composition early in the C18. In the centre a tower (summerhouse?); to the l. and r. the wall makes three segmental curves.

ALMSHOUSES, 1719–22, for two men and two women. One-storeyed, central gable, the windows still mullioned.

QUARRIES *see* Middleton p. 185.

HOPWELL HALL

Five-bay, two-and-a-half-storey, brick mansion with broad giant angle pilasters. The bulgy top cornice, the moulded stone window frames, and the doorcase with open segmental pediment and pilasters with sunk panels all characteristic of the inscribed date 1720. A lower three-bay wing to the W.

HORSLEY

ST CLEMENT. A fine all-embattled church with a spire on a hill. The spire is broached and not high (two tiers of dormer windows), but the view of the E end is quite splendid. The interior is wide and light with N and S aisles, the S arcade on tallish circular piers, the N arcade octagonal. The arches are double-chamfered, the whole looks early C14. Of the same date probably the S doorway and the tower (*see* the tracery of the bell-openings and the S doorway with head-stops to the label). The tower has angle buttresses. Most of the windows are Perp, segment-headed of two and three ogee-arched lights, including the clerestory windows. A two-light window opens above the chancel arch, an unusual feature. All this Perp work and the whole of the crenellating is connected with a re-dedication in 1450. Sedilia C14 or C15, with cusped ogee arches and plain shields in the spandrels (cf. Breadsall). – FONT. Big, Perp, octagonal. – PLATE. Chalice, C16 or C17, says the local guide book.

HULLAND

CHRIST CHURCH, 1851, by *Mason* (GR). Neat rectangle with embattled W tower. No aisles. All windows lancets of two lancet lights with the spandrel pierced. E window three-light intersected. Box pews, two-decker pulpit, W gallery on cast iron columns, flat ceiling, whitewashed—i.e. nothing altered. – PLATE. Brass Almsdish with St George and the Dragon, probably German, *c.* 1600; given to the church in 1936.

IDRIDGEHAY

ST JAMES, 1854–5, by *Stephens* (GR).

SOUTH STITCH. An uncommonly good timber-framed house with closely set uprights and no decorative bits. The interior well preserved too.

ILKESTON

A town singularly devoid of visual attractions.

ST MARK. A big stately church now, but chiefly owing to a bold enlargement of 1907 which made out of a nave three bays long one of double that length and shifted the W tower to a new position at the same time. Of the original building of *c.* 1200 there remain the three E piers between nave and S aisle, circular with transitional capitals with small upright leaves and unmoulded pointed arches. When the N arcade was built in the C14 with octagonal piers and double-chamfered arches, the authorities wanted their church to be considerably higher than the Norman church had been, and so about 5 ft were added to the Norman piers and the new N piers were made that much longer. A clerestory was not found necessary. But before then the W tower* was built, as its rather low arch towards the nave with semicircular responds and dog-tooth ornament shows. That must have been early in the C13. It was followed by the chancel; *see* the excellent Sedilia and Double Piscina which is datable *c.* 1280 by the foliage capitals, the head label-stops, and the bar tracery of the Piscina (with a quatrefoil in a circle). The exterior of the church is terribly over-restored, the E window, for example, is entirely of 1855 (by *Walker*), but the tracery of the original (E) parts of the two aisles, though renewed, represent what was there: fine three-light windows, the three lights lancet-shaped and stepped, with pointed trefoils in the heads and much cusping, i.e. typical of the early C14. Of the late C14 the N chancel chapel (Chantry of St Peter). Its piers and arches are delicate and many-shafted. The capitals are small and decorated with bossy leaves. – SCREEN. Remarkable early C14 stone screen, each division of one light only with a cusped ogee arch and a large quatrefoil in each spandrel. Very light and transparent. The lower parts C19. – PLATE. Chalice given in 1622. – MONUMENT. Fairly well preserved effigy of a cross-legged knight, presumed to be Sir William de Cantelupe † 1309. 19a

ST BARTHOLOMEW, Hallam Fields, 1895, by *Currey*. Brick, a pretty composition with an almost detached NW tower with saddle-back roof.

* Top parts remodelled in the C19. Originally the church had a spire.

ST JOHN THE EVANGELIST, Nottingham Road. Designed 1894 by *Currey*. Brick with lancet windows, no tower but a turret in the angle between nave and N transept.

WESLEYAN CHAPEL, Bath Street, 1849. Brick, of three bays, still in the Georgian tradition.

INGLEBY

PAGAN CEMETERY containing over fifty burial mounds in Heath Wood. Recent excavations suggest a date between A.D. 800 and 950.

IRONVILLE

Built by the Butterley Iron Company *c.* 1850. There is well-spaced factory housing, long rows of plain brick cottages, and there are quite an ambitious church of 1852, two schools of 1850, and a monument of 1854 in the recreation ground.

KEDLESTON

ALL SAINTS. In spite of its Norman S doorway (one order of colonnettes, with beakheads biting into them, arch with zigzag, and defaced tympanum with traces of beasts) this is essentially a late C13 church, cruciform with crossing tower, which is rare in Derbyshire. The transepts have their original N and S windows of three stepped lancet lights, the chancel new windows, except for one small cusped lancet, but original S doorway, Piscina, and the springers of the arch of a recess replaced by a Perp one. The top parts of the crossing tower are Perp. The E end was classicized late in the C17; *see* the pedimented sundial and the two vases to the l. and r. The N aisle was added by *Bodley* in 1906–13 as a memorial to Lord Curzon of Kedleston, Viceroy of India. Sumptuous wrought iron grilles by *P. Krall* inside, stained glass by *F. C. Eden*, and a MONUMENT of gleaming white marble with two recumbent effigies and an elegant white woman, life-size, standing at the head end. By *Sir B. Mackennal*. – FONT, BOX PEWS, COMMUNION RAILS, all *c.* 1700, the font baluster-shaped on four scrolly feet. – FAMILY PEWS in the chancel, *c.* 1700. – COMMUNION RAIL, *c.*

1700. – PAINTINGS. Holy Family by *Giampetrini*. – Madonna by *Pier Francesco Mola*.

OTHER MONUMENTS. Coffin-shaped slab with foliated cross, C13. – Twin quatrefoils with large heads of a knight in chain mail and a lady wearing a wimple, sunk in the oddest way into the floor of the crossing. They no doubt commemorate the builders of the church. – Effigy of Sir John Curzon † 1406, in a recess in the chancel S wall. – Excellent alabaster tomb-chest for Sir John Curzon † *c*. 1450, effigies of husband and wife, against the front wall of the chest five figures, three of them seated saints, the other two standing angels. – Brass to Richard Curzon † 1496, and wife. – Sir John Curzon † 1686, large epitaph, shockingly bad. The main part divided into two panels by a black column. Flanking columns as well. In the panels frontal demi-figures, each accompanied by an angel in whole figure. In the *predella* seven frontal busts of children between draperies. – Sir John Curzon † 1727, obelisk with portrait medallion surrounded by a wreath of cherubs' heads. Standing putti l. and r. – Sir Nathaniel Curzon † 1737, an ambitious composition, but unsigned. Standing wall monument with obelisk and at its foot husband and wife in Roman attire seated with an urn between. Sir Nathaniel Curzon, 1763, by *Rysbrack* to *Robert Adam's* design. Yet not very satisfactory. Rusticated pyramid, and in front of it the upright figures of Sir Nathaniel, his wife, and two sons.

KEDLESTON HALL. The most splendid Georgian house of Derbyshire, in extensive grounds with a long undulating lake to the N, and to the S the slope upwards of a hill which tends to deprive the house of some of its effect on that side. The house was designed by *Matthew Brettingham* *c*. 1758 and then redesigned in its centre block in 1761 by *James Paine*. Paine's centre block is oblong with a large and tall hall at r. angles to the N front, a staircase and semicircularly projecting drawing room behind, three large rooms on the E and four smaller ones on the W, and semicircular one-storeyed colonnades projecting from all four angles and ending in two-and-a-half-storeyed angle 54a pavilions. The colonnades and angle pavilions are Brettingham's The two N ones were built, and then the centre begun to Paine's plan. The great N portico raised above the rusticated basement storey and reached by a double staircase is also by Paine. It has six giant Corinthian columns, a commanding if not specially imaginative motif. But in 1760 *Robert Adam* was called in, and to him is due the much more original S front. This has as its centre a motif derived from Roman triumphal arches, four detached Corinthian columns standing close to the wall and each carrying its own piece of projecting entablature. Above this is an attic with a date plate of 1770 and statues on the four pieces of entablature. The motif possesses just that 'diversity of form' and 'advance and recess' of which Adam wrote in 1773 that they 'add greatly to the picturesque' of an architectural composition. Between the columns also the motifs are more varied than in the centre of the N front. The less emphasized parts to the l. and r. of the centre have only window pediments on brackets, whereas Paine had given them attached columns. Adam is unquestionably less grand, but he is more elegant and, in spite of the great size of the block, more intimate. Inside Adam accepted Paine's main idea for the Great Hall, that is the use of detached giant columns along the walls, an idea derived from Lord Burlington's Assembly Rooms at York and Kent's Holkham. The Hall of Kedleston is one of the most magnificent apartments of the C18 in England, about 67 by 37 ft in size, and 40 ft high, with the fluted Corinthian columns of pink English alabaster 25 ft high, and a generously coved ceiling with stucco decoration and three central skylights. The stucco here was carried out (by *Joseph Rose*) only in the seventies. The fireplaces have elaborate overmantels. The character of this adornment is somewhat different from that of the architecture which is, like all early Adam work, just a little more robust than his later designs. Giant columns so consistently used would have appeared too massive to Adam in the seventies. From the far end of the Hall the Rotunda is immediately reached, the room

54a

54b

55

replacing Paine's projected staircase (Adam's is W of the Hall and less conspicuous) and drawing room. The Rotunda is fitted into square outer walls by means of corner niches, again a typical motif of Imperial Roman architecture. The room is domed, and the coffering of the dome and its central skylight are also clearly of Roman derivation. The spatial effect in moving from the Hall into the Rotunda is delightful; for the Rotunda is considerably higher (62 ft high; diameter 42 ft). The paintings of ruins are by *Hamilton*, the grisaille panels between them by *Rebecca*. In the niches are cast iron vases on pedestals disguising Adam's central heating arrangements. The pilasters flanking the doorways are of blue scagliola.

To the l. of Hall and Rotunda are, taken from N to S, the Music Room (white with an organ designed by Adam and a fireplace inlaid with blue-john), the Drawing Room, 44 by 28 by 28 ft (with a gorgeous Venetian window of alabaster, alabaster doorcases, a fireplace flanked by large standing female figures and furniture designed by Adam), and the Library (quieter in its architecture and with Tuscan columns for the doorcases instead of the Corinthian ones next door). On the other side of Hall and Rotunda lie chiefly the Dining Room (facing N, with an apse at the W end into which fit curved tables, a white ceiling with painting, by *Zucchi* and *Angelica Kauffmann*, a fireplace with termini caryatids, and a monumental wine cooler of jasper in the form of a bath), the Staircase, the State Bedroom (with its fantastic bed, the four angle posters of which are carved in the form of palm trees), and the State Boudoir (facing S, the spatially most complex room, in so far as the part nearest the Rotunda is divided off by a wall, opening in the middle in a somewhat lower tripartite screen with a pierced segmental arch above the entablature, a very characteristic Adam motif). Below the Entrance Hall is a low five-aisled Hall at ground floor level.

In the grounds is an elegant BRIDGE across the lake by *Adam* (drawing dated 1761), a BOAT HOUSE to the W of the Bridge and a small BATH HOUSE *c.* ½ m. to the E. The

N GATES have Tuscan columns and a pediment. The church lies so close to the house that it seems to hide behind the NW colonnade and pavilion.

KILBURN HALL

Partly Jacobean and partly dated 1712. The latter work is remarkably conservative, still with gables. Quoins and stone lintels to the windows. Much renewed and added to after 1900.

KILLAMARSH

ST GILES. The interest of the church is the Norman S doorway (one order of colonnettes, capitals with leaves, arch with zigzag in intrados and extrados). The Late Perp S window should also be noted in which all curved forms of Gothic arches have gone straight. W tower Perp (diagonal buttresses, battlements, pinnacles). – STAINED GLASS. C15 Virgin in a chancel S window. – Chancel E window by *Warrington*, 1845 (TK).

KIRK HALLAM

ALL SAINTS. Two Norman beakheads preserved in the porch; the FONT also Norman, tub-shaped with arcade of intersecting arches. Dec chancel windows (straight-headed) and Sedilia and Piscina. Perp W tower, short and ashlar-faced. – COMMUNION RAIL. C18.

KIRK IRETON

HOLY TRINITY. C18 gateway into the churchyard. Embattled W tower low, broad and unbuttressed: obviously early. Blocked W doorway. Small low church with two-bay Late Norman S arcade (piers circular and with simplified leaves, arches lopsided two-stepped, quite illogical) and slightly later N arcade (piers circular with moulded capitals, arches single-chamfered). Chancel-arch and arches into the chancel chapel Perp. These parts are embattled on the S side, the nave and aisles are not.

The only more ornate detail in the church is the C14 doorway from the chancel into the vestry, with thin shafts and the voussoirs decorated with big fleurons.

KIRK LANGLEY

ST MICHAEL. Early C14 chancel (Sedilia with pointed trefoiled heads, lancet window, N doorway) N. aisle also early C14 (windows, arcade) W tower Perp, ashlar-faced with angle buttresses connected at the top, below the battlements, by a horizontal band. – TOWER SCREEN, apparently *c.* 1300, *see* its simple geometrical tracery. – PARCLOSE SCREEN. Perp, with original tracery motifs. – PLATE. Silver-gilt Set consisting of Chalice of Gothic shape, Paten and large Flagon; London-made, 1640–1.

Several good brick houses in the village, e.g. the gabled Vicarage dated 1655, a Georgian house next to it, and another on the main road, with broad doorway with attached Tuscan columns and stone-dressed window above.

KNIVETON

ST MICHAEL. Small; just nave and chancel and W tower. The latter C13, unbuttressed with small lancet windows, battlements and a short spire. S doorway, Norman on the plainest imposts. Label with two stops (one of them a beakhead). The keystone a bear, the whole evidently tampered with (cf. Hognaston). All windows are renewed. – FONT. of the Ashbourne type, but the trefoil motif pointed.

LADYBOWER RESERVOIR

The name applies to a group of connected reservoir lakes which form a splendid enhancement of the natural beauties of Derbyshire. The purpose of the reservoirs is to supply water for Derby, Leicester, Nottingham, Sheffield, and some smaller local authorities. They consist of the two upper NE parts with their two forbidding castellated dams, Howden Dam and Derwent Dam, begun in 1906 and 1907 and completed with their respective reservoirs in 1912 and 1916. These were followed by the Ashop Diversion or Compensation Works (1921–30) and finally the Ladybower proper, with its grass-embanked dam (1935–45). The filling of the reservoir submerged DERWENT WOODLANDS Church and DERWENT HALL.

LANGWITH

HOLY CROSS, Upper Langwith. Nave and chancel; no tower. Chancel C13, *see* one long lancet window. S porch with big pinnacles, vaulted inside with transverse arches (cf. Ault Hucknall, etc.). Most of the windows Perp.– PLATE. Small simple bronze Censer, C15.

LANGWITH BASSET CAVE, Upper Langwith. Old Stone Age habitation.

LEA HALL *see* DETHICK

LEAHURST *see* DETHICK

LEA WOOD *see* DETHICK

LIFF'S LOW *see* YOULGREAVE

LITTLE CHESTER NR DERBY

The Roman station of Derwent—at the crossing of the Icknield Way which runs through Derbyshire from Burton-on-Trent to Chesterfield and on to York. The camp was 615 by 540 ft in size, much larger than the other Derbyshire camps.

In OLD CHESTER ROAD a few old houses: No. 83 with some mullioned windows, School Farm with large medieval stone chimneys (Stone House Prebend) and the handsome brick house opposite.

LITTLE EATON

ST PAUL. Built 1791, but all that is visible now is a modernization in the Norman style of 1837 (with embattled W tower). N aisle Victorian.

The village has a neat little centre with rows of stone cottages on three sides. SW of the church a handsome mid-Georgian brick house of three bays and two and a half storeys, with quoins, rusticated window lintels, a pedimented doorway and l. and r. of it Venetian windows.

LITTLE HUCKLOW

HOUSE with date-stone 1661. Yet the windows are low and mullioned and have hoodmoulds, oddly double-stepped (cf. Unstone 1657). At the back is a projecting spiral staircase; so the structure of the house is perhaps older.

LITTLEOVER

ST PETER. Plain Norman doorway (with replaced shafts) in the W wall. Otherwise the exterior mostly over-restored. Bellcote and S aisle are C19. N aisle C14 (octagonal piers, double-chamfered arches). The chancel early C14 (*see* its windows). – MONUMENT. Sir Richard Harpour † 1635 and wife, epitaph with kneeling figures facing each other across a prayer desk. In the *predella* the children.

COUNTY INFANTS' SCHOOL and COUNTY SECONDARY SCHOOL. Among the recent standard steel and brick schools provided by the County Education Department (*see* Introduction, p. 33).

LITTON

Those interested in the development of the architectural style in Derbyshire houses will find one of 1723, still with the old low two-light windows, but with a doorway with pediment on corbels and regular quoins, and another of 1768 with a segmental pediment to the doorway and an arched window above it, but the other windows even now still of the three-light mullioned type.

LOCKO PARK

Large stone mansion overlooking an ornamental lake. The original part early C18, nine bays wide, three storeys high with emphasis by rusticated giant pilasters on the angles and the angles of the five-bay centre. Top balustrade. Low short projecting wings, that on the W side older than the house. It contains the chapel which was built in 1669, but has been remodelled internally. The other wing was added *c.* 1750 to match the chapel. Fine early C18 staircases with thin twisted and non-twisted balusters. Stained glass by *Powell's*, *c.* 1900. The house was much enlarged in a restrained Italianate style *c.* 1850–60: a symmetrically placed tower and E porch. etc. More additions on the E side 1896. Pretty S Lodges.

LONG EATON

ST LAURENCE. Behind the Market Place. The low and broad church makes a pretty picture, with its separate N aisle and nave roofs and its SW tower. This picture is C19. It belongs to *Street's* rebuilding of 1868. He made the old nave his S aisle and thereby displaced the old W tower. The tower is ashlar-faced with diagonal buttresses and has the recessed spire behind battlements which is so frequent in Derbyshire. The old nave has a Norman doorway with one order of colonnettes and in the voussoirs an inner order of beakhead and a second order of large chain-links. In the old chancel also a few Norman fragments of a doorway (zigzag, shaft). The windows are of the C14, straightheaded.

ST JOHN THE EVANGELIST, College Street. By *Sir Charles Nicholson*, designed 1916. Brick (English bond) with stone dressings. Incomplete. The chancel and the SW tower not yet built. Interior with slim piers and a prettily painted roof typical of Nicholson's work.

DERBY ROAD WESLEY CHURCH. By *Brewill & Baily*, 1903–4, in the enterprising and fanciful style of these architects and of Methodist architecture about 1900.

TRENT COLLEGE, 1866–8, with Chapel of 1874 by *Robinson* of Derby and more later buildings. The Chapel was re-modelled inside by *A. E. Richardson* in 1949.

LONGMOOR PRIMARY SCHOOL. One of the recent standard schools of the County Education Department, *see* Introduction, p. 33.

LONGFORD

ST CHAD. Close to the house. The oldest part is the Norman three-bay N arcade with circular piers, many-scalloped capitals and unchamfered two-step arches. The fourth arch is early C14, as is the chancel, *see* the tall two-light windows, the Sedilia and Piscina and the low N recess. The E window, however, dates from 1843. The S and N aisles are *c.* 1300 (*see* the windows, lancets of two-lancet lights with pierced spandrel, also three light intersected). At the same time the S arcade was altered. Its piers are still the Norman ones, but the arches are double-chamfered, and the capitals are an ugly makeshift. The clerestory with battlements is C15. So is the fine ashlar-faced W tower with angle buttresses and two large two-light bell openings on each side (cf. Youlgreave and North Wingfield). – CHANCEL SEATS with a few old poppy-heads. – MONUMENTS. A whole alabaster corner in the S aisle, with effigies laid on the floor: Sir Nicholas Longford † 1810 and wife. – Then three Knights, one of them under a recess in the S aisle. The latter Sir Nicholas Longford † 1357, the others, probably Sir Nicholas III † 1402 and Sir Nicholas IV † 1429. – Mutilated effigy in the chancel recess. – Sir Edward Coke † 1733, plain large pyramid in relief. – Thomas William Coke † 1842, tall epitaph with Dec canopies and marble portrait bust. – Anne Amelia Countess of Leicester † 1844, large marble epitaph with angel taking her to heaven; unsigned.

LONGFORD HALL. Brick with stone dressings. Burnt out 1942 and now under partial reconstruction. The main façade (W) very peculiar. Evidently a Tudor front (similar to the former Risley Hall) was remodelled about 1700. The result is a façade 15 windows long and between them symmetrically arranged four big projecting chimney shafts carrying Tudor chimneys. The work of 1700 consisted of the introduction of sash-windows, quoins and top balustrade with vases. The S front has two far projecting wings and a recessed one-storeyed range to connect them. The former courtyard behind this is now partly pulled down. The S Gates probably by *Bakewell*. Nothing seems known of the building history of the house.

LONG LEE *see* ROWORTH

LONG LOW *see* TIDESWELL

LONGSTONE

ST GILES. N aisle lancet windows, C13. Of the same century the S doorway. W tower early C14, unbuttressed and with an ogee-headed lancet window on the W side. Perp battlements and pinnacles. Perp clerestory and other windows. The church was restored, it is said, very carefully, by *Norman Shaw* in 1873. The six-bay arcades inside C14. The chief pride of the church is its Perp woodwork. Original ROOFS with bosses in nave, chancel, and aisles. The aisles of lean-to type, nave, and chancel simply braced, without tie-beams. – PARCLOSE SCREEN in the S aisle with a broad flat top-frieze of not at all usual design. – STAINED GLASS. Wright Memorial (E) window, 1873, good. – BRASS. Roland Eyre, 1624, two small kneeling figures facing each other across two prayer-desks.

LONGSTONE HALL, 1747. Extremely attractive completely plain three-bay brick house with quoins and parapet. The windows are widely spaced and the effect is entirely due to proportions.

CRESSBROOK, *see* p. 102.

THORNBRIDGE HALL, *see* p. 232.

LORDS SEAT *see* CASTLETON

LULLINGTON

ALL SAINTS. Old only the W tower with diagonal buttresses and a broach spire with two tiers of dormer windows, one low down, one high up. The spire was taken down and rebuilt in 1766.

MACKWORTH

ALL SAINTS. On its own in a field. W tower, ashlar-faced, Perp with angle buttresses connected at the top below the battlements by a horizontal band. Recessed spire with one tier of dormer windows. The bell openings altered in the C19. S aisle with two-storeyed porch and Perp windows, N aisle windows also Perp except for the W window which is typical of *c.* 1300 (lancet consisting of two lancet lights with pierced spandrel). The W tower is supposed to have had defensive purposes, as it has only a small door into the nave and none to the outside, and also very small openings in its lower stages. N and S aisles, both C14; that of the S side has characteristically earlier capitals than that of the N. The approximate date of the S aisle indicated by the finely moulded low recess in the S wall: early C14. In the chancel the plain Sedilia prove that it is also no later than the early C14. The niches at the E end of the N aisle and the canopy in the same aisle are supposed to be old but altered in the restoration of 1851. – Lots of lavish Victorian and later alabaster decoration, e.g. the Neo-Dec Vestry door surround of 1886 and the fantastic LECTERN of 1903 with its vine twining round the stem and ending in leaves and grapes below the bible support. – CHEST, 1640. – MONUMENT. Edward Mundy † 1607, alabaster effigy on tomb-chest with figures of children on the front wall.

CASTLE. Only the front wall of the GATEHOUSE survives, erected between 1495 and 1500. The gateway has a four-centred arch. Above, one upper storey with cusped straight-headed two-light windows under hood-moulds. Above the upper storey battlements and gargoyles. No turrets.

MAM TOR *see* CASTLETON

MAPLETON

ST MARY. An C18 stone building with a W tower crowned to one's shocked surprise by an octagonal dome with a lantern. The W porch was originally more ornate and attached to the S wall. The nave has arched windows. The interior is disappointing.

CLERGYMENS' WIDOWS' ALMSHOUSES, W of the church. 1727. A fine brick house with ample stone dressings. Five bays, two storeys, hipped roof, quoins. The centre bay projects and is flanked by giant rusticated pilasters. Doorway with Gibbs surround and triangular pediment. Windows with stone frames.

MARKEATON HALL NR DERBY

1755, brick with restless stone dressings, rather ugly in design. The Torrington Diary of 1789 comments unfavourably on the 'flaming red' colour. E front with five windows very close together and canted bays flanking them. Big pediment above the five-bay centre. S front with an asymmetrical canted bay, W side nine windows wide with five-bay pediment and a curved double staircase up to the main entrance. To the N of the NW corner a contemporary Orangery runs towards W.

MARKLAND GRIPS *see* CLOWNE

MARSTON-ON-DOVE

ST MARY. C13 chancel, wide, with lancet windows and small S doorway with one order of colonnettes. Early C14 S aisle, windows with flowing tracery, two-bay arcade with tall quatrefoil pier and double-chamfered arches. Ashlar-faced C14 W tower, no battlements, recessed spire with three tiers of dormer windows. The N side of the nave altered in the C15, when the clerestory was built. – The church possesses the oldest BELL of Derbyshire (1366; cast by *John of Stafford* at Leicester).

MARSTON MONTGOMERY

ST GILES. Nave with pyramidal bellcote dating from 1875. Beneath it in the W wall of the church a small Early Norman window. On the S side of the church the S doorway Norman with one order of colonnettes and a tympanum with an incised cross. The S chancel doorway also Norman. The chancel windows and the nave S window late C13, lancets or intersected tracery. Inside, the chancel arch is Norman, plain; the N arcade has circular piers with plain moulded capitals and still single-chamfered arches. – FONT. Plain Norman.

MANOR FARM. Half-timbered, not outstanding.

MATLOCK

Matlock consists of the old Matlock village, Matlock Bank, and Matlock Bath, which is chiefly the Matlock of to-day.

ST GILES is the church of old Matlock, on a bluff with the Village street on one side and the river making one of its frequent bends not far from it. The church itself has its Perp W tower with diagonal buttresses, the rest was rebuilt in 1859 (chancel) and 1871 (nave). – FONT. Norman, very big, ribbed at the angles and with little crescents along the upper border.

The RECTORY to the W of the church is late C18. Between it and the church WHEATSHEAF FARM, 1681, with a symmetrical front with windows of mullion-and-transome-crosses. Church Street prettily bends round by the church. No one can feel the nearness of modern Matlock here.

MATLOCK BATH lies to the S of Matlock village. The Old Bath, of wood lined with lead, was made in 1698. In the course of the C18 a New Bath of stone was constructed, 'a handsome house', says Bray in 1777. Torrington in 1789 complains of the growing popularity of Matlock: 'The quiet and society of the place is lost.' Lysons in 1818 calls it a favourite summer resort. By then a road had been blasted from Cromford through Scarthing Nick, the New Bath Hotel (for 50 visitors) and the Temple Hotel (originally an appendage to the Old Bath) existed, and Museum Parade or SOUTH PARADE was probably just about being built, a row of honest, solid, attractive houses, though of no special architectural merit. Architectural ambitions came in only with the PAVILION, unimaginative and not too costly spa architecture of *c.* 1885.

The church of HOLY TRINITY was built in 1842 by *Weightman & Hadfield* (s aisle and enlargement of chancel 1873).

Matlock Bank is reached from Matlock Bath by DALE ROAD (Dale Cottage, 1820, with pretty, elaborate wooden trellis-work around the porch and centre). Across the river Derwent by a medieval stone BRIDGE, C15, four pointed arches, massive break-waters, widened 1904 the modern town rises up the hill to culminate in SMEDLEY'S HYDRO, the therapeutic establishment started by John Smedley in the early fifties. It is a large complex of buildings, with a private church with spire, now the engine house, a castellated half of *c.* 1855 and a larger Italo-Frenchy part of 1885, the latter by *Statham*. The success of the Hydro was enormous. In 1867 Smedley treated 2000 patients, and there were another nine competitive establishments at Matlock Bank.

The church up here is ALL SAINTS, 1883-4, by *Healey* (GR). It has an E window with STAINED GLASS by *Morris & Co.*, 1905.

MAYFIELD BRIDGE *see* ASHBOURNE

MELANDRA CASTLE

¾ m. WNW of Glossop

Roman Fort, built at a point near the hills yet readily accessible from the plains. Originally of earth and wood, later substantially and skilfully remodelled in stone. Usual symmetrical design and lay-out of such small forts, i.e. four gates (one in the middle of each side), four towers (one at each corner set back from the rampart faces) and a ditch of simple type. Dimensions: 398 ft long, 368 ft wide. Area just over 2 acres. Last excavated in 1942. Finds from the site consist mainly of bricks and sherds and are now in Buxton Museum. The fort (whose Latin name is unknown) was probably not occupied after C2, and seems to have been an Agricolan fort held continuously until the building of the Antonine Wall.

MELBOURNE

ST MICHAEL AND ST MARY. The church is one of the most ambitious Norman parish churches of England, and its interior is as impressive and as well preserved as any. But its exterior is unfortunate. Not only does a TITHE BARN stand within a few yards of the W front, but the two W towers are incomplete, and their C19 pyramidal roofs start no higher than the ridge of the nave roof. That in itself is far from handsome, and it is made worse by the excessive heightening of the crossing tower which was carried out after 1602. As has come out in these preliminary remarks, the church possesses a two-tower façade, a unique feature amongst Norman parish churches, and a crossing tower as well. It has in addition a nave of six bays and aisles and transepts. All this is Norman with the exception of the aisle windows and the E window. This is due to an alteration of the chancel which originally ended in an apse. The transepts also had apsidal E chapels of which the entrance arches remain. But there were no chancel aisles, with or without apses, i.e. the plan was not that of so many Romanesque churches of Normandy and England (with a stepped E end) – the plan usually known as Cluny II and first transferred to Normandy with the Cluniac reform at Bernay – but rather that of the Romanesque style of the German C10 and C11 (e.g. Gernrode and Goslar in the Saxon territory and St Pantaleon at Cologne, Hersfeld, and Laach farther W). It is not entirely absent in Normandy (Domfront, *c.* 1050), but rare, and its existence at Melbourne may be one of the several C10–C11 survivals of architectural connexions between the Holy Roman Empire and England.

6

No building dates are known for Melbourne and most of the details look C12, but the plan may well have been drawn up before 1100. The living of Melbourne went to the Bishop of Carlisle, when the see was founded in 1133.

The sumptuous interior of the nave and the W parts are certainly younger than that date.

The nave has tall circular piers of four feet diameter, standing so close together that the arches are strongly stilted to give sufficient height. The bases have angle-spurs (also not an early motif), and the capitals are many-scalloped.* The arches are thickly zigzag-decorated, a somewhat barbaric but very strong effect. On the capitals stand coupled wall shafts as if transverse arches and perhaps vaults had originally been intended.‡ If so, they were not carried out; but there is a clerestory with small arched windows (with nook-shafts on the exterior) and a wall-passage with tripartite stepped openings towards the nave: again a motif familiar from cathedrals and large collegiate churches, but unique in parish churches. This upper part is preserved only on the N side. On the S side there are C13 pointed twin-openings instead and twin pointed windows.

The crossing again is most remarkable. It has arches to all four sides, standing on twin demi-shafts. Most of these have broad cushion capitals, but some on the E side are enriched by capitals with flat foliage scrolls interspersed with grotesques and human figures. The capitals of the E transept apses also had flat decoration. Inside the crossing tower above the arches are three tiers of openings. The lowest of them opens into nave and transepts, and to the E this and the higher ones opened into an upper storey of the chancel: once more an extremely unusual motif. The three tiers of openings are vertically connected by attached shafts, as if here also vaulting had been intended. Outside, the Norman parts of the crossing tower the broad buttresses are also shafted. The chancel windows have nook-shafts inside as well as outside. Outside, the chancel still reveals the beginning of the former apse, and also the beginning of a blank arcading outside the former upper storey.

* Except for the last four to the W on the N side and the W respond on the S side which have embryonic volutes as well.

‡ Which is no necessity; for such shafts with no other motif but to articulate a wall had been quite usual in C11 Normandy (cf. e.g. Jumièges as early as *c.* 1030–60).

As for the exterior of the aisles, the most noteworthy features are the two small doorways, both with one order of colonnettes, but that on the N side with a more elaborate moulding of the voussoirs. The aisle windows, as has already been said, are Perp replacements, but the lower parts of the broad Norman buttresses survive.

The W front would be impressive no doubt, if it had been completed. It has a central W portal of four orders of colonnettes with zigzag voussoirs, a window above converted in the C15, and the two W towers with very broad flat buttresses. The inside arrangements of the W parts deserve special notice. Immediately behind the front are three very roughly groin-vaulted rooms, two square underneath the towers and one rectangular between them. The latter carries on a broad arch with rich zigzag voussoirs, open to the nave, a gallery or balcony also open to this nave. This is a motif known, for example, from C11 buildings in Normandy and elsewhere in France. The three vaulted rooms are interconnected by arches on coupled shafts, and the square ones communicate with the aisles by arches on very simple imposts.

MONUMENTS. In the S transept, now Vestry. C13 slab with foliated cross. – Early C13 effigy of a knight, damaged, wrongly placed in a C15 arched recess. – Three crude C17 alabaster slabs.

MELBOURNE HALL. Immediately E of the church, a big stone-mansion rather forbidding-looking, except from the E. The architectural details reveal at least three building phases. The back (N) side shows the mullioned and mullioned-and-transomed windows of a C16 or early C17 building. Enlargement must have taken place in the late C17, *see* the S side. To its N is a seven-bay two-storeyed house with mullion-and-transome-cross, i.e. late late C17, windows. The house is a square block of two storeys with a very deep S COUR D'HONNEUR (now glazed over and made into a billiard room). This is much as at Shardlow in 1684. The windows go with such a date (mullion-and-transome-cross). The walls are of big rough stonework. Then, about 1725, the E front was converted into a fine seven-bay façade with three-bay pediment, and door and windows on the ground floor with Gibbs surrounds. The S door at the far end of the Cour d'Honneur also received a Gibbs surround, and four rather odd additional doors from this Court to the E and W were added. Originally the S door led no doubt into a Screens Passage. To its E indeed the Hall survives, though redone in the C18.

The GARDENS to the E were laid out by *London* and *Wise*, the Royal Gardeners, before the house was remodelled. A letter of 1696 has been published referring to two drafts by Mr Wise 'to suit with Versailles'. The garden is not at all big, but its composition makes it appear larger. It is divided by three main avenues leading down gently with some broad staircases to a pond at the far end of which

52 stands an exquisite wrought-iron ARBOUR, of *c.* 1705–10, by *Robert Bakewell* of Derby. There are many contemporary lead figures in the garden, and to the l. and the r. of the main composition long yew tunnels. To the S a later serpentine lake.

MELBOURNE CASTLE. Licence to crenellate was given to Robert of Holland in 1311. Later the castle came under the Duchy of Lancaster. It was a large many-towered group of structures, when it was engraved in 1733, although it had been dismantled in 1460. Now only an ivy-grown wall stands high up behind the buildings of CASTLE FARM, a good gabled brick house partly C17 and partly *c.* 1800.

Other pretty brick buildings in the main streets of Melbourne, domestic as well as commercial (CASTLE MILLS, said to be of *c.* 1860). At the foot of Potter Street one long thatched timber-framed house, in Chapel Street the BAPTIST CHAPEL of 1750, enlarged in 1833, stucco-fronted and pedimented.

MICKLEOVER

ALL SAINTS. Low W tower with angle buttresses, chancel early C14 (*see* the window with intersected tracery), S aisle C14: all much renewed.

OLD HALL. Timber-framed with brick infilling, the S side with twin gables. No fancy timber decoration.

MENTAL HOSPITAL, 1849, by *Duesbury*, surprisingly sober Neo-Tudor structure with shaped gables and mullioned and transomed windows. Symmetrical S front with three symmetrically placed thin towers.

MIDDLETON NR WIRKSWORTH

HOLY TRINITY, 1844, by *Newton* (GR). No tower, no separate chancel. Stone. Castellated gabled porch. Perp straightheaded windows.

Between Middleton and Wirksworth are the HOPTON WOOD QUARRIES, amongst the most exciting pieces of rock-scenery in the county. Sheer walls of great height rising quite close to the road.

MILFORD

Milford owes its fame to Jedediah Strutt, who founded the mill here about 1780 and resided at Milford House (seven-bay stone house with a three-bay pediment, altered). The date of the present mills seems unrecorded.

Other buildings of interest are the STONE BRIDGE of 1790 with its two elegant segmental arches, the pretty, airy SUSPENSION BRIDGE of 1826, the former WESLEYAN CHAPEL of 1842, the BAPTIST CHAPEL of 1849 (both stone and classical), and the church of HOLY TRINITY by *Moffatt*, 1848 (E.E. style, lancet windows, SW turret).

MINNINGLOW HILL *see* WINSTER

MONYASH

ST LEONARD. In a dip between exposed high moors. Founded *c.* 1198. Of the earliest building period the Sedilia and Piscina with segmental arches decorated with dog-tooth, the shafts with crude stiff-leaf or crocket capitals. The chancel arch is contemporary. The imposts rest on stiff-leaf capitals and these on head corbels. In the chancel lancet windows, renewed. Also of about the same time the S doorway and the lower parts of the tower, *see* the tower arch towards the nave. The tower is unbuttressed and has lancet windows. The tower stair starts in a most unusual way from the S aisle. The tower battlements and the spire with two tiers of dormer windows are later. The church has S and N transepts (cf. Ashbourne, Bakewell, etc.). The former was founded as a chantry in 1348, the latter was rebuilt on the old foundations in 1887. The windows of the transepts and the aisles are mostly straightheaded. Yet their tracery is still essentially Dec, *see* especially the one big four-light window in the S aisle and the smaller N aisle windows. Their date may well be as late as *c.* 1375. Of the same time probably the nave arcades. Pretty timber tracery, probably of the C19, in the outer walls of the S porch. – FONT. Octagonal bowl on quatrefoil stem decorated with animals. – PARISH CHEST, big, iron-bound, perhaps as old as the C13. – PLATE. Chalice, 1726.

MORLEY

ST MATTHEW. The church is important in several ways, for its architecture, its monuments, and its stained glass. It stands away from the village, but close to a large stone outbuilding of the former HALL (with mullioned windows) and not far from the handsome five-bay, early C18 RECTORY. The oldest part of the church is the Norman S arcade of two bays with circular pier with scalloped capital and unmoulded arch. The E respond has sparse leaves in the capital. The N arcade has the same piers but very elementary moulded capitals, probably of the early C13. The chancel seems to be early C14 (*see* the renewed E window and the S window high up). The chancel arch is tall and of fine proportions (double-chamfered). The S porch with its handsome external doorway also seems to be early C14. The rest of the building history is exceptionally well documented by brass inscriptions. The N chancel chapel with its four-centred arch to the chancel was added by Ralph de Stathum, who died in 1380, the W tower by his widow Goditha and her son, who died in

1403 (inscription on their brasses in the S chancel floor: 'qui campanile istud et ecclesiam fieri fecerunt'), the S chancel chapel by John Stathum who died in 1453. The W tower has a round SW stair turret, angle buttresses with many set-offs, Perp detail and a recessed spire, the S chancel chapel an irregular arch to the chancel. C15 also is the clerestory. The windows of N and S aisles are straightheaded of three and four ogee-arched lights. – TILES. Many original floor tiles in the N chancel chapel which was built *c.* 1370. – STAINED GLASS. This came to Morley from Darley Abbey at the time of the Dissolution. It had there been used to glaze the new cloister of 1482. The glass was repaired and much added to in 1847, but enough remains of the original work to make Morley the most rewarding place in the county to study late medieval stained glass. Most of the glass is in the N chancel chapel, in the two N windows. The more westerly one has chiefly scenes from the legend of St Robert of Knaresborough, the other stories from the Invention of the Holy Cross. In the E window an original figure of St Ursula, the rest Victorian.* – MONUMENTS. A larger number of medieval monuments than in most Derbyshire churches. They are the following in chronological order: John Stathum † 1453 and wife, brasses, kneeling; above their heads a St Christopher (N chapel). – Thomas Stathum † 1470, and two wives, brasses of the three figures with scrolls leading up to figures of St Christopher, St Anne, and the Virgin with Child. On a tomb-chest (S aisle, N side). – Henry Stathum † 1480, and three wives and children, brasses on tomb-chest under a cusped depressed arch between chancel and S chapel. – John Sacheverell † 1485 on Bosworth Field (*see* inscription) and his wife, the Stathum heiress, brasses also of the children (S wall of the S chapel). – Henry Sacheverell † 1558 and wife, brasses on tomb-chest (between chancel and N chapel). – Katherine Babington † 1543, tomb-chest with recumbent effigy and kneeling figures against the tomb-chest (N 25b

* The Harriet Jervis Memorial Window, † 1875, in the N aisle, is by *Burlison & Grylls.*

chapel), aesthetically the best monument in the church. The effigy as well as the kneeling figures are competently and sensitively carved. The monument might well be in Westminster Abbey. – Four incised slabs to Sacheverell children, in the N chapel floor, 1625, 1626, 1638, 1639. – Jacynth Sacheverell † 1656 and wife, recumbent alabaster effigies, kneeling children against the big tomb-chest (N chapel). – Henry Sacheverell † 1662, big tomb-chest with polished black marble top; no effigies (N chapel). – Jonathas Sacheverell † 1662, and wife, epitaph (S chapel) with two frontal demi-figures holding hands; two angels pull away draperies from them; very poor workmanship (cf. Kedleston). – William Sacheverell † 1691, big tomb-chest with polished black marble top; no effigies (N chapel). – Robert Sacheverell † 1714, big pedestal with free-standing urn, urns at the angles, etc., very Baroque and not at all elegant (N chapel).

MORLEY MANOR (formerly Hayes Lodge), asymmetrical Neo-Tudor house of moderate size, by *Bodley* 1900.

MOATED MOUND. Curious earthen mound, probably a fortified dwelling or other stronghold.

MORLEY PARK FARM *see* BELPER

MORTON

HOLY CROSS. Perp W tower with diagonal buttresses and eight pinnacles on the battlements. The rest 1850 except for the N arcade of circular piers with double-chamfered arches. The capitals as well as the filleted E and W responds are typical late C13.

Close to the church a handsome C18 stone house with a central Venetian window.

MOSBOROUGH HALL *see* ECKINGTON

MUGGINTON

ALL SAINTS. The W tower is Norman, unbuttressed, but for one big buttress placed at a later date against the middle of the W wall. It half-covers traces of a round-headed doorway also visible from within. The tower arch to the nave had semicircular keeled responds and a pointed unchamfered arch, *i.e.* early C13. But above this is a small deeply splayed evidently earlier window. It may well be of the C11. On the upper floor on the N side bell-openings with Norman arches but C13 twin openings underneath them. Norman corbel-table above. The top later. S doorway and W window of the S aisle look C18. The small SE doorway is late C13 and the S doorway early C14. The S arcade need not be later. Perp S chancel chapel, the piers and responds have their capitals decorated with big individual leaves, heads and shields. Perp roofs. – FONT. Perp, hexagonal, with pointed quatrefoils; re-tooled. – PEWS. Plain and honest, dated by an inscription 1600. Some later box-pews. – SCREEN. C15, of single-light openings with ogee arches and between them and the straight tops of the individual divisions Perp panel tracery. – MONUMENTS. Good large brasses on a tomb-chest to Nicholas Kniveton † 1400 and wife. The brass figures of *c.* 1475.

HALTER DEVIL CHAPEL, 1½ m. N. 1723, enlarged 1890. Attached to a farmhouse. Stone-faced with doorway, two arched front windows and parapet. The chapel was built by Francis Brown, a farmer, who one night swore he could ride into Derby even if he had to halter the Devil. When he found his horse in the field and tried to halter it in the dark, he found that it had horns. Brown fainted and the Devil disappeared in a flash of lightning.

NETHERSEAL

ST PETER. Mostly 1877. But Perp N tower with diagonal buttresses, and inside the following C13 features: a four-bay arcade with octagonal piers, double-chamfered arches and very elementary moulded capitals, chancel two-light C13 windows with nook-shafts placed high up in the wall. – MONUMENT. Incised slab to Roger Douton † 1500, rector of Netherseal.

NETHERSEAL HALL. Plain nicely proportioned parallelogram, two-storeyed with mullion-and-transome-cross windows. The window frames finely moulded, the doorframe also. The date seems *c.* 1700; yet in Derbyshire the date 1751 displayed on the façade may be correct. Much C19 addition.

NEWBOLD

ROMAN CATHOLIC CHAPEL. Doorway with almost completely defaced Norman tympanum. Windows Perp, no windows on the N side. Roof with bosses on the tie-beams. The chapel is only 36 by 18 ft. It was granted by James II for Roman Catholic worship and sacked by a Protestant mob in 1688. The pediment-like gable with its pinnacles may be part of the restoration after that event.

GREEN FARM. Dated 1678, but still gabled and with mullioned windows.

NEWBOLD HOUSE. C18, stone, five bays, two storeys, with pedimented doorway.

NEW BRAMPTON NR CHESTERFIELD

ST THOMAS, 1830–2, by *Woodhead & Hurst* (GR). The Commissioners' type with rather narrow W tower crowned by clumsily big pinnacles. The tower is flanked by entrance bays, nave without aisles, and tall lancet-like three-light windows. Chancel 1891.

MANOR HOUSE. Just a few mullioned windows and a summerhouse with ogee top remain.

NEWHAVEN

NEWHAVEN HOUSE HOTEL. Quite large, with a five-bay front, a nicely unexpected porch, and a big canted bay window round the corner. Painted white with black quoins and window frames. According to *The Beauties of England and Wales* (1802) the inn had been built 'lately' by the Duke of Devonshire.

NEW MILLS

ST GEORGE, Church Road, 1839. Big church with wooden galleries inside, thin lancet windows, and a W tower with spire.

ST JAMES THE LESS, 1880, by *W. Swinden Barber* (GR). – STAINED GLASS. Crucifixion by *Kempe* 1880, Four Evangelists 1888.

CONGREGATIONAL PROVIDENCE CHAPEL, Mellor Road, 1823, with a broad gabled front and arched window. The centre window of the Venetian type.

METHODIST CHAPEL, St George Road, 1810, with a broad gabled front, arched windows, and a lantern.

The Chapel faces the valley and opposite is a group of characteristic C17–C18 cottages, gone slummy. The HIGH STREET starts from here into the centre. In it the BULLS HEAD, with a typical symmetrical C18 front (low mullioned windows) and the WESLEYAN SUNDAY SCHOOL, 1844, with arched windows.

LADYSHAW HOUSE, dated on the barn 1759. In spite of this date, the windows are still low and mullioned, but they have now broad unmoulded frames and are arranged symmetrically, and the doorframe is arched and of blocks of alternating size.

OLLERSET HALL, Low Leighton. The usual L-shape, with gable and low mullioned windows of four lights. Datestone 1529 renewed, perhaps for an original 1629.

NEWTON OLD HALL *see* TIBSHELF

NEWTON SOLNEY

ST MARY. Plain Norman N doorway and bits from a more decorated Norman doorway built into the tower N wall. N aisle with lancet windows. On the N side they are coupled and have heads inside at the springer between the two. W tower short with recessed spire with one row of dormers. The interior mostly C14 (low octagonal piers, double-chamfered arcade arches). Perp the straightheaded chancel windows and the clerestory. – MONUMENTS.

Headless Knight of mid C13 date. – Cross-legged Knight, very effaced. – Alabaster Knight of *c.* 1375. – Sir Henry Every † 1709, very well carved semi-reclining figure in Roman attire. – Tombstone in the churchyard to Thomas Gayfere † 1827, mason in London who restored Westminster Hall and Henry VII's Chapel.

BLADON CASTLE. Large brick-built house of *c.* 1801, overlooking the valley with a long symmetrical crenellated front. All windows pointed. Walls with little bastions. Originally the structure was entirely a sham (known as Hoskins' Folly), later it was converted into living quarters.

NINE LADIES *see* STANTON MOOR

NORBURY

14b ST MARY. Norbury church is one of the most rewarding of Derbyshire because of its wooded position, because of the variety of its parts, and because of the noble grandeur of its chancel. The rest of the church is comparatively small, and especially short. The chancel is 46½ ft long, the nave 49 ft. Width and height and the absence of a chancel arch towards the nave also contribute to create an impression of splendid breadth. The windows are tall and large, three-light on the N and S sides and five lights at the E end. Their tracery is entirely out of the ordinary, with a stylized flower at the main meeting point in each window, both on the inside and the outside. The tracery is based on intersection and pointed quatrefoils and trefoils, i.e. Early Dec motifs; but it has (in the E window) just a few hard Perp uprights. There are no flowing forms. Below the windows runs blank arcading, without any ogee motifs. The date goes with all this. The chancel was erected by Henry Kniveton, Rector of Norbury from 1349 to 1395, probably in conscious competition with Bishop Norbury's immediately preceding work at Sandiacre (*c.* 1345). Building may have gone on from about 1355 to 1365 or 1370. Externally the chancel has saw-teeth-like crenellations and big buttresses. Do these in conjunction with the shafts (triangular section) running up to the roof inside (a timber roof of the later C15) tell of a projected vault? The nave has a N aisle added by Nicholas Fitzherbert († 1473). This has octagonal piers and double-chamfered arches. Nicholas Fitzherbert also built the chapel E of the S tower. His grandson John Fitzherbert († 1513) erected the tower and the chapel W of it. The nave has a Perp clerestory. The whole S side of the church is embattled, the N side, less of a show-front, is not. The C15 and C16 windows are of three lights, consisting of cusped lancets under a four-centred arch. – FONT. C15, octagonal, with elementary tracery, etc., panels – SCREEN. With one-light openings; thin tops, ogee arches, and Perp panel motifs behind and above them. – CHANCEL SEATING. With poppy-heads; the fronts with blank arches with Perp tracery also some elementary Flamboyant motifs. – Excellently preserved fragments of two SAXON CROSSES, mainly crisp interlacing, but also one small figure. The work belongs to an C11 group which includes Two Dales and Hope. – STAINED GLASS. An uncommonly large amount of C14 and C15 glass survives. That of the E window was originally in the nave and N aisle. The chancel side-windows have geometrical ornament only. The colour is disappointing, all grisaille, save the borders. The large and smaller figures in the E window are also mostly colourless. Smaller more colourful figures in the SE chapel (three saints and the kneeling family of the donor below). – MONUMENTS. Incised slab to a Woman. – incised slab to Henry Prince, Rector of Norbury, † 1500, with a chalice. – Stone effigy of a cross-legged Knight. – Nicholas Fitzherbert † 1473, good alabaster effigy on tomb-chest with standing figures under ogee arches. – Sir Ralph Fitzherbert † 1483 and his wife, another big alabaster tomb-chest, this one with standing figures holding shields which stand on the ground; also under ogee arches. The feet of Sir Ralph rest on a lion, but under one of his soles crouches the tiny figure of a bedesman (cf. e.g. Strelley, Nottinghamshire). – Brasses to Sir Anthony Fitzherbert † 1538 and wife, their children kneeling below.

23b 24

NORBURY HALL. Immediately to the W of the church. The façade is early C18 brick with quoins and segmentheaded windows. The house represents part of a range between two courts of a large medieval manor house. The stone range behind it to the NE whose back faces the churchyard is the remains of an older building in the Inner Courtyard, perhaps the Hall. Its upper windows of *c.* 1300 seem to be original. The doorways are all later (one dated 1682). The building would deserve closer study.

NORMANTON NR DERBY

ST GILES, 1861. The only fragment from the previous church is a Norman carved stone from a lintel, almost unrecognizable (S porch).

NORTH LEES

1¼ m. N of Hathersage

44a Impressive, small, towering, C16 and C17 manor house of a branch of the Eyre family. The front belongs to the later period. It is three-storeyed above a basement in the sloping ground, with a chimney in the centre and four-light mullioned windows on the l., three-light mullioned and transomed windows on the r. The latter belong to the principal rooms of the house, which lie above each other and face S with six-light mullioned and transomed windows. Very little of plaster decoration is left in their decaying interiors. At the back of the house an older tower with spiral staircase and Perp doorcases. The house is embattled with semicircular merlons. It plays a part in *Jane Eyre* (as Marsh End or Moor House).

Across two fields to the W are scanty remains of the ROMAN CATHOLIC CHAPEL built by special permission of James II in 1688 and soon afterwards sacked by Protestants.

NORTH WINGFIELD

ST LAWRENCE. The best piece of the church is the big, tall, Perp W tower with angle buttresses, two two-light bell-openings on each side, a frieze of shields above and then battlements. The most interesting piece is the Norman N transept E window, big, with quite elaborately moulded jambs and voussoirs and odd very sparsely decorated capitals. The arcade to the aisles consists of two circular piers with plainly moulded capitals and double-chamfered arches (the arch to the transept similar) and then two more Perp bays, their capitals with large shields set upside down, a very odd thing, as the tower arch has capitals of the same kind with the shields set correctly (the arch with concave chamfers). The chancel dates from the C14 (E window with ogee reticulation, ogee-headed recesses inside and outside). So does the N vestry which has a window of unusual tracery (exactly as at Whitwell). The body of the church was embattled in the C15; the aisle windows are all Perp too (but S aisle rebuilt 1860, N aisle heavily restored 1872, clerestory windows 1872). – The Perp S porch is covered by a pointed tunnel-vault with transverse arches (cf. Ault Hucknall, etc.). The nave roof has old tie beams and broad trefoil tracery above, C14 according to Cox (cf. Ault Hucknall). – FONT. 1662, with scarcely any decoration. – SCULPTURE. Defaced relief of the Martyrdom of St Lawrence, under cusped broad flat ogee arch, C15 (S aisle). – Many MONUMENTS, throughout in a very bad state of preservation: foliated cross slabs in the S porch; fragmentary stone effigy of a knight in the chancel recess (late C13?); priest, *c.* 1300, S porch; knight in the outer chancel recess.

CHANTRY HOUSE, now Inn, S of the church, some C15 masonry and very small upper windows. A chantry was founded in 1488.

RECTORY, W of the church, five-bay Georgian, stone, with segmental pediment above the central doorway.

WILLIAMTHORPE COLLIERY, ¾ m. NE. Pithead baths, 1940s, by *J. W. M. Dudding*, in that sound contemporary style which was favoured by the Miners' Welfare Committee.

NORTON (YORKSHIRE)

Church and Hall are across the border, but THE OAKS is in Derbyshire, a plain nine-bay, two-and-a-half-storey house with Tuscan porch. It was built in 1827.

OCKBROOK

ALL SAINTS. The chancel of the old church is said to have been rebuilt by Thomas Pares who died in 1805. Is it not later? His MONUMENT and, as a symmetrical group, those of Mary Pares † 1823 and Thomas Pares † 1824 are on the S wall. Mary Pares's is above a doorway and crowned by a figure of Christ rising. The three monuments are by *Westmacott*. The chancel windows have typical neo-C13 tracery of the period about 1800. The E window is of three lights, intersected and with coarse STAINED GLASS. – The nave was rebuilt in 1835, without the former aisles, with a flat ceiling and a W gallery in two parts, on cast iron columns. – FONT. Norman, tub-shaped, with interlaced arches. – SCREEN from the Wigston Hospital at Leicester, fine, slender, delicate workmanship, with tall one-light openings, ogee tops with much crocketing and panelled tracery in the spandrels. The W tower is the only other medieval survival, unbuttressed, C13, with a somewhat later plain broached spire.

MORAVIAN SETTLEMENT, founded 1750. The Chapel of 1751–2 and the adjoining houses are of brick, a neat very handsome group. The chapel is of five bays and has three arched windows and two arched entrances to the l. and r. Pediment and white timber cupola above. Original wooden organ gallery, pulpit opposite.

OFFERTON HALL

1¼ m. W of Hathersage

Interesting house, partly C16 and partly 1658. Note the difference between the three-light mullioned window still with arched tops to the individual lights and the upright windows with mullion-and-transome-cross, also the difference between the windows under individual hood-moulds and under continuous string-courses.

OGSTON HALL NR STRETTON STATION

An exceedingly instructive building, more composite than any other of its size in the county. A parallelogram with an irregular inner courtyard, Victorian at first sight. In fact there is a low W range wholly pre-Reformation, probably of *c.* 1500, according to the evidence of the moulded beams. At its S end was the Hall. At the N end of this range a few C16 windows (mullioned, but no arched cusped lights). The N range has, it seems, masonry of the same early period, and in addition a gateway; but this is not *in situ*. Then on the S side a further building went up in the C17, *see* the four-light window with a transome which appears above a Victorian bay window. It has a straight hood and should in Derbyshire be dated *c.* 1650. There is indeed in the garden a date-stone, obviously not in its original position, which carries a date 1659. Inside, contemporary panelling on the ground floor, and on the second floor a former external window, an oval of a type found in other places in Derbyshire in C17. Against it an Elizabethan staircase which can hardly be *in situ*. The next stage in the building history is represented by a bit just N of the previous building, with windows still mullioned, but now of upright shape, i.e. late C17. The N wing ends on the E with a coachhouse extension dated 1694. Again two generations later it was felt that the C17 house was no longer serviceable, and a completely new house was erected in the SE corner facing E. This was of five bays and two storeys with a hipped roof and is dated 1768 (architect probably *E. Stanley* of Chesterfield). This seems at first no longer to exist, but it is all there, only hidden by a Victorian veneer. Even the doorcase with Tuscan columns and a metope frieze survives behind a Victorian porch. The quoins can also still be seen without difficulty. Finally the C19 added, besides the porch, bay windows, a piece between the ancient Hall and the 1659 block, a Gothic tower, etc. Most of the work was done in 1864 by *Hine* of Nottingham, but further amendments were made in the nineties. The whole is an ideal object lesson in dating.

OLD BRAMPTON *see* BRAMPTON

OLLERSET HALL *see* NEW MILLS

OSMASTON

ST MARTIN, 1845, by *Stevens*. Big and solid, inside correct and rather cold. The facing material is smallish rock-faced stones.

OSMASTON MANOR. Large Neo-Tudor mansion of 1846–9, by *Stevens*. Irregular grouping, grey stone, the chief accent a tower 150 ft high. Extensive Italianate terraces with palm house, loggia, and another tower.

In the village the lords of the manor of Osmaston have apparently done a good deal of building, notably a number of picturesque brick cottages with thatched roofs and bargeboards.

OSMASTON-BY-DERBY

ST OSMUND. This small church was pulled down in 1951. For the new St Osmund (London Road) *see* Derby, p. 115.

MIDLAND REGION TRAINING COLLEGE, 1937, by *W. H. Hamlyn*, in a friendly Neo-Georgian style, with a slightly Swedish angular lantern that goes well with it.

OVERSEAL

ST MATTHEW, 1841, by *Thomas Johnson* (GR). Aisleless stone building with W tower, lancet windows, and five-light E window with Late Geometrical tracery.

In the village some nice brick houses; one with a pediment is a former NONCONFORMIST CHAPEL.

OVERTON HALL

The country house of Sir Joseph Banks. It looks earliest C18. On the E side there are still the typical C17 windows with mullion-and-transome-cross. On the S side segmental door pediment. The S front is of five bays and two and a half storeys with parapet. Stables, etc., further SW. The house is not specially shapely. A great variety of coniferous trees in and near the grounds.

PADLEY

MANOR HOUSE. The foundations of the N and W ranges and, above ground, the Hall range, survive, the latter converted in 1933 into a Roman Catholic chapel (to commemorate the arrest in 1588 of two priests hidden in the manor house. This belonged at the time to the Fitzherberts to whom it had come by marriage from the Eyres who had built it. The Hall was 32 by 17 ft in size, and above it on the upper floor lay the original Chapel. Two doorways into the Hall remain and parts of the hammerbeam roof with angels against the hammerbeams. The windows much renewed.

PARK HALL, BARLBOROUGH

Handsome C17 house of three storeys with three straight gables, two symmetrical castellated bay windows, and a central castellated porch. The building looks as if it might be of the middle of the century.

PARK HALL *see* HAYFIELD

PARWICH

ST PETER, 1873, by *H. Robinson.* In the tower the original N doorway and chancel arch. Norman tympanum with various animals, the Lamb carrying a cross, and a stag, each standing on a serpent. Above the lamb a bird, above the stag a pig and a lion.

PARWICH HALL. Five-bay house of three storeys with the

centre bay projecting. It is said to have been completed in 1747. An outer staircase leads up to the doorway which has Tuscan pilasters and rustication of alternating size. Segmentheaded windows, except for the first floor middle window which has a pediment. Quoins at the angles and at the angles of the centre projection. Later l. wing.

PEAK CASTLE *see* PEVERIL CASTLE

PENTRICH

ST MATTHEW. The arcades late C12 or *c.* 1200 (circular piers, single-chamfered round arches), the tower ground floor of the same date. The rest essentially Perp, embattled W tower, nave, S aisle, and S porch. All windows Perp, in the chancel more elaborate than otherwise (E window of five lights). – FONT. Rather puzzling. The foot is dated 1662, the top of different stone and with an unusual motif of low arches. Is it really Norman, as Cox says? – MONUMENT. Edmund Horn † 1764, graceful Rococo epitaph, without effigy; trophies of canon, anchor, etc., signed *A B fecit*.

PEVERIL CASTLE

34a By far the most important castle in the county, in fact the only one of importance. William the Conqueror made William Peveril bailiff of the Royal Manors in NW Derbyshire and gave him the land for Peveril Castle. The castle was built by Peveril, at once, it seems, of stone, which is unusual. The strength and scale of the work are explained by the wealth of lead in the neighbourhood. Of the C11 work the N curtain wall towards Castleton survives almost complete, though much repaired. Its characteristic Early Norman herringbone masonry can easily be detected. It is understandable that this wall was the chief concern of the early builders; for Peveril Castle is wonderfully protected by nature towards the whole E (Carr Dale) and W (Peak Cavern) and a large part of the S. The N slope is steep enough, but not rocky. So attacks were expected from here or a narrow ridge at the back, where now the

Keep is, but where originally probably a bridge and the gateway had been built. Also of the C11 seem to be an orientated building in the SE corner of the steeply rising site, *c.* 36 by 25 ft, which may have been the chapel, and some older structures to the W of the chapel, comprising probably the original hall. The W curtain wall is attributed to the early C12.

The Keep was erected by Henry II in 1176, *c.* twenty years after the Peveril estates had been confiscated. There are documents to ascertain the date of the erection of the Keep. It stands on the highest point of the site, in a splendidly commanding position, and its walls survive to the top. They were ashlar-faced inside and out. They are strengthened by the typical angle and middle buttresses of the time of Henry II. Access was by an outer wooden staircase. The main room was on the upper floor, with relatively large windows and two mural recesses. One of these contains a garderobe. The Hall had an open timber roof. The roof line against the outer walls is clearly marked. The walls are carried up higher and ended with a wall-walk and parapet and one angle turret which carried the staircase up.

Of the same date as the Keep is probably the new GATEWAY in the NE angle. At present only its double-chamfered arch can be recognized, but it had originally zigzag decoration in the arch similar to that of Castleton Church below. Of C13 additions only two need mention, the new Hall in the NW corner which has an open hearth as well as a fireplace at the dais end, with angle colonnettes, and two circular towers on the S side visible from below the castle. Their interest lies in the fact that Roman brick (probably from Brough) is extensively used.

During the C14 the castle lost its importance, and in the C17 it was in ruins.

PINXTON

ST HELEN. Of the medieval church only the unbuttressed C13 W tower and the very beginning of the nave remain (on the N side one small lancet window). On the S side of the tower a two-light Dec window has been incongruously inserted. In 1750 a large church was built at r. angles to the old one, with arched windows and a plain Venetian E window. To this in 1939 an aisle and a porch were added. – PAINTING. Annunciation attributed to *Guido Reni*. The painting was presented by the Pope to General Manley who commanded his guard and given in 1902 to the church by General Coke of the Coke family of Brookhill Hall. – STAINED GLASS. S transept window by *Morris & Co.*, 1870–1.

PLEASLEY

ST MICHAEL. Norman chancel arch with double billet frieze on the label and two roll-mouldings in the arch. The rest mainly C13; long aisleless nave. – FONT. Norman, circular, with seated figure. (Virgin?)

QUARNDON

ST PAUL. 1874, by *Giles & Brooklands* (GR), tasteless and restless, rockfaced, with SW broach spire.

Of the old church farther S nothing remains but an ivy-covered crag of tower-walling.

RADBURNE

ST ANDREW. In the grounds of Radburne Hall, with a fine spreading-out yew tree to the W. – The chancel Sedilia are early C13, the nave and N aisle windows early C14 (nave S side one three-light intersected and cusped window, and two small pretty Tudor windows higher up to its l. and r.). NW tower Perp, ashlar-faced, with diagonal buttresses. The N arcade of three bays has hexagonal piers and double-chamfered arches. – Bench-ends and benches from Dale Abbey with poppy-heads with faces and tracery, late medieval. – W PEW. Front of linenfold panelling with motif of big grapes and vines. – MONUMENTS. Coffin-shaped C13 slab with foliated cross. – Incised slab to Peter de la Pole † 1432 and his wife, quite good in the draughtsmanship. – Alabaster tomb-chest with recumbent effigy of John de la

Pole and wife, † 1491. – Incised slab to Radulphus Pole † 1454 and wife. – Standing wall monument to German Pole, erected 1684, with big sarcophagus in relief and big urn on it, under segmental pediment with putti; no effigy. By *Grinling Gibbons* (*see* J. D. A. & N. H. Soc. 1951). 32a

RADBURNE HALL, built *c.* 1750 by German Pole, red brick, placed on an eminence. Seven bays, stone-faced basement storey and two main storeys. An open staircase leads up to the main doorway with segmental pediment on attached Corinthian columns. The first-floor windows with alternating segmental and triangular pediments. The E and W sides of three bays with a central Venetian window. The Entrance Hall with a pair of coupled columns at the back, a fine fireplace with caryatids on one side and a large niche for a statue opposite. Behind it, in the middle of the other side an oblong room, also with good Rococo plaster. Sopraporte and portraits by *Wright* of Derby (dated 1771, 1772) and a pair of the rare large mythological pictures by *Mortimer*.

RENISHAW HALL

57b Built by George Sitwell about 1625 and still the seat of the Sitwells. The original house survives as the core of a much larger structure chiefly the work of Sitwell Sitwell about 1800. The Carolean core is entirely in the Jacobean style, in plan of H-shape. It is clearly recognizable on the S (garden) side. In the middle of the recessed centre is oddly a chimney-stack. On the N side, the area between the two arms of the H has been filled in by an entrance hall with a Gothic porch. The additions of 1793 to 1808 have converted this small compact house into one that is long, rambling and castellated, in spite of its Georgian windows. Inside, the parlour has still its original plaster ceiling with thin ribs. But the most handsome of the rooms decorated before the present generation of owners are the Dining Room of 1797 (by *Joseph Badger* of Sheffield), oblong with an apsed end, the Drawing Room of 1803 and the Ballroom of *c.* 1808 with its anteroom re-modelled with somewhat formidable formality by *Lutyens* in 1909. The chimneypiece in the Ballroom was designed by *Chambers* c. 1772 and taken to Renishaw from Albany in London.

The gardens were re-made with the greatest application and cost by Sir George Sitwell about 1890. Of the time of Sitwell Sitwell the STABLES of 1794, which, as is so often the case, are, with their broad Tuscan archway, more monumental than the house to which they belong. A GOTHICK ARCH on the Barlborough Drive to the E, and a polygonal Gothick CONSERVATORY (1808) in the gardens to the SW.

REPTON

Hrewpandun was the capital of Mercia under King Penda. Here, in 653, his son married the Christian daughter of King Oswy of Northumberland. The first Bishop of Mercia, Diuma, founded at Repton a monastery for men and women under an abbess. The foundation date was *c.* 660. The buildings were destroyed by the Danes in 875. The abbey was never re-established, but a new church was built *c.* 975. It was dedicated to St Wystan. His body was the chief object of worship. The C10 church survives independent of, though physically close to, the Augustinian Priory which was founded in 1172 and whose fragments have become part of Repton School.

ST WYSTAN. The C10 church was cruciform and had a crossing-tower. The chancel, inner transept angles at the NE and SE, and the crypt are one of the most precious survivals of Late Saxon architecture in England. The CRYPT is small (15 by 15 ft by 9 ft in height), reached by curved narrow staircases from the transepts, and has very rude groined vaults on four columns (according to Clapham added in the C11). The columns have capitals which are simply blocks with tapering sides. Along the shafts a spiral band runs up: a motif unique in England. The chancel is tall and decorated by the narrow vertical strips of rectangular section which are to be found in so much Late Saxon work (Bradford-on-Avon, etc.). Also of the

5b

C10 are the two columns now placed inside the S porch. They come from the E end of the nave. In the C13 lancet windows were put in to replace the smaller original windows. In the C13 also the aisles were rebuilt (SW lancet, traces of NW lancet). In the early C14 the aisles were widened (octagonal piers and double-chamfered arches with only small chamfers, windows, also chancel E window). Of the same date is the W tower and spire which were completed in 1340. The tower has angle buttresses, battlements with tiny pinnacles, and a recessed spire rising with two tiers of dormer windows to a height of 212 ft. The C15, however, altered the tower windows. Also C15 the castellated clerestory, the timber roof and the pretty two-storeyed porch. A curious piece of tracery design is the four-light straightheaded S window of the S transept. Its upper part consists of a row of lozenges: that is a straightsided, and thereby really un-Gothic motif. – PLATE. Chalice of 1548 or 1549. – MONUMENTS. Alabaster effigy of a Knight, *c.* 1400. – Incised alabaster slab to Gilbert Thacker † 1563 and wife. – Francis Thacker † 1710, epitaph with frontal bust between columns carrying a scrolly pediment.

THE PRIORY consisted of the church, the cloister, the ranges around the cloister containing in the usual way the Chapter House on the E side, the Refectory on the far or N side, and the Prior's Lodgings and Hall with Cellars beneath on the W, and in addition various buildings a little away from this compact group. It deserves special notice how close the Priory buildings were placed to the old church. Repton School is now entered through the PRIORY GATEWAY, not a proper gatehouse, but simply an arch in a buttressed piece of wall. To find one's way through the remains of the Priory one must remember that the range immediately to the E of the church, containing the School Library and Sixth Form Room above the recently installed Museum, is the W range of the CLOISTER, the War Memorial Garth is the cloister, and the Pears Memorial Hall stands in the place of the nave of the church. Excavations and research have shown the survival of characteristic bits of the first work, i.e. the work of 1172–*c.* 1200 which was still untouched by the new Gothic style. The MUSEUM is the Cellars. The circular piers are a replacement of the original ones. The room was as far as one can see never vaulted. But to the S of it, between the cellars and the church was a tunnel-vaulted Entrance Corridor or SLYPE or Outer Parlour. In its place is now the Elizabethan staircase. Above the Slype was another also tunnel-vaulted room, probably the PRIOR'S STUDY. Here a deeply splayed window (W wall) survives and remains of another have been found. S of this room, in the place of the Library and Sixth Form Room, was the PRIOR'S HALL or Great Hall, rebuilt *c.* 1400 and with a fine open timber roof of which fragments still exist. N of the Hall were no doubt kitchens, strategically placed between it and the REFECTORY. The latter room also stood on an undercroft which seems to have been unvaulted, but had to its E a small rib-vaulted room and then a Slpye. The wall which now represents this range is a C16 reconstruction.

The most interesting remains are those of the CHURCH, lower masonry courses of the E and S wall of the outer S Chancel Chapel and the N Chancel Aisle as well as of the solid Pulpitum erected at the W end of the choir under the E arch of the crossing tower. In addition there are stumps of piers of varying and characteristic sections, all clearly belonging to the C13. They are all based on the quatrefoil but vary the type imaginatively, in chronological order thus: Nave E half main thick shafts keeled and in each of the diagonals a cluster of three thin shafts, Nave W half main shafts unkeeled and only one (detached) shaft in each of the diagonals, S transept main shafts filleted and the diagonals as if the core of the pier were an octagon, Choir main shafts keeled, diagonal shafts attached and unkeeled. All these forms are not connected with local Derbyshire traditions.

Of buildings away from the cloister the most important is that part of the Headmaster's House known as PRIOR OVERTON'S TOWER. It is in fact of an importance considerably more than regional. It represents the remains of the Prior's new lodgings to replace the inadequate accommodation of an earlier age. Overton was made prior in 1437. The tower containing his Study on the first floor is built of brick with two corbelled-out angle turrets, and can be called one of the most ornate pieces of early domestic brick architecture in England. The style is more Hanseatic than English, with its two very tall, blank, cusped two-light arches into which the one-mullion one-transome windows on two floors are let in. The top cornice is of typical 'billet' kind. The Study has fine carved beams with ornamental bosses.

THE SCHOOL. We must now deal with the alterations and additions made for Repton School, which was founded by Sir John Port in 1556. He left money for the school at Repton as well as the hospital at Etwall and lies buried there. The School first took over the Prior's Range of the cloister group and converted it for its uses. The outer gables, the four-centred doorway and the inner staircase are indeed Elizabethan. About 1680 the Headmaster's House received a new façade towards the Priory. It has windows with wooden mullion-and-transome casements and a segmental pediment over the door. The main changes, however, took place only in the C19 – the usual pattern of the English public schools which, for all their venerably remote foundation dates, were as a rule of very inconsiderable size before the Victorian era (Repton *c.* 100 scholars early C19, *c.* 50 about 1850). The rapid growth of the school under Dr Pears (1854–74) and after is not matched by buildings of high architectural merit. Names of architects and dates will be sufficient: CHAPEL by *Stevens* of Derby 1857 (apse 1867, N Aisle, N Transept and Antechapel 1904–5, S Transept and Porch 1929); PEARS MEMORIAL HALL, by *Sir Arthur Blomfield* 1883–6, and decidedly pretty with its open arcades on the lower floor, its Neo-Tudor windows, gables, tower, turrets and rock-faced surfaces; NEW HOUSE (outside the school precincts on the l., going up the Burton Road), by *W. A. Forsyth*, 1909.

THE TOWN forms a pleasant background to the school, though it has no individual buildings calling for special notice. The wide main street runs from the church and priory gateway S towards the restored Cross. It then splits and on the one branch, the road from Swadlincote, two houses may be noted: TUDOR HOUSE, a symmetrical timber-framed house with central porch, and THE GRANGE, an early C18 five-bay, two and a half storey brick house with stone trim, pedimented doorway and original iron garden gates.

RIBER

High above to the E of Matlock RIBER CASTLE formed an ideal eye-catcher for the poetical visitors of the Baths. But the embattled Castle with its four angle towers and its embattled curtain walls with its own angle turrets was built as late as 1862–8 – a surprising case of posthumous romanticism, due to *Mr Smedley's* unerring sense of publicity values. The castle was built to his design as his residence, though it is now a boys' prep school. Its size is 145 by 110 ft.

After the ostentatious picturesqueness of the Castle RIBER HALL and the MANOR HOUSE are happy surprises, both of the genuine, unselfconscious picturesqueness of minor Elizabethan and early C17 architecture in the county, stone, with low mullioned windows, and gables. The Manor House especially makes a most felicitous picture. It has a date-stone 1633.

RIDDINGS

ST JAMES, 1832, by *Francis Bedford* (who built some of the Waterloo churches in London). A handsome building for its date. Stone, narrow W tower with spire, nave with buttresses carrying pinnacles, and coupled lancet windows. Straight-ended chancel. White interior, no aisles, W gallery on cast-iron columns.

RINGWOOD HOUSE *see* CHESTERFIELD

RISLEY

ALL SAINTS. Built by Michael Willoughby in 1593; *see* the date above the N doorway. Consecrated only in 1632. N aisle 1841. The doorway still four-centred, with a hood-mould. The S windows interestingly posthumous-Gothic, i.e., with intersected tracery but roundheaded. The W tower unbuttressed, of two stages only, with roundheaded two-light bell-openings, the two lights of lancet shape. – FONT. Alabaster, octagonal on a tapering shaft, with strapwork decoration. – SCREEN. Still purely Gothic, though of a minimum kind.

LATIN HOUSE, to the E of the church, one of the best of its time in the county. Dated 1706 above the door in the big segmental pediment on big acanthus brackets. The house is of brick, in chequerboard pattern with blue bricks on the ground floor, simply red brick on the upper floor. Generous stone trim. The ground floor windows have wide eared frames, big keystones with female faces and an entablature projecting above the keystones. The upper floor is similar, though more delicate. Stone quoins and hipped roof.

SCHOOLS, E of the above house. Founded in 1583 and built in 1718. A delightful group. The master's house (five-bay, two-storeys) with a shell-hood over the door stands back in the middle. The two schoolrooms are to the l. and r. nearer the street but parallel to the master's house. They are identical in design, each with four tall windows with one wooden mullion and two wooden transomes. The only decoration is simple brick friezes.

RISLEY HALL. Of the original hall nothing remains but a castellated gateway on a terrace by the moat. In present use a long outbuilding with mullioned windows and at right angles to it a Georgian house with a Late Georgian porch.

ROSLISTON

ST MARY. Tiny unbuttressed W tower with plain broach spire. The door and windows ogee-headed. The church itself is of 1819, aisleless with the typical lancet windows, a lancet porch, and the larger windows equally typically lancet-shaped with two lancet lights and pierced spandrel. An unusual addition a transome at the springing points of the arches of the two lights. The E end and a group of two single and one two-light lancet under a pediment-like gable.

ROWORTH

LONG LEE. An exceptionally fine farmhouse, in the original C17 state, with all its farm buildings. The house itself is dated 1663 on the porch. It is of T-shape and has low, long mullioned as well as mullioned and transomed windows. One outbuilding with similar windows has the date 1679. No signs yet of a move away from Tudor traditions.

LITTLE MILL INN. This is dated 1781. Now at last windows of Georgian shape without mullion and transome have become accepted.

ROWSLEY

ST KATHERINE, 1855, by *Salvin Jnr* (GR), in the Norman style. – Anglo-Saxon CROSS-HEAD with curling ends, an interesting specimen dated mid C9, by Sir Thomas Kendrick. – MONUMENT. Tomb-chest with the recumbent effigies of Lady John Manners † 1859 and a child, by *Calder Marshall.*

PEACOCK HOTEL, 1652, but still entirely in the Jacobean tradition, with symmetrical gables l. and r., and mullioned and transomed windows. The door has a semicircular pediment.

ROWSLEY BRIDGE. Early C17, widened in 1925 from 16 to 40 ft. Five pointed arches.

ROWTOR *see* BIRCHOVER

ST BRIDE'S *see* STANTON-BY-BRIDGE

SANDIACRE

ST GILES. The most interesting church in its neighbourhood, with remarkably rich piece of the Norman as well as the Dec style. Of the Norman church the S doorway, the chancel arch and two windows remain. The S doorway is of three orders with capitals with volutes and scallops and an arch with three roll-mouldings. The two windows are big and curiously high up so that they were later lengthened below. They have nookshafts inside and out. The chancel arch has thick semicircular responds as well as several orders of shafts. The capitals have leaves, heads, scallops, and volutes. The frieze also has upright leaves and a diaper band above and extends along the E wall of the nave. To this Norman nave of quite sizeable proportions a taller chancel was added, only 6 ft shorter than the nave. This was presumably a gift of Bishop Norbury of Lichfield, who held the prebend of Sandiacre from 1342 to 1347. The chancel is buttressed with big crocketed pinnacles on the buttresses, and a quatrefoil frieze above the tall windows. These are of three lights on the N and S sides, of six on the E side. The tracery is manifold, but on the S chiefly of three odd three-pointed stars similar to the so-called Kentish tracery but characterized by the points being specially long and concave-sided.* The N windows have flowing leaf shapes, the E window tracery also consists of them, but they are multiplied by necessity of the greater width.‡ In the nave at the time when the chancel was built a four-light S window was opened out to give more light to the Norman nave. In date between the nave and the chancel lies the W tower, short and unbuttressed, with small lancet windows, no battlements and a spire with low broaches. The date of this is C13. The Perp style added the small clerestory. No furnishings of importance.

SAWLEY

ALL SAINTS. Norman chancel arch with much wall exposed above. Very wide nave. Arcades of octagonal piers

* This tracery is somewhat baffling. Lysons in 1819 illustrates it, the Rawlins drawing of 1822 shows clearly that it is not there, the Meynell Langley drawing of the 1820s less clearly that it is not there, but the Browne drawing of about the same time again shows it.

‡ This window also was put in only after 1822 (Rawlins).

with late C13 to early C14 capitals and double-chamfered arches. Late C13 chancel with typical tracery (lancets of two lancet lights with pierced spandrel) especially fine the five-light E window (arches upon arches; e.g. Lichfield Chancel Aisles).* The N aisle has windows of three lancet lights, the middle one higher than the others. The S aisle has a single smallish lancet as its W window, the other windows, with elongated ogee reticulated tracery. This is Dec. Perp clerestory, embattled, as is the S aisle. Perp W tower (different stone). Angle buttresses and the spire recessed behind battlements. Inside, the tower is open to the nave in an opening not larger than a door. Inside the chancel two specially noteworthy features in the chancel – a solid stone-screen just W of the W wall separating a back vestry (cf. Tideswell) and a kind of bay window, deep and with panelled sides and four-centred vault. It is a CHANTRY CHAPEL and holds the alabaster effigy of John Boothe † 1496, Treasurer of Lichfield Cathedral (cf. the similar recess in the S Chancel Aisle at Lichfield). Other Boothe MONUMENTS. Ogee-headed recess in the chancel N wall (panelled back-wall) with tomb-chest with small brasses of Roger B. † 1467 and his wife and children. – Under the chancel arch big tomb-chest with larger brasses of Robert B. † 1478 and his wife. – E end of N aisle brass to Richard Shylton † 1510 and wife. – Next to this stone effigy of a priest taken in from a tomb-recess outside. – PULPIT. 1636, still in the Jacobean tradition, with handsome tester with pendants. – SCREEN. Perp with single-light openings. Also fragments from another screen. – STALLS, partly old.

SCARCLIFFE

ST LEONARD. Norman S doorway with one order of colonnettes, one roll-moulding in the arch, and a lintel with ill-assorted wheels, stars, saltire crosses. Norman chancel doorway renewed. C13 W tower rebuilt in 1842.

* But from the Rawlins Manuscript it looks rather as if this were a C19 alteration.

The detail not reliable. C13 lancet windows in the chancel N and S walls. Embattled nave S side with late C16 or C17 windows (the tall one C19). The windows on the N side of the same style but smaller.

SCROPTON

ST PAUL. 1856, by *Ferrey* (GR). The W tower has the alien motif of a pyramid roof. – MONUMENT. Nicholas Agard and his two wives, *c.* 1520. On the front wall of the tomb-chest angels holding shields under ogee canopies, and plain panels with shields.

SHALLCROSS HALL *see* TAXAL

SHARDLOW

ST JAMES. 1838, it is said, by *Stevens*. Stone-faced. Aisleless interior, tall lancet-like windows with Perp tracery. Embattled W tower without pinnacles.

SHARDLOW HALL. Fine seven-bay garden front, of brick, bays 1 and 7 quoined l. and r. Doorway with Gibbs surround and pediment. The date according to rainwater-heads is 1726. But the entrance side is dated 1684 and is stone-faced, very severe, with a receding centre and projecting side-parts. The windows have still hood-moulds and these are connected by horizontal courses. Heavy parapet, no visible roof (cf. Eyam). To the l. and r. of this main block stone-faced Palladian wings, three-bays, one-storeyed with arched windows, and then two-storeyed pavilions with pediments. The odd thing is that the garden front is not also stone-faced.

SHELTON LOCK PRIMARY SCHOOL. One of the recent standard steel and brick schools erected by the County Education Department (*see* Introduction, p. 33).

SHIRLAND

ST LEONARD. Essentially a C15 church. W tower with diagonal buttresses and eight pinnacles on the battlements (cf. Morton), embattled clerestory with pinnacles, embattled aisles, windows Perp throughout, that at the E end of the chancel quite unusual (if correctly renewed): three lights under four-centred arch with the centre light reaching up higher than the side-lights, and a little panel tracery above all three. S porch vaulted with pointed transverse arch (cf. Ault Hucknall, etc.). – PAINTING. Crucifixus and Magdalen, small in original altar frame, looks North Italian, mid C15. – MONUMENTS. Big ogee-headed recess in the chancel N wall with tomb-chest with many shields; the effigy has disappeared. – From another tomb-chest only an alabaster panel with four thin long kneeling figures remains (chancel S wall). – Tomb-chest in the N aisle with three fine large cusped and embellished quatrefoils and on the top incised slab of John Revell † 1537 and wife and children. – John Revell † 1708, sumptuous epitaph of wood with fruit, flowers, etc., and many cherubs' heads.

SHIRLEY

ST MICHAEL. W tower and N aisle 1861 and 1842 respectively. C14 chancel (with Perp E window), C14 S aisle (with an arcade of octagonal piers and double-chamfered arches; the windows C19). The W gallery on cast-iron columns and the box-pews no doubt of 1842. – In the N aisle E wall outside a badly preserved carved stone from a Norman lintel (beasts and birds). – PLATE. Paten of *c.* 1500.

SMALLEY

ST JOHN THE BAPTIST. Of the building of 1793 nothing survives. Additions and alterations 1844, 1862, and again (the pretty, nearly detached, short W tower with pyramid roof) 1912. – Radford Memorial Window, 1882, with good STAINED GLASS.

SMISBY

ST JAMES. Small church with W tower, nave and S aisle, and chancel. The aisle arcade has three bays with circular piers hardly taller than four and a half feet. Double-chamfered arches. The chancel E window is of three lights, broad with rather coarse Dec tracery. Most of the other windows are C16 or C17, straightheaded with one mullion or one mullion and one transome (S aisle E). – PANELLING of the E end, linenfold pattern, from Ashby-de-la-Zouch Castle. – MONUMENTS. Alabaster effigy of Joan Comyn of Smisby, mid C14; must originally have been of good quality. – Incised alabaster slab of W. Kendall † 1500 and his wife. – Epitaph to Henry Kendal † 1627 and wife, with large kneeling figures facing each other across a prayer desk. Kneeling children below (nine sons and seven daughters, the swaddled babies upright and incongruously mixed up with the kneeling figures).

LOCK-UP, close to the Tournament Field: brick, polygonal, with spire and ball on top.

SNELSTON

ST PETER. Only the NE tower is old, with diagonal buttresses, battlements, and pinnacles. The church, of nave and chancel only, is of *c.* 1825, altered 1884.

SNELSTON HALL, a spectacular piece of romantic Gothicism. By *Cottingham*, 1827. With two show-fronts, both completely asymmetrical, very pinnacled: a miniature Alton Towers. Like Alton Towers the house is to be demolished. There is never much hope for the preservation of C19 fantasy in the C20.

SNITTERTON HALL

1¼ m. W of Matlock

A gem of an Elizabethan manor house. Symmetrical front embattled and gabled with broad shallow projections on the sides and six-light and four-light mullioned and transomed windows. The doorway asymmetrically placed, flanked by crude fancy Ionic pilasters and with a lintel decorated with flower motifs. In front of the house a small formal garden. The garden wall with its arched door is flanked on the l. and r. by square pavilions or summer-houses. One of them has recently fallen down. 38b

SOMERCOTES

ST THOMAS. 1902, by *P. H. Currey*. Handsome E front, the four-light window with a big mullion running right to the top. Angular bell-turret to the r., on the aisle.

METHODIST CHURCH, Birchwood Lane, 1853. Brick with a pretty embattled W tower and lancet windows. Not at all Nonconformist in appearance. The church was given by John Smedley (*see* Matlock).

SOMERSAL HERBERT

ST PETER. 1874, by *C. J. Neale*, of Mansfield, of good solid design. – FONT. Norman, tub-shaped, with blind arcade of intersecting arches and above a border of lozenges overlaid with intermittent circles. – STAINED GLASS. N chancel window by *Kempe* 1896. – MONUMENT. Priest with chalice in his lap below his folded hands.

38a SOMERSAL HALL. A most felicitous picture of Elizabethan half-timbering. The entrance side in particular has four gables grouped so that a broad low one on the l. is matched by two small ones on the r., higher by one overhanging half-storey. The fourth gable in the middle of intermediate height and width. The timbering chiefly narrow uprights. More decorative motifs in the gables. In the entrance two inscription tablets of 1564. – SW block of brick 1712. – Much added in 1899.

SOMERSALL HALL *see* CHESTERFIELD

SOUTH NORMANTON

ST MICHAEL. C19 W tower. Nave with N and S aisles, the S aisle 1878, the N aisle with a three-bay arcade on thin, coarse octagonal piers. Late Perp N windows. N chancel chapel opening by one arch into the chancel. In the chancel N wall (originally S wall) is the only interesting 8b piece of architecture in the church, the doorhead of the vestry door, pointed trefoiled with dogtooth decoration and the two cusps in the shape of a kind of stiff-leaf fleurs-de-lis. The shafts in the jambs of the doorway are filleted. Its date must be *c.* 1250–75. – PLATE. Chalice and Paten 1645; Flagon C17; two Patens given 1713 and 1714. – MONUMENT. Robert Revel † 1714, epitaph with two standing putti, not good.

SOUTH WINGFIELD

ALL SAINTS. The church lies on its own, half a mile E of the village and a mile NNE of the Manor House. The body of the church is C13 (*see* the arcade of five bays with circular piers, characteristic capitals (occasional nailhead decoration) and a keeled respond. The W tower is of different stone and Perp (diagonal buttresses). In 1803 the windows of nave and aisle were all re-done, arched and unmoulded. The chancel except for the bare masonry of the walls dates from 1877. – FONT. Plain, big, Norman, of tub-shape.

WINGFIELD MANOR HOUSE. Neither the picturesque nor the strictly architectural traveller should miss Wingfield Manor House. Its tall ruins with the chief tower standing to a height of 72 ft are an extremely dramatic sight. It is a larger complex of buildings than Haddon Hall, and it was all built within twenty years and never much altered after. The manor came into the hands of Ralph Lord Cromwell in 1440. He was extremely rich, Lord Treasurer, Warden of Sherwood Forest and Constable of Nottingham Castle. He began building at once and on the largest scale. Wingfield is 416 ft long and over 256 ft wide. Like Haddon it consists of two courts. 35

Of the Outer (S) Court the GATEHOUSE with a large and small entrance survives in the SE corner and next to it a big BARN. What we see to-day of the E and W ranges is their inner and outer wall respectively. The range dividing the S from the N court has a S front towards the outer court which is more or less symmetrical, certainly an attempt at regularity. The gateway, again with one large and one small entrance, is flanked by square turrets. At about equal distances from these follow big projecting chimneys. A second chimney on the l. is balanced by a porch (?) on the r. The symmetry is, however, in the end effectively overturned by the Great Tower riding on the W extremity of this range.

The W and E ranges of the Inner Court are destroyed. The N range contains the State Rooms, the Hall with bay-window at the dais end and porch, and to the l. of this an apartment as large as the hall but placed at r angles so that it projects far to the N. This apartment is supposed to have contained the Solar or Parlour on the upper floor. The range ends to the l. (W) with Kitchen and Offices, a confused group of rooms projecting yet a little farther N than the Parlour.

The architectural details deserve as much notice as the planning. The Hall rests on a vaulted UNDERCROFT with five octagonal piers along its centre line and heavy ribs with typical Perp mouldings (wavy curves). The HALL is 72 by 36 ft in size. The Porch leading into the former Screens Passage has fleuron decoration in the jambs of the arch, an upper chamber and battlements decorated by shields above a quatrefoil frieze. The Hall itself has three windows of moderate size with depressed pointed arches of almost straight sides. The bay is tall and relatively narrow, buttressed and also crowned by battlements above a quatrefoil frieze. The bay-window tracery is remarkable in that it still preserves some traces of the Dec past (ogee and leaf shapes): a warning to those trying to date church windows on insufficient evidence. To the N the original windows have been altered in the C17 into two tiers of mullion-and-transome-cross windows.

The greatest surprise is the S window of the Solar or Parlour, a very large four-light transomed window with panel tracery, the arched panels starting higher for the inner than the outer lights. Above it an oculus window with three cusped spherical triangles with tracery. Perp three-light and two-light windows with a minimum of panel tracery W of the Parlour on the first floor and simpler Perp windows in the same part of the range to the N. Similar windows in the outer court on the E side and in the tower.

Ralph Cromwell sold the estate to the second Earl of Shrewsbury. His descendants often resided at Wingfield. The fourth Earl died here. The sixth Earl accommodated Mary Queen of Scots at the manor house three times in 1569, and again in 1584. In the Civil War it changed hands twice and was finally dismantled in 1646. It has been a ruin since. In 1774 masonry from the house was used in the building of WINGFIELD HALL, W of the old manor house.

SPARROW PIT BARROW *see* CHAPEL-EN-LE-FRITH

SPINKHILL

ST MARY'S COLLEGE. The nucleus is a private house of the C17, much altered for the school in 1842 (*A. Hansom*). Wings were added in 1859. The R.C. CHURCH is of 1845. The New School was built in 1876 by *Clutton*. Further enlargements 1902 and 1912 (*C. & C. M. Hadfield*). The War Memorial Chapel is by *Adrian G. Scott* and was completed in 1930: pale brick with a dome over the crossing.

PARK HALL, ½ m. E (*see* p. 199).

SPONDON

ST WERBURGH. A largish church, well placed above the street. It would be architecturally unusually interesting, if it had not been so thoroughly restored, first in 1826 and then again in 1892. It was completely rebuilt after a fire in 1340, in which year the inhabitants were granted exemption from taxes while the rebuilding went on. W tower with spire recessed behind battlements, as usual in Derbyshire. Large nave with three-bay arcades to the wide aisles. Octagonal piers, double-chamfered arches, fairly finely moulded capitals. The chancel has ogee-reticulated windows, the aisle E windows fanciful flowing tracery of different designs. All three E windows are of five lights. The N aisle N windows have again reticulated tracery, the S windows of the S aisle flowing forms. – In the chancel N wall a low recess for a tomb or Easter Sepulchre and a stone lectern built into the wall (cf. Chaddesden, Crich, Etwall, Taddington).

Several good Georgian brick houses, the best THE HOMESTEAD, five bays, two and a half storeys, with quoins and a central 'Venetian' entrance and arched windows above it, the upper one reaching into the pediment.

STAINSBY HOUSE NR SMALLEY

Plain nine-bay, two-and-a-half-storey house of stone with three-bay pediment.

STANAGE EDGE *see* HATHERSAGE

STANLEY

ST ANDREW. Small Norman doorway on the S side, E of it a small C13 lancet window. The chancel E window of three stepped lancet lights, early C14. The rest mostly *c.* 1875. Nave, chancel, bellcote.

STANTON-BY-BRIDGE

ST MICHAEL. Small and low with a C19 bellcote. Interesting Saxon remains, especially the long-and-short work at the SE angle. Norman S doorway (one order of colonnettes, and zigzag in the arch), Norman W window and wall, Norman chancel arch. The rest is later C13, *see* the chancel S window (bar tracery with quatrefoil in circle) and the N aisle windows. The arcade inside is of three bays, low, with octagonal piers and double-chamfered arches. – MONUMENTS. Recess with effigy of Priest, *c.* 1400. – Incised alabaster slab to William Sacheverell † 1558 and separate slab with kneeling children (from the front of the tomb-chest). – A second badly preserved incised alabaster slab.

ST BRIDE'S FARM, 1½ m. S. In the outer wall next to the door a tiny Norman Tympanum with a quadruped in profile, not an unusual representation.

STANTON-BY-DALE

ST MICHAEL. Chiefly *c.* 1300, *see* the chancel windows (with three stepped lancet lights), the N aisle N and W windows and the three-bay N arcade. The S doorway has a tympanum with a rude cross which may be Norman. The W tower with buttresses covering the angles, battlements and crocketed pinnacles. Handsome S porch, tunnel-vaulted with thick transverse arches (cf. Ault Hucknall, etc.).

VILLAGE CROSS, slim, octagonal, on substructure.

ALMSHOUSES E of the church, 1711. With their plain brick gables they look a good deal older.

STANTON HALL, C18, three-bay centre with rusticated stone lintels to the windows and giant angle pilasters. Other parts castellated.

STANTON-IN-THE-PEAK

HOLY TRINITY. 1839, with spire and transeptal chapels. Inside as gifts of members of the Thornhill family a HOLY WATER STOUP, Italian, bronze, dated 1596, and a TABERNACLE, of very good Florentine Quattrocento style, with praying angels in three tiers above each other, used to hold a dedication inscription of the church. – MONUMENT. Henry Bache Thornhill † 1822, an imitation of the Florentine Quattrocento, very skilfully done, probably *c.* 1860–70.

STANTON HALL. A composite building with one gabled bay remaining of the C16 or early C17, then a broad, fine eight-bay, one-and-a-half-storey house with original sash-windows and top balustrade, dated 1693, and then an addition of 1779 (Tilley) or 1799 with a semi-circular porch and a three-bay pediment above, five by five bays.

STANTON OLD HALL, now a farmhouse, still gabled and with mullioned windows, yet dated 1667.

STANTON WOODHOUSE, C17 or a little earlier. Much altered. But the two-light windows with the individual

STOKE ON-TRENT PUBLIC LIBRARIES

lights ending triangularly instead of in pointed arches are apparently original.

STANTON MOOR (Prehistory, etc.) (*see* below).

STANTON MOOR

TOWER on Stanton Moor Edge. The tower was erected in 1832 in honour of Earl Grey to commemorate the Reform Bill.

HARTHILL, ½ m. W of the Nine Ladies, is a Bronze Age STONE CIRCLE consisting of six stones, the tallest of which is no less than 17 ft high. Two smaller stones stand 75 yds S of this circle.

ANDLE STONE, 1½ m. N Winster. A large stone block believed to have been part of a stone circle. 250 yds W of it is the DOLL TOR STONE CIRCLE (Bronze Age) of which only six stones remain. Cremation burials were found at the foot of four of them. The most prominent antiquity on the moor, with an attendant member known as the KING'S STONE, 30 yds to the W. The circle dates from the Bronze Age and some of the stones have been removed for building purposes.

On the S side of the moor is a huge natural boulder known as the CORK STONE. A round barrow near the Cork Stone has been left open to show its concentric rings of stones round the inner cast. The moor is lavishly studded with barrows, many of which cluster round the 1832 Tower. Excavated barrows all yielded Bronze Age primary burials by cremation.

STAPENHILL NR BURTON-ON-TRENT

ST PETER. 1880, by *Evans & Jolly*, a large and interesting design with a tall SW tower inspired by the tower of Magdalen College, Oxford, but with oddly 1900-looking detail, for example, the corbelled-out buttresses at the angles between the angle-buttresses, the concave-sided top gables of the buttresses, and the straightheaded windows of several ogee-headed lights.

STAVELEY

The village, with its large, friendly C 20 housing estates, winds along to the S of the large Staveley Iron Works.

ST JOHN THE BAPTIST. C13 W tower with W door, tall W lancet window, tower arch to the nave with keeled semicircular responds. The upper parts are Perp (different stone), the battlements and pinnacles of 1681. The doorway also C13, with one stiff-leaf capital and renewed arch. The S aisle Perp, *see* its arcade and windows. The N aisle of 1887. The most interesting part of the church is the Frecheville Chapel (S chancel aisle) dated in the glass (cf. below) 1676: two bays, latest Perp windows. The chancel clerestory is a C19 addition. – STAINED GLASS. A splendid window of heraldic display, big, fat, scrolly foliage and cherubs. By *Giles*. – MONUMENTS. On the N side of the chancel two memorials to Peter Frecheville † 1503, one a tomb-chest with brass effigy in armour, erected during his life-time, the other a coarse Perp wall recess with kneeling figures of brass against the back wall. – On the S side of the chancel incised alabaster slab to John Frecheville † 1509. – In the N aisle a curiously crude ogee-headed recess with figures above each other in the flanking buttresses. The style is Perp. – In the Frecheville Chapel large epitaph with semi-reclining figure of Christian Frecheville who died in childbed, in 1653. She is shown contemplating her baby. Two putti pull away curtains to the l. and r. – John Lord Frecheville † 1682, standing wall monument with a big bulgy base and a bulgy sarcophagus with two putti on it. No effigy.

RECTORY. Formerly Staveley Hall. Built in 1604, although the exterior tells little of that. But some wall panelling survives inside. The exterior was made classical in the C18 and then again more nearly Jacobean in the C19. The window pediments on the garden side are still those of the C18.

To the W of the church the former SCHOOL with octagonal

master's house. The style is typical of the 1840s. The school was indeed established in 1844.

GRAMMAR SCHOOL, NETHERTHORPE, ½ m. E. Now part of the County Secondary School. The original building of *c.* 1572 still exists, gabled, with an asymmetrical porch and three-light mullioned and transomed windows.

STEETLEY

STEETLEY CHAPEL is by far the richest example of Norman architecture in Derbyshire. Yet it is only 52 ft long and 15 ft wide. The lavish, almost ostentatious display of mid C12 decoration must be connected with some special purpose of the chapel; but manorial history has not so far yielded an answer. The chapel consists of a nave, a slightly narrower and lower chancel, and a yet a little narrower and lower apse. The nave is oblong, the chancel square, the apse provided with a short oblong W bay. There are elaborately ornamented arches between nave and chancel and chancel and apse, and the apse is in addition vaulted, a tunnel vault over the oblong bay and a semi-sphere over the apse proper. The two parts are separated by a transverse arch of relatively complex profile (three roll-mouldings and two ridges between) and two ribs of the same profile run against it. There is no keystone or boss, where they meet. The arch and the ribs are strengthened (or emphasized) outside by buttresses. The apse receives its light through three windows with nook-shafts outside. At the height of their cill a band of scrolly ornament runs round the apse. A corbel-table supports the roofs of apse, chancel and nave.

7

The nave was roofless right through the C19 and probably earlier. A restoration took place in 1880 (*J. L. Pearson*), and although it was careful, a certain amount of what we see at present is Victorian and not Norman. That applies in particular to the S portal. Of its four orders of colonnettes, two were at the time of Lysons' *Magna Britannia* of 1818 so completely defaced that he does not illustrate them. Of the inner orders one has medallions, the other foliage scrolls. The corresponding arches are decorated with zigzag and simplified beakhead. The gable dates from 1880. The nave has two very narrow W windows and one on the S side, and a small and insignificant N doorway.

Much better preserved naturally are the two chancel arches and the apse. The chancel imposts have four shafts each. The capitals display, besides the usual scallops, foliage scroll-work, animals (a double-headed lion) and scenes (St George and the Dragon, Adam and Eve). The chancel W arch with zigzag and crenellation and a kind of crescent-motif on the label is more elaborate than the E arch which is plain except for a billet frieze on the label.

There are few Norman churches in England so consistently made into show-pieces by those who designed them and those who paid for them.

STOKE HALL

$1\frac{1}{2}$ m. NW of Curbar

Quite a stately stone mansion, five by five bays, two and a half storeys. Doorway with Tuscan columns, the head connected with the frame of the window above. Coach-house and stables across the road. Dated 1757 on rain-water-heads. Fine fireplaces inside.

STONEY MIDDLETON

ST MARTIN. A rarity, if not a visually very satisfying one. To the low unbuttressed Perp W tower (C19 doorway) in 1759 a new church was added which is octagonal with an ambulatory and a lantern story on piers. The roof of the lantern unfortunately is almost exactly the height of the tower. The ambulatory has circular windows, the lantern tripartite semi-circular ones, the chancel a tall arched window with two mullions and one transome continuing the string-course round the building which also runs above and below round the circular windows. The open timber roof is C19.

STONEY MIDDLETON HALL. Elizabethan or Jacobean with a symmetrical front with two gables; much re-modelled, probably early in the C19.

In the village the style of the C18 windows of the church can be found in several houses.

STUBBING COURT

1½ miles W of Wingerworth

Seven-bay, two-storeyed stone house with central pediment and pedimented doorway. The date is said to be *c.* 1700, with older portions at the back.

STYDD HALL *see* YEAVELEY

SUDBURY

ALL SAINTS. Over-restored. Low W tower with diagonal buttresses and a top balustrade with short pinnacles. Inside arcades of three bays, on the N sides on circular piers, on the S side on octagonal ones. Capitals with nail-head decoration. Double-chamfered arches, i.e. *c.* 1300 and a little later. Of about the same time the opening from the chancel into the Vernon Chapel (octagonal pier without capital). – STAINED GLASS. E window, 1850, given by Queen Victoria and Prince Albert and made, it is reported, by a German artist. – Memorial windows to the sixth Lord Vernon 1885 by *Burlison & Grylls*. – MONUMENTS. Defaced effigy to a Woman, *c.* 1300. – Defased effigy to a Woman, her heart in her hands. – John Vernon † 1600, and wife Mary (who built Sudbury Hall); alabaster; she lies on a tomb-chest, he behind and above her under a shallow arch rising between baluster columns. – Margaret Vernon † 1675; urn on a free-standing pedestal. – George Charles Lord Vernon † 1835 and his wife, Grecian twin stelae in relief, with profile heads and drapery over the stelae. By *J. Francis* of London. – Two Vernon children † 1862, epitaph with pretty oval showing the two asleep and a few trails of blossom around them. – Augustus Henry Lord Vernon † 1885, elaborately Neo-Quattrocento epitaph.

48a SUDBURY HALL. Sudbury Hall is uncommonly satisfying to the eye in its outside and inside and at the same time uncommonly interesting and instructive in its architectural history. It was begun *c.* 1613 by Mary Vernon and left unfinished at her death. The upper storey and the entrance frontispiece and nearly all the interior features were added by George Vernon between 1670 and 1695. The building is of comfortable moderate size (C19 additions on the W side), brick-built with diapering of dark brick in both storeys. The plan is of a usual Elizabethan and Jacobean type, the E-type with central porch and somewhat projecting wings. On the river-side (for the gardens slope down to the river) the wings do not project but are marked by bay-windows. The windows are mullioned of three or four lights and with two transomes. George Vernon seems to have built new stables E of the house before he decided to complete it. They are dated 1664 and have still the low mullioned windows and the straight gable of Tudor tradition. About 1665 he turned to the house. Building accounts are happily preserved so that the work and its executants can be followed. The upper storey differs from the Jacobean custom in several characteristic ways. The quoins are flat below, in relief above. The window tracery has in some windows been replaced by an odd design, in its very oddity typical of the mid C17 transition. Each light ends in a round arch above which runs a transome and above the transome is a horizontal tracery oval. It is evidently an attempt at achieving novelty without abandoning tradition entirely. Tracery as such is traditional, the round arch and the oval are classical. The mixture resembles contemporary work at Oxford. The hipped roof, balustrade and cupola are more uncompromisingly of the new style, similar to Coleshill, Clarendon House London, and other such buildings. The most conspicuous innovation is the frontispiece marking the Jacobean porch. It has coupled columns and broken pediments on two floors and is of a decidedly Baroque depth of relief and liveliness of contrast. It is the work of *Sir William Wilson* (1641–1710), sculptor and architect of Sutton Coldfield near Birmingham.

Inside little is left of the Jacobean building phase, chiefly the arched doorways of Screens Passage, and Hall (now dining room). Of the Carolean period the most gorgeous room is the Staircase in the projecting W wing (no doubt not the original Jacobean position). It has a wooden balustrade with luxuriantly carved foliage by *Edward Pierce*, the sculptor of the best portrait of Christopher Wren which we possess, and an equally luxuriant, breathtakingly skilful plaster ceiling by two craftsmen from London, *Bradbury* and *Pettifer* (1675–6). The ceiling paintings are by *Laguerre* and were added later (1691). The same combination of artists appears in the Parlour (Saloon) S of the staircase (1675–6 and 1691–4). The Drawing Room follows E of the Parlour on the S front. Here also *Bradbury* and *Pettifer* and *Laguerre* were engaged, but *Pierce* was replaced by *Grinling Gibbons* himself. His overmantel carvings arc miraculous, but so are *Pierce's* carvings in the Parlour. On the upper floor the chief rooms are the Queen's Room with a rather more Jonesian fireplace of 1670 by *Wilson* (cf. Wilton House) and plasterwork by the local craftsman *Samuel Mansfield* (1675), and the Long Gallery filling the whole S front: a conservative feature. The ceiling here is again by *Bradbury* and *Pettifer* (1676).

48b

To the N of the house some distance away an EYE CATCHER, a brick parallelogram with angle turrets and a turreted sham gatehouse, built probably *c.* 1800, perhaps with the use of some other structure.

In the village, an unusually pretty brick village, consisting chiefly of one long street, George Vernon in 1671 built the INN, a symmetrical composition with slightly projecting outer bays, straight gables and a segment-headed central carriageway. The windows are in the Tudor tradition. Several ranges of contemporary cottages near by.

SUTTON-ON-THE-HILL

ST MICHAEL. C14 W tower; the spire rebuilt in 1831. The rest of the church of the same date, save for the C14 aisle arcade with octagonal piers and double-chamfered arches. Heads and leaf-motifs on the label-stops. – MONUMENT. Judith Sleigh †1634, standing wall-monument with, instead of an effigy, a coffin carved in black stone, complete with its handles. Back architectural with arch.

SUTTON HALL. Castellated front with two canted bays and Gothick sash-windows.

SUTTON SCARSDALE

SUTTON HALL, now a ruin facing the depressing untidiness of open-cast coal mining. The house was built by *Smith* of Warwick (*see* All Saints, Derby) in 1724 and was easily the grandest mansion of its date in the county. Stone, two-storeyed, with giant fluted pilasters throughout. The straight main front, to the E, has a pedimented centre where the pilasters are replaced by attached columns and angle pavilions where the pilasters are coupled. The principal entrance was on the N. The doorway has a Gibbs surround. On that side some of the rooms still show traces of their once gorgeous decoration, a delight which people middle-aged now can still remember *in situ*. To see some of it now, one must go to the Philadelphia Museum. The back (to the W) has two projecting wings with a relatively narrow courtyard between (cf. Melbourne Hall). An outbuilding to the W of C17 date. 53a

ST MARY. Incongruously and picturesquely close to the Hall. Poignant contrast between the low embattled and pinnacled E parts of the church and the desolate grandeur of the Hall. – Perp W tower with diagonal buttresses. Some C14 windows (the two-light S window however is C19), a C14 S porch and C14 N arcade to aisle and chancel aisle. – COMMUNION RAIL. C17. – MONUMENTS. John Foljambe † 1499, incised slab. – Samuel Pierrepont † 1707, epitaph with bust in roundel, not good.

SWADLINCOTE

EMANUEL CHURCH. 1848, by *Stevens*. Aisleless stone building of modest size. No tower, polygonal apse, lancet windows.

GRANVILLE PITHEAD BATHS. 1941, by *J. W. M. Dudding*, one of the many modern structures erected by the Miners' Welfare Committee.

SWARKESTON

ST JAMES. So much restored in 1876 that only the SW tower and the Harpur (SE) Chapel are now worth recording. The chapel contains two alabaster MONUMENTS consisting of tomb-chests with the recumbent effigies of Richard Harpur † 1577 and his wife, and Sir John Harpur † 1627 and his wife, the latter of much superior workmanship. In addition in the chancel tomb-chest with effigy of John Rolleston † 1482 and his wife; against the front wall of the chest two angels and between them two attractive panels with the kneeling children. – FONT. Norman, plain. – A few small Norman fragments built into the E aisle wall.

46b SWARKESTON BRIDGE. Though much restored (e.g. shortly before 1802; *see* the *Beauties of England and Wales*) still a remarkable example of medieval public works. The bridge and causeway, altogether three quarters of a mile long, probably date from the C13 and C14. Seventeen old arches remain, though the actual span across the river is only 414 feet. The arches are depressed-pointed and ribbed underneath.

SWARKESTON HALL. Rectangle of stone, with a front of three gables and a central doorway with four-centred head. The windows symmetrical and mullioned. The date may be *c.* 1630.

46b SUMMER HOUSE. An extremely odd structure probably of Jacobean date, connected with the big Harpur mansion which stood at Swarkeston. The function of the building is not clear. It overlooks THE CUTTLE, a kind of rectangular enclosure with a low fence. The Summer-House is also known as the Grandstand (cf. The Stand at Chatsworth), and it is assumed that bull-baiting and similar sports took place in the arena. The house has two angle towers with bulbous tops and a crenellated three-bay centre with a loggia on the ground floor (Tuscan columns, and, strangely enough, depressed ogee arches). The first floor windows have one mullion and one transome each. The large room behind them is in ruins. – The mansion has gone, though Swarkeston Hall is no doubt connected with it.

SWARKESTONE LOWS, round barrows.

TADDINGTON

ST MICHAEL. Not large, but in a fine position with its N side overlooking the high country around, and of some architectural interest. The W tower early C14 throughout; the arch towards the nave with double-chamfered imposts and double-chamfered arch without any intervening capitals, the windows small and ogee-headed, the spire broached, with big broaches starting directly on the tower without any battlements. The dormer windows altered in the C19. The rebuilding of the rest of the church followed, inspired perhaps by Tideswell. Nave with tall four-bay arcades. Octagonal piers, E responds on head corbels. The chancel arch exactly contemporary with these, and the chancel, if smaller than Tideswell, yet clearly of the same type, i.e. tall straightheaded N and S windows, and a very large E window with elaborate flowing tracery. The aisle windows also with flowing tracery, though of course more modest. No battlements at all. The whole considerably restored in 1891. – BIBLE SUPPORT of stone in the chancel (cf. Chaddesden, Crich, Etwall, Spondon). – PLATE. Small Chalice and Cover, 1568. – CROSS SHAFT in the churchyard with zigzag and saltire cross decoration. Is it Norman? – BRASS to Richard Blackwall † 1505, wife and children.

FIVE WELLS TUMULUS, 1½ m. W. Bronze Age. Round barrow. This consists of an unusual central cist now roofless, containing two burial chambers of limestone slabs.

TANSLEY

TANSLEYWOOD MILL. Dated 1799 by coins found buried in the walls. Big and tall. Unarched casement windows, cast-iron pillars, timber beams.

TAPTON HOUSE *see* CHESTERFIELD

TAXAL

(St Leonard now called St James. c16 w tower with later c17 turrets. The body of the church 1825, restored 1889 (chancel enlarged). Aisleless, originally with galleries. – Jodrell epitaphs in the chancel.

In the village a c17 stone-built Inn.

Shallcross Hall. Early Georgian, seven-bay, two and a half storey stone house with two later two-bay deep symmetrical projecting pavilions. A few windows remain of the Elizabethan Hall.

Yeardsley Hall, 2 m. n of Shallcross Hall. c16, L-shaped, most of the windows modernized.)

THE HOLT *see* DARLEY DALE

THORNBRIDGE HALL

½ m. s of Great Longstone

Spectacular Neo-Tudor mansion, castellated, with a tall asymmetrically placed tower. In the entrance hall the grand Buffet Fountain from Chatsworth, by *Samuel Watson*.

THORPE

St Leonard. The church marks the entrance to Dovedale. It overlooks a hilly skyline and manifold green slopes. Short Norman w tower, unbuttressed, with big quoins. The w doorway blocked, the twin bell-openings badly preserved. Corbel table and later battlements. The nave of Norman masonry too, *see* a small lancet in the s wall. Another small window c13 of two lights. Perp window in the chancel. The e window is new. – Font. Plain Norman. – Communion Rail. Elizabethan. – Plate. Chalice and Paten, given 1710. – Monument. John Millward † 1632, badly preserved, with standing figures against the tomb-chest.

TIBSHELF

ST JOHN THE BAPTIST. On a hill overlooking the surrounding mining scenery. W tower with diagonal buttresses Perp. The rest by *Bodley & Garner* 1887–8.

NEWTON OLD HALL, 1 m. S. 1690. Small with symmetrical three-bay front of mullioned windows. The side to the street irregular and perhaps older. Staircase with twisted balusters.

TICKNALL

ST GEORGE. 1842, by *Stevens*. Good honest simple Gothic Revival. W tower with the recessed spire usual in the Perp style of this part of the county. W gallery on cast-iron columns. Aisle arcades with octagonal piers. – MONUMENTS. Effigy of a Civilian holding his heart in his hand. – Incised alabaster slab to John Frances, knight in armour, *c.* 1375.

The previous church stood farther S, and picturesque fragments of the W tower and the E end (three-light window with intersected tracery) survive. S of this the HARPUR ALMSHOUSES built in 1772, a long two-storeyed brick building with central pediment and angle quoins.

LOCK-UP. Circular with polygonal spire roof.

TIDES LOW *see* TIDESWELL

TIDESWELL

ST JOHN THE BAPTIST. One of the grandest of Derbyshire parish churches, impressive from far, though lying with the little town in a sheltered dip between the high lands around, and impressive from near, though the churchyard has no old trees, the railings are a rather rigid early C19 cast-iron pattern and the houses around are low, grey, and not specially attractive.* To the architectural historian the chief interest lies in the fact that Tideswell 14a

* Except perhaps the GEORGE HOTEL in the square to the SE of the church, which has Venetian windows throughout and was much praised by late C18 travellers.

church was apparently built without major breaks in the course of about seventy-five years during the C14. The chancel may have come first. But of this only the chancel arch remains. Its imposts are exactly like the nave piers halved. The nave and aisles are of five bays with piers taller than usual in Derbyshire and of a section unique in the county: quatrefoil with, in the diagonals, narrow grooves between narrow ridges. The vigorously rising arches also are of unusual section: step, quarter-roll, step, quarter-roll, step. Their labels start from head, leaf, etc., stops. They reach right close to the clerestory. The fifth of the arches on the N and S open into transepts of two bays. To date these earliest parts of the new church one has to study the windows and their tracery. This is flowing throughout, i.e. Dec, i.e. *c.* 1320–50. Nave and aisles and the contemporary, two-storeyed S porch (vaulted inside) are embattled.

It cannot now be said for certain whether the chancel had been built *c.* 1325 and was *c.* 1360 no longer regarded as adequate, or whether it had been begun *c.* 1340 and been interrupted by the Black Death. The fact remains that the roof line of the old chancel is still visible, and that about 1360 a new higher chancel was erected, which is one of the three or four finest in the county, of the same type as Sandiacre, Norbury, and Chaddesden. It has an E window still completely Dec with flowing tracery just like that of the transept windows. But its chief characteristic is its very tall and broad straightheaded three-light windows on the N and S separated by buttresses with pinnacles* and with tracery neither Dec nor Perp: namely, simply pierced quatrefoils standing on the trefoiled heads of the individual lights. These are almost archaic motifs, but the straightheadedness is of course a turn towards the new ideals of the Perp style. Inside, the chancel is high as well as wide. The Sedilia, although each seat is ogee-headed, have also quatrefoil decoration in the spandrels.‡ There

* The S transept also has pinnacles on its buttresses.

‡ A Piscina in the E wall of the S transept has very similar decoration, which also shows how close in date the W and E parts of the church are.

are two flat ogee recesses in the N wall. In front of one of them is the brass to John Foljambe who died in 1383 and of whom the inscription says 'multa bona fecit circa fabricaciounem huius ecclesiae'. That presumably dates the chancel as *c.* 1360–80. Other notable features are the screen wall to the W of the E wall which divides off a vestry behind the altar (cf. Sawley) and the niches for statuary on this screen wall (with tall canopies) and to the l. and r. of the E window.*

The W tower came last, but the masonry does not look as if it were much later than the rest of the church. Yet it is now fully Perp, in the style which by then had become nationally accepted. The W window is indeed one of the largest in the county, five lights only, but very tall, and with panel tracery of a usual pattern. The tower has angle buttresses, battlements, and eight pinnacles. Of these the four angle ones are developed into proper polygonal angle turrets with pinnacles on: an ambitious but in effect somewhat heavy conception. The tower arch towards the nave is of immense height. Its capitals and mouldings are also Perp.

ROOF. Nave with heavy tie-beams and broad cusped trefoil tracery above. No doubt original. – N aisle 1632–5. – FONT. Perp, octagonal, with shields and simple panels. – CHANCEL SEATS. Now in the N transept. Of no special ornamental merit. – PEWS. Perp pew fronts now in the N aisle. They may originally have served another purpose. The present pews date from 1824–7. – TOWER SCREEN. Designed by *Oldrid Scott*, 1904. – PANELLING. S porch, upper chamber, made of parts of C17 pews. The date 1632 occurs (cf. Castleton, Hope). – STAINED GLASS. E window, Tree of Jesse unusually sensitive, designed by *Mr C. G. S. Foljambe* (cf. *The Buildings of England, Nottinghamshire*) and made in 1875 by *Heaton, Butler, & Bayne*. – W window by *Hardman & Powell* 1907. – PLATE. Chalice given 1683; Paten dated 1724; Flagon dated 1738; Dutch brass Almsdish.

MONUMENTS. The church is rich in pre-Reformation

* Again a similar niche in the SE corner of the S transept.

monuments. The oldest are two defaced stone effigies in the N transept, late C13 and C14. – The big brass to John Foljambe † 1383 has been mentioned above (Chancel). It is the earliest brass and one of the best in the county. – Sir Thurstan de Bower † 1423, good alabaster effigy on a modern tomb-chest (S transept). The naming is more than doubtful; for the man is in armour and Thurstan de Bower was a yeoman who had made much money out of lead-mining. He was one of the founders of the Guild of St Mary at Tideswell (foundation charters 1384 and 1392) which held the present Lady Chapel as its Guild Chapel. – Brass with figure of God holding Christ Crucified and divers shields, on the lid of a modern tomb-chest whose openings reveal a stone cadaver underneath: Sampson Meverill † 1462 (chancel). – Brass to Sir Robert Lytton † 1483 and wife, the figures about 28 in. long (S aisle). – Brass to Bishop Pursglove † 1579, still entirely in the pre-Reformation tradition of the composition of brasses (chancel).

LONG LOW, 2 m. NE. Round barrow.

TUP LOW, 2 m. NE. Round barrow.

TIDES LOW, 2 m. N. Round barrow.

BATHAM GATE, 3 m. NW. Remains of a Roman road.

TISSINGTON

From the triangular Green one enjoys a picture of exquisite beauty: a few quiet stone houses on two sides (one Georgian of three bays), on the third, raised, well up a green slope, the church, and a little back to the S the Hall, which reveals its extent and character as one approaches it.

ST MARY. Sadly Normanized in 1854 (N aisle added) to match the broad square unbuttressed Norman W tower. It is this tower, fortunately, which is chiefly visible from the Green. In its S wall is one slim window with a roll-moulding. The S doorway is Norman too; one order of colonnettes with one scallop and one primitive volute capital, billet-frieze in the label, and a tympanum with two little standing figures to the l. and r., a double diaper frieze between them and the main field decorated by a plain chequer-board pattern and a cross distinguished by diapers in its five chequer-board fields. The tower arch to the nave is large (renewed?). The chancel arch is also Norman, single-stepped with one order of zigzag in the voussoirs of the arch. – FONT. Norman, tub-shaped, with incised animals, also a snake; very barbaric. – TWO-DECKER PULPIT. – COMMUNION RAIL. *c.* 1600, very finely turned, not at all a usual English pattern. – PLATE. Chalice and Paten, 1732 and 1734. – MONUMENTS. Francis † 1619 and Sir John Fitzherbert † 1643, with their wives. Standing wall monument with kneeling figures in two tiers, the father and his wife facing each other below, the son and his wife above. Outer columns, below intermittently rusticated Ionic, above black Corinthian: top with achievement and obelisks. – In the chancel various Fitzherbert epitaphs, e.g. Mary † 1677 and Martha † 1699, the latter by *Francis Bird.*

TISSINGTON HALL. Plain square medium-sized Jacobean house with an E porch, walled garden in front of it, and squat garden gate. The façade is plain with upright mullion-and-transome-cross windows and a parapet. No gables, no visible roof. To the N of the house a little away and not in axis with it a contemporary outbuilding, much restored. In the C18 the S front towards the terraced back garden was remodelled in the classical style with a bay window in the centre and a loggia open on the ground floor. A library wing was added on that side *c.* 1910 by *Arnold Mitchell.* The largest room is the Hall on the ground floor placed centrally and at right angles to the façade, that is in the new position first established a little earlier at Hardwick. In the Hall contemporary panelling (with intersected arches) and an elaborate fireplace and plasterwork in the new Gothick taste of *c.* 1750. In the Dining Room on the upper floor specially handsome panelling with fluted pilasters.

56

TRUSLEY

ALL SAINTS. 1713. Small, of brick, with short nave, lower chancel and W tower. The windows are arched, with stone surrounds; the tower has C19 battlements. The W front has a straight top to the aisles and the tower rising equally straight from it. The entrance with a scrolly pediment as at Barton Blount near by. – BOX PEWS, three-decker PULPIT, COMMUNION RAILS, and baluster-shaped FONT: all original.

HALL. Of the Tudor house one part still stands, the brickwork mainly in stretcher courses, flat stone quoins, the windows converted into sash. Also a separate Elizabethan summer-house on its own, with pyramidal roof. Much Victorian adding, restoration (1902) and recent Neo-Georgian tidying up.

TUP LOW *see* TIDESWELL

TWYFORD

ST ANDREW. Norman chancel arch, narrow with zigzag ornament. W tower unbuttressed, with lancet window below, Perp above with spire recessed behind battlements. Chancel with Dec windows. Nave remodelled in brick in the C18 and now prettily overgrown with ivy. May no purist insist on its removal.

UNSTONE

MANOR FARM. Just NW of the railway bridge at the Dronfield end of Unstone: L-shaped gabled manor house of 1653. The windows are mullioned, also mullioned and transomed, and under hood-moulds. The door surround was apparently altered in the C18. The inscription above the door is quite legible but also quite incomprehensible.

WEST HANDLEY OLD HALL, 1½ m. ENE. Small Jacobean or later C17 house.

VIATOR'S BRIDGE *see* ALSOP-EN-LE-DALE

WALTON-ON-TRENT

ST LAURENCE. Perp W tower with diagonal buttresses overlooking the river. The interior has a Late Norman arcade of some interest. The two circular piers and the two responds have capitals all with very stylized small upright leaves and all different. The arches are of two steps, the big inner one unmoulded, the outer one slightly chamfered. The chancel is C13 with one lancet window on the S side and trefoiled Sedilia. The S transept (large squint to the chancel) was the Waley Chantry, founded in 1334. It has a low S recess with a defaced effigy. The windows on the E side of a big rather coarse Dec variety. – MONUMENT. Thomas Bearcroft † 1680, demi-figure of a divine between twisted columns.

WALTON HALL. *c.* 1720. Brick house of seven bays and two and a half storeys with top parapet. The garden side has giant angle pilasters, the river side angle pilasters and additional pilasters between the second and third and fifth and sixth bays. On the garden side a simple central doorway with segmental pediment.

WENSLEY (SOUTH DARLEY)

ST MARY. Neo-Norman 1843, by *Weightman & Hadfield* (GR).

WEST HALLAM

ST WILFRID. Nave and two aisles. The N arcade has octagonal piers and the most elementary moulded capitals; hard to date. The S arcade more usual C14. The chancel arch with semicircular responds clearly early C14. The chancel E window is renewed, but its flowing tracery (three lights) would go well with the arch. The S aisle windows (renewed) of two lights flowing but straightheaded, later C14, if a copy of the original. The other windows Perp. Perp W tower. – Elizabethan COMMUNION RAIL. – PLATE. Two brass Almsdishes, probably Dutch C17. – MONUMENT to Walter Pontwell

† 1598 and wife, recumbent alabaster effigies on tomb-chest with two panels in the front wall containing the children standing upright.

WEST HANDLEY OLD HALL *see* UNSTONE

WESTON-UPON-TRENT

ST MARY. Essentially a C13 church, prettily placed near the river. W tower with recessed spire and Perp windows. The interior exceptionally impressive for a church of its size, thanks to the surprisingly tall circular piers with moulded capitals and double-chamfered arches. They give a noble uprightness to the whole. The nave is not long (three bays), the chancel lower than the nave. The chancel windows are small lancets with inner chamfered arches. The S doorway to the chancel is contemporary; the E window is new. The S aisle has windows of three stepped lancet lights uncusped, and an E window also of three lancet lights but with an unfoiled circle above the lower middle lancet. The N aisle windows are C14 (with ogee details). – Special features are the dogtooth course below the battlements and the pretty timber-framed S PORCH, added early in the C17. – FONT. Dated 1661 of the type with elementary decorated panels as usual in Notts around Southwell. – PULPIT. Jacobean. – MONUMENT. Fragments of a large monument to Richard Sale † 1615 with kneeling figures. Above this in an oval a skeleton with pick and shovel and the inscription: 'Ecce nosce te ipsum. Ut sum tu eris'.

30b

WET-WITHENS MOOR *see* EYAM

WHALEY BRIDGE

The typical small industrial North Country town which is missed out in practically all guide-books because of no artistic, historical, or architectural interest. Yet, as one walks through, there are a few eminently characteristic, if not beautiful buildings.

JODRELL ARMS HOTEL. Along the main road, *c.* 1800

with additions of *c.* 1850 in conjunction with the situation close to the new railway. The additions comprise a heavy Tuscan porch and minimum-Elizabethan gables. – METHODIST SUNDAY SCHOOL, 1821, simple and friendly with arched windows, and next to it the WESLEYAN CHAPEL, rebuilt 1867, still classical, but debased (*see* the pediment which has become a low-pitched gable and the overdone rustication). – MECHANICS INSTITUTE, 1876, preposterous Frenchy style with bits of incised ornament. – The church of the SACRED HEART (R.C.) dates from 1903 and has an ugly small S tower with thick buttresses. It goes octagonal on top and ends in a spirc.

WHESTON

WHESTON HALL. The front mid Georgian with a recessed centre and two-bay side wings projecting from the centre in two steps (a type of plan which may easily be much earlier: cf., for example, Ham House, Surrey). The first step has arched windows, the centre of the recessed part a pedimented doorway. Above it an upright oval window. One side of the house has recently collapsed, the other is clearly older than the front: three gables and mullioned windows. The back shows the two building periods together, one side with four-light hood-moulded C17 windows, the other like a complete five-bay Georgian house with central doorway.

VILLAGE CROSS, to the W of Wheston Hall: C15. Preserved complete with its cusped head with clumsy renderings of Christ Crucified and the Virgin. The shaft stands on four steps: the whole is *c.* 11½ ft high.

WHITEHAUGH

1¼ m. NW of Chapel-en-le-Frith

Gabled, with hood-moulded low mullioned windows. Above the entrance a recent inscription *A.K.* 1559, not reliable.

WHITWELL

ST LAWRENCE. The church is equally important for its contribution to the Norman and Dec styles in Derbyshire. As to the former we see a W tower, originally unbuttressed, with an original W doorway (one order of colonnettes, leaf capitals, zigzag in the arch), a window above and the blocked bell openings, replaced by higher Perp ones, when the battlements and pinnacles were added. Also Norman is the masonry of the whole nave (*see* the fully preserved clerestory, a rarity, and the corbel-table above), the masonry of the whole chancel also revealed by the corbel-table, the plain S doorway and the interior of the nave in its predominant features, i.e. the circular piers, very simply moulded capitals, and round arches with single-stepped profiles. The E responds are keeled, a usual late C12 feature in this part of the county. The tower arch looks earlier (unmoulded arch on the simplest responds), and that goes well with the evidence of the W doorway. The chancel-arch on the other hand, with keeled shafts, waterleaf side by side with scalloped capitals and finely detailed arch mouldings is clearly on the way towards the E.E., although the arch is still round. – The second great building period of the church was the time from *c.* 1300 to *c.* 1350. To this belong the chancel and the two transepts: *see* the geometrical tracery of the chancel with such no longer quite classical motifs as unencircled quatrefoils, encircled trefoils (exactly as at North Wingfield) and sharply pointed trefoils and quatrefoils (i.e. *c.* 1300), the Sedilia and the niche opposite (aumbrey? miniature Easter Sepulchre) with delightful openwork cusping, ogee elements, steep gables and much crocketing (an offshoot probably of the Notts-Lincs workshops of Hawton, etc.), the flowing tracery in the N transept N and S transept S windows, and the ogee recess in the N transept with its openwork double-cusping.*
FONT. Norman, plain tub-shape. – PANELLING in the

* It should, however, be said that the chancel E and S windows are not in their present form in the Rawlins Manuscript.

chancel, Jacobean. – MONUMENTS. Sir Roger Manners † 1632, standing wall monument, recumbent effigy in armour under shallow arch between two black columns.

N of the church WHITWELL MANOR HOUSE. The Hall of the manor house is now the school hall. Three-light and six-light mullioned and transomed windows.

WHITTINGTON

ST BARTHOLOMEW. 1896, by *C. R. Rollinson.*

A handsome C17 farmhouse to the W of the church with gables and three- and four-light low mullioned windows.

WILLERSLEY CASTLE *see* CROMFORD

WILLINGTON

ST MICHAEL. Pretty, modest W tower of 1824 with quoins and no pinnacles. S doorway Norman with defaced tympanum. The lancet windows in the chancel, and coupled lancets in the S wall are C19. The interior is aisleless and has white plaster ceilings in nave and chancel, no doubt of *c.* 1824. Also of that date the addition of a N transept. – FONT. C18, baluster, richly acanthus-ornamented. – COMMUNION RAILS. Cast iron.

WILLIAMTHORPE COLLIERY *see* NORTH WINGFIELD

WILNE

ST CHAD. Outside the village, fairly close to the river Derwent. W tower, the lower part C13 with rectangular stair turret, the upper part later. Embattled, but no pinnacles. Nave and S aisle separated by octagonal piers with double-chamfered arches. The aisle windows of three lancet-lights of which the centre one is higher than the others, i.e. *c.* 1300. S porch Perp with very pointed stone tunnel vault with transverse arches (cf. Ault Hucknall, etc.). S aisle and chancel embattled. The windows on the N side of the nave Dec. Small C15 clerestory. – FONT. Part of a circular Saxon Cross with carvings of dragons and birds. – CHEST. With chip-carved roundels on the front. – PLATE. Chalice 1566–7. – MONUMENTS. Hugh Willoughby † 1491 and wife, incised alabaster slab, nave floor, large figures, badly preserved. – Hugh Willoughby † 1514 and wife, brass with kneeling figures.

The main interest of the church is the WILLOUGHBY CHAPEL at the E end of the S aisle. This was established in 1622. It has its original STAINED GLASS, with large figures in strong colours, probably Flemish. It also has very pretty floor TILES. The MONUMENT for which the chapel was founded is that of Sir John Willoughby † 1622, a big standing wall-monument of alabaster with small kneeling figures against the tomb-chest, two recumbent effigies, a big coffered arch between coupled columns, plenty of strapwork decoration of the back wall, and a top achievement. The workmanship is not good. – To its l. Ann Cray *née* Willoughby † 1688, also standing wall-monument, black pedestal, large white urn with white putti to the l. and r.

WINDTHORPE HALL *see* CLAY CROSS

WINGERWORTH

ALL SAINTS. The interest of the Church lies in its Norman remains, the low, completely plain, small, unmoulded early chancel arch on the plainest imposts, three-bay S arcade, higher, with circular piers, simply moulded capitals, and round single-chamfered arches, and the S doorway, of rather narrow proportions, with one order of colonnettes and no ornamentation. There are in the outer S wall also the remains of another round arch. The chancel has C13 lancet windows. The rest, including the W tower (diagonal buttresses, no battlements), the clerestory and all the battlements, is Perp. In 1783 the Hunloke family added on the N side a family MAUSOLEUM, an entirely plain parallelogram without decoration. – FONT. Norman, plain big tub. – ROOD LOFT. A rare survival. It does not stand on a rood screen but is affixed to the wall above the low Norman chancel arch. The underside projects in a straight diagonal, not coved. It is decorated with ribs and bosses at wide intervals. The beam at the foot is moulded; crenellation at the top. – MONUMENT. Effigy of Priest, C13, a chalice lying below his folded hands.

Of WINGERWORTH HALL only minor and outbuildings are preserved. The Hall itself, completed in 1729, was pulled down after an existence of about 200 years.

STUBBING COURT, *see* p. 226.

WINSTER

ST JOHN THE BAPTIST. Plain W tower of 1721 with segment-headed windows. The rest 1842 and again altered in 1883. The latter alteration (by *A. Roland Barker*) is quite remarkable. It made the church two-aisled with tall slim quatrefoil shafts along the middle. The easternmost of these is connected with the chancel arch by two arches thrown diagonally across to the NE and SE: a surprising and successful effect. – FONT. A puzzling piece; circular, tub-shaped bowl on a conical foot. The carvings of a style that could be a Tudor imitation of Norman.

The town has good houses, both above the church (stables and outhouses of WESLEYAN CHAPEL of 1837 with Venetian windows l. and r. of the door), and along the main street (one Early Georgian five-bay stone house with giant pilasters to single out the centre bay, and top balustrade; the doorway late C18). The chief building of Winster is the MARKET HALL with an originally open ground floor on pointed arches and an upper floor of brick with gabled ends and windows of one mullion and one transome, evidently late C17. Past the Market Hall several more houses worth noticing, e.g. one dated 1754 which has still the traditional low two-light windows, but now systematized by being placed between horizontal string courses running all along the front. Also a Palladian house with two Tuscan porches and between them on the ground floor and the upper floor a Venetian window. The date no doubt mid C18.

MINNINGLOW HILL, 3 m. SW of Winster. Large burial

mound on the top of a hill. Beside it is another much smaller cairn. Both are round, and date from the Bronze Age. Five burial chambers were found inside the larger mound when it was excavated.

WIRKSWORTH

ST MARY. An impressive church of the ambitious type of Ashbourne, 152 ft long, with a crossing tower and spire and transepts. The chancel with aisles. Nothing survives necessarily older than 1272, the date when the Dean and Chapter of Lincoln, to which Wirksworth belonged, appointed the first special vicar for the church. Of that time the tall N and S windows of the chancel and the less tall lancets in the W wall of the N transept. They look influenced by Ashbourne.* The other windows have to be examined with caution. In their present appearance they all belong to *Sir George Gilbert Scott's* restoration of 1876. The restoration also added the clerestory and kept and made historically probable-looking the E transept aisles added in 1820 to house galleries for a fast-growing congregation. They confused the appearance of the E parts of the church considerably. The chancel E window incidentally dates from 1855, i.e. before Scott. The other windows and their tracery are Dec (S aisle; probably by *Scott*) or Perp (W, N aisle, N transept N, S transept S). The S porch is roofed with pitched stone slabs. The crossing tower is C13 below, and early C14 above. It has a quatrefoil frieze instead of battlements and the exceptional feature of a 'spike' instead of a spire proper. The interior tells of the late C13. There are first of all the four arches of the crossing tower with their massive supports (*see* for example, the occasional use of nailhead ornamentation and the keeling or filleting of shafts). The arcades between nave and aisles belong to a slightly later building phase: three bays, quatrefoil shafts with fillets, double-chamfered arches; E responds slimmer and with shaft-rings. The nave is wider than the chancel.

* Also the large chancel Piscina.

The furnishings of the church take us back much further than the present building. In Anglo-Saxon times Wirksworth was dependent on Repton. The Anglo-Saxon COFFIN LID of *c.* 800 found in 1820 must have been from the sarcophagus of an important saint buried here. It is one of the most interesting sculptural remains of its date, embellished with stories from the life of Christ, in short, stumpy figures coarsely carved with schematic parallel reeding of the draperies. Upper tier: Washing of the Disciples' Feet, Cross with Lamb and the Symbols of the four Evangelists (originally no doubt the centre of the slab), Burial of Christ, Descent into Hell, the Body in the Tomb. Lower tier: Adoration of the Child?, Ascension (below the Cross), Annunciation, Raising of Jairus's Daughter. Sir Thomas Kendrick compares the style of the figures with that of the Rothbury Cross. – Next in time is a large number of NORMAN ARCHITECTURAL FRAGMENTS in the N transept N wall, S transept S wall and S transept W wall, also one in the N aisle wall. They deserve close study and might yield quite some information on the lavish appointment of the predecessor of the C13 church. 4

FONTS. One Norman, a large, plain, impressive cauldron, the other of 1662, octagonal, with the usual style of carving of the 1662 fonts, and a series of florid initials. – MONUMENTS. Foliated Cross with Sword and Forester's Horn (N transept). – Brasses to Thomas Blackwell † 1525 and wife. On the same panel the figures from another Blackwell brass (N transept). – Anthony Lowe † 1555, the best monument in the church, already completely in the new Renaissance style. Tomb-chest with putti and fine panel of kneeling children on the W side, effigy in armour (does it belong?) and back-plate against the wall with short fluted Corinthian pilasters and cornice (chancel). – Incised alabaster slab to Ralph Gell † 1564 with two wives and children (N chancel aisle). – Tomb-chest of Anthony Gell † 1583, with good alabaster effigy, inscription on a plate against the wall and copious strap-work decoration of the chest. 26

THE TOWN

THE TOWN. Around the churchyard to the E of the church the PRIESTS' HOUSE, C15 and C16, derelict, small, raised on steps with square-headed four- and six-light windows; GELL'S BEDEHOUSES, 1584, of two storeys, with three-light mullioned windows and gabled ends; and the GRAMMAR SCHOOL, also founded 1584, but rebuilt in 1828 in a pretty Neo-Gothic style with battlements and crocketed pinnacles, and small-paned window casements. More substantial C18 stone houses (e.g. the VICARAGE) N of the church. Church Street leads to the main street of the town: COLDWELL STREET. Turning to the E down the hill on the l. the OLD MANOR HOUSE, gabled early C17 with Georgianized side projections (inside an early C17 plaster ceiling), and lower down the STABLES, etc., of Wirksworth Hall, late C18 with semi-circular windows and pediment and lower projecting wings with semi-circular windows. Up Coldwell Street to the W one should first turn into Chapel Lane to the MOOT HALL, rebuilt one-storeyed in plain ashlar work in 1814. It is the place in which the Barmote Courts are held, the prerogative of Wirksworth which was the centre of English lead-mining. It is known from literature that the Romans and Saxons mined here. In the Hall is the 14-pint oblong measuring vessel for the lead. It has an inscription referring to the third year of Henry VIII. – Back into Coldwell Street and up to THE VAULTS, a picturesque early C19 group, whitewashed with dark brown trim (Piper's Delight), then a late C18 brick house and the RED LION (mid Georgian, brick, painted white, with archway, Venetian window above and semicircular tripartite window above that) facing into the MARKET PLACE. Next to the Red Lion across the road to Middleton, No. 18, a fine mid-Georgian five-bay stone house, doorway with steep pediment. To the l. of this a one-bay brick addition with Venetian windows on both main floors and flanking giant pilasters. Round the corner in DALE END a broad gabled house of *c.* 1630 with mullioned windows (derelict). Farther out the OLD HOSPITAL (Babington Guest House), gabled, irregular. On a recent porch the quite probable date 1588. – The Market Place spreads down the hill and opens to the W into the wide WEST END (No. 1, late C18 three-bay brick house). Down the hill St John's Road leads to the S. Off it at the end of Causeway the GATE HOUSE, an independent house in its garden: C17 (mullioned windows at the back), with a late C18 brick front.

Wirksworth is attractive as an *ensemble* rather than by means of individual houses (as, for example, Ashbourne is). The visual effect which one remembers is of the differences of levels, the curved course of the two main streets and their ascent towards the crown of the Market Place.

(GREENHILL. C17 gabled house with mullioned windows)

WOODTHORPE HALL *see* HOLMESFIELD

WOODVILLE

ST STEPHEN. 1846, by *Stevens*, stone, in the Norman style, with SW turret and apsed E end.

WORMHILL

ST MARGARET. Almost rebuilt in 1864. Only the base of the narrow unbuttressed W tower is medieval. The top is inspired by the Rhineland Romanesque style (or by Sompting, Sussex).

OLD HALL FARM. C16–C17, with mullioned windows under hood-moulds, probably the old Manor House, before Wormhill Hall was built.

WORMHILL HALL. Dated 1697 on a rainwater head, and a good example of the style of its date in Derbyshire. H-shaped, with quoins and a segmental pediment above the doorway. The windows with mullion-and-transome-crosses under straight hoods. In the projecting wings of the front the window hoods are connected by flat string courses.

YEARDSLEY HALL *see* TAXAL

YEAVELEY

HOLY TRINITY. 1840, by *J. Smith* (GR). Small brick church with lancet windows and a pretty little embattled brick W tower.

STYDD HALL, 1 m. W. Interesting remains of a Preceptory of the Knights Hospitallers, founded *c.* 1190. One wall of the C13 chapel with lancet windows, their labels on head-stops. Shafts between the windows. The present house stands on medieval stone foundations, but is Elizabethan or Jacobean, brick and stone, tall and square, almost tower-like, with mullioned windows and battlements. Gothick bay windows added in 1840.

YOULGREAVE

ALL SAINTS. One of the most impressive churches of Derbyshire. Externally the impression is dominated by the broad, big and tall Perp W tower (angle buttresses with many set-offs, big W door, big W window, two tall two-light bell-openings on each side, battlements and eight pinnacles, tall and wide arch towards the nave) and by the crenellation of the rest of the church. Internally the capital quality of the church is its very wide nave with its interesting three-bay arcades. The S arcade is Late Norman at its sturdiest: circular piers, capitals many-scalloped or even scalloped in two tiers, double-chamfered round arches. The N arcade is a little later, also circular piers, also Norman capitals, but with volutes and heads in various combinations, and pointed double-chamfered arches and head label-stops. The W respond is even keeled.* The S doorway can hardly be as early as the S arcade. When the W tower was built, it was placed considerably farther W than the W end of the Norman nave. The two were connected by an aisleless part. The windows are mostly Perp, especially chancel E (five lights). The S aisle windows are of typical designs of *c.* 1300. The restoration of 1870 (by *Norman Shaw*) was

* The blocked N doorway belongs to the date of the N arcade.

on the whole satisfactorily done. The plain clerestory windows are dated C17 by Cox, but may well be Early Tudor, i.e. of the time of the well-preserved nave roof. – FONT. Big, circular, with a few motifs (animals, fleurs-de-lis pointing to *c.* 1200. Its remarkable feature is the addition of a separate projecting side stoup. – SCULPTURE. Fine small arched panel with figure of a man in long frock, Norman (N nave wall). – STAINED GLASS. E window by *Burne-Jones* (*Morris & Co.*), 1878. – Chancel S window by *Burne-Jones*, 1894. – N aisle E window and nave S window by *Kempe*, 1893, the former a specially good example of his manner. – MONUMENTS. Cross-legged bearded Knight holding his heart in his hands (cf. Darley Dale), *c.* 1325 (chancel N wall). – Alabaster effigy of Thomas Cokayne † 1488, on tomb-chest, of exceptionally good quality, but also exceptionally small size (how young was Thomas Cokayne when he died?). The tomb-chest on the long sides with two standing angels separated by a tracery panel (instead of the more usual two panels and three angels). – Exquisite oblong alabaster panel to Robert Gylbert † 1492, his wife and children. In the centre seated Virgin, r. and l. the kneeling figures first of husband and wife, then of the seventeen children. – Frideswide Gilbert † 1603, small brass figure. – Roger Rowe † 1613, fairly large, one of the usual epitaphs with kneelers, the children below the parents in the 'predella'.

17a

25a

In the Market Place a big plain lumpy circular Conduit Head of 1829. To the NW OLD HALL FARM, 1630, gabled and with mullioned windows, and below the OLD HALL of 1650 (date on panelling inside). The Old Hall has somewhat projecting symmetrical wings with five- and six-light mullioned windows and gables. Just behind the CONGREGATIONAL CHURCH, at Middleton-by-Youlgreave, is the tomb of Thomas Bateman, C19 gentleman of means and indefatigable excavator of Derbyshire's innumerable barrows. The tomb is amusingly surmounted by a stone model of a Bronze Age cinerary urn. Bateman's collections and his beautifully written and illustrated MSS are now housed for the most part in the museum at Sheffield.

HERMITS CAVE. At the end of a footpath branching off the path which runs between Gratcliffe Rocks and Woods and Robin Hood's Stride. Rudely carved Crucifixus in the cave.

ARBOR LOW, $2\frac{3}{4}$ m. W. The most famous of Derbyshire antiquities. Early Bronze Age sanctuary, consisting of a stone circle about 250 ft in diameter enclosed by a rock-cut ditch 4 ft 6 in. deep and outer bank 6 ft high. There are two opposite entrances. None of the monoliths are now standing. There are forty stones, the largest 13 ft long. One stone lies in the centre of the circle. In appearance the site seems a smaller version of Avebury and Stonehenge. As usual with this class of monument, the sanctuary stands at the centre of a thick agglomeration of barrows, clustered for reasons of piety round the sacred edifice. The two lanes which lead to Arbor Low, called Long Rake and Green Lane, may be ancient trackways.

Close to Arbor Low stands an impressive tumulus known as GIB HILL, the largest round barrow in the county, 15 ft high. It contained an Early Bronze Age burial and was thrown up from material excavated during the building of the sanctuary itself. The mount covered four smaller barrows.

At END LOW, 2 m. S of Gib Hill, is another prominent barrow. At LIFF'S LOW, 2 m. S of End Low, Bateman found a hunter, complete with stone arrow heads, axes, knives, woad, pottery, a red deer horn, and two huge boar's tusks.

Near Arbor Low on the Ashbourne road is a small barrow from which Bateman recovered the helmet and decorated leather cap of an Anglo-Saxon chieftain.

GLOSSARY

ABACUS: flat slab on the top of a capital (q.v.).

ABUTMENT: solid masonry placed to resist the lateral pressure of a vault.

ACANTHUS: plant with thick fleshy and scalloped leaves used as part of the decoration of a Corinthian capital (q.v.) and in some types of leaf carving.

ACHIEVEMENT OF ARMS: in heraldry, a complete display of armorial bearings.

ACROTERION: foliage-carved block on the end or top of a classical pediment.

ADDOSSED: two human figures, animals, or birds, etc., placed symmetrically so that they turn their backs to each other.

AEDICULE, AEDICULA: framing of a window or door by columns and a pediment (q.v.).

AFFRONTED: two human figures, animals, or birds, etc., placed symmetrically so that they face each other.

AMBULATORY: semicircular or polygonal aisle enclosing an apse (q.v.).

ANNULET: *see* Shaft-ring.

ANTIS, IN: *see* Portico.

APSE: vaulted semicircular or polygonal end of a chancel or a chapel.

ARABESQUE: light and fanciful surface decoration using combinations of flowing lines, tendrils, etc., interspersed with vases, animals, etc.

ARCADE: range of arches supported on piers or columns, free-standing; or, BLIND ARCADE, the same attached to a wall.

ARCH: round-headed; i.e. semicircular pointed, i.e. consisting of two curves, each drawn from one centre, and meeting in a point at the top; Segmental, i.e. in the form of a segment; pointed; four-centred, *see* Fig. 1(*a*); Tudor, *see* Fig. 1(*b*); Ogee, *see* Fig. 1(*c*); Stilted, *see* Fig. 1(*d*).

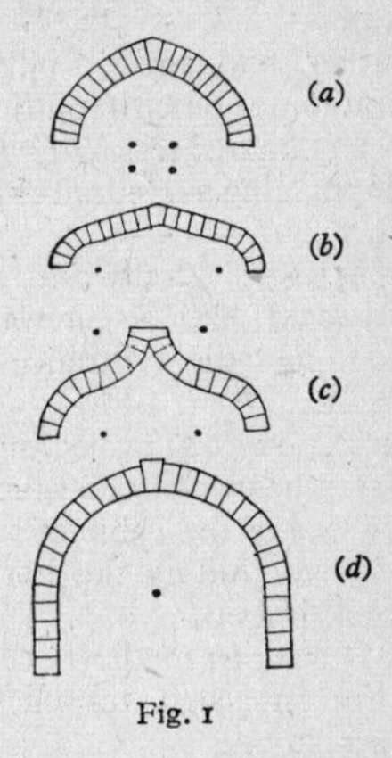

Fig. 1

ARCHITRAVE: lowest of the three main parts of the entablature (q.v.) of an order (q.v.) (*see* Fig. 11).

ARCHIVOLT: undersurface of an arch (also called Soffit).

ARRIS: sharp edge at the meeting of two surfaces.

ASHLAR: masonry of large blocks wrought to even faces and square edges.

ATRIUM: inner court of a Roman house, also open court in front of a church.

ATTACHED: *see* engaged.

ATTIC: topmost storey of a house, if lower than the others.

AUMBREY: recess or cupboard to hold sacred vessels for Mass and Communion.

BAILEY: open space or court of a fortified castle.

BALDACCHINO: canopy supported on columns.

BALLFLOWER: globular flower of three petals enclosing a small ball. A decoration used in the first quarter of the C14.

BALUSTER: small pillar or column of fanciful outline.

BALUSTRADE: series of balusters supporting a handrail or coping (q.v.).

BARBICAN: outwork, constructed like a gateway, defending the entrance to a castle.

BARGEBOARDS: projecting decorated boards placed against the incline of the gable of a building and hiding the horizontal roof timbers.

BASILICA: in medieval architecture an aisled church with a clerestory.

BASTION: projection at the angle of a fortification.

BATTER: wall with an inclined face.

BATTLEMENT: parapet with a series of indentations or embrasures with raised portions or merlons between (also called Crenellation).

BAYS: internal compartments of a building; each divided from the other not by solid walls but by divisions only marked in the side walls (columns, pilasters, etc.) or the ceiling (beams, etc.). Also external divisions of a building by fenestration.

BAY-WINDOW: angular or curved projection of a house front with ample fenestration. If curved also called bow-window; if on an upper floor only also called oriel or oriel window.

BEAKHEAD: Norman ornamental motif consisting of a row of bird or beast heads with beaks pointing downwards and biting usually into a roll moulding.

BELL-COTE: turret usually on the W end of a church to carry the bells.

BILLET: Norman ornamental motif made up of short raised rectangles placed at regular intervals.

BLOCK CAPITAL: Romanesque capital cut from a cube by having the lower angles rounded off to the circular shaft below (also called Cushion Capital) (Fig. 2).

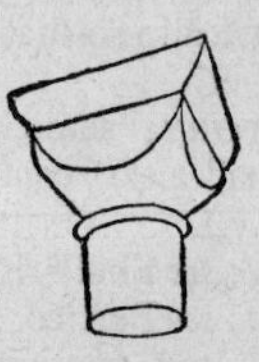

Fig. 2

BOND, ENGLISH or FLEMISH: *see* Brickwork.

BOSS: knob or projection usually placed to cover the intersection of ribs in a vault.

BOW-WINDOW: *see* Bay-Window.

BOX PEW: pew with a high wooden enclosure.

BRACES: *see* Roof.

BRACKET: small supporting piece of stone, etc., to carry a projecting horizontal.

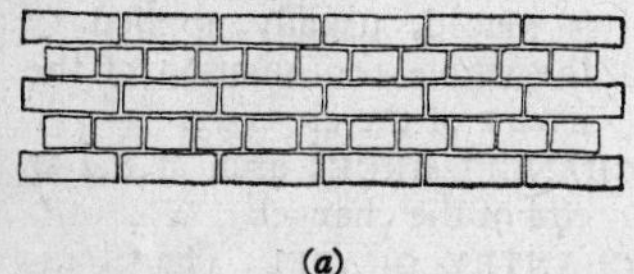

(*a*)

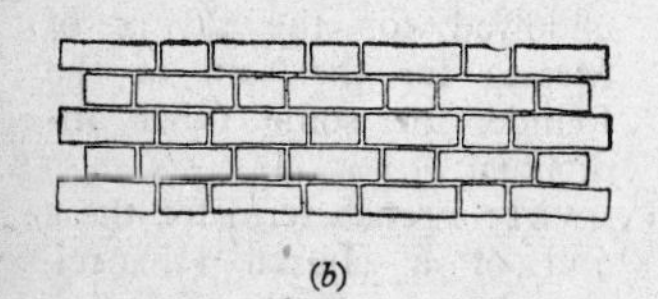

(*b*)

Fig. 3

BRICKWORK: *Header:* brick laid so that the end only appears on the face of the wall. *Stretcher:* brick laid so that the side only appears on the face of the wall. *English Bond:* method of laying bricks so that alternate courses or layers on the face of the wall are composed of headers or stretchers only (Fig. 3*a*). *Flemish Bond:* method of laying bricks so that alternate headers and stretchers appear in each course on the face of the wall (Fig. 3*b*).

BROACH: *see* Spire.

BROKEN PEDIMENT: *see* Pediment.

BUTTRESS: mass of brickwork or masonry projecting from or built against a wall to give additional strength. *Angle Buttresses:* two meeting at an angle of 90° at the angle of a building (Fig. 4*a*). *Clasping Buttress:* one which encases the angle

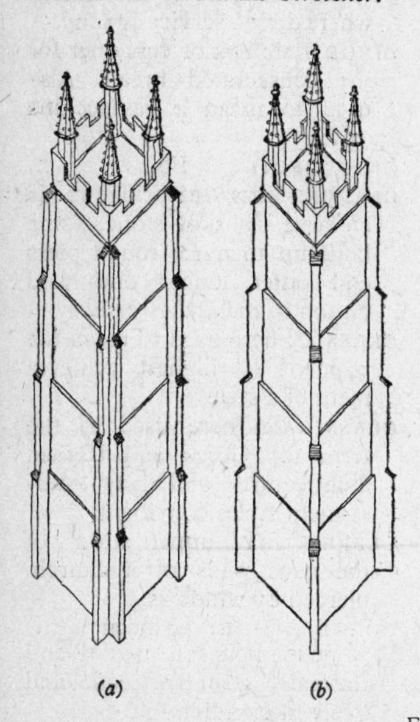

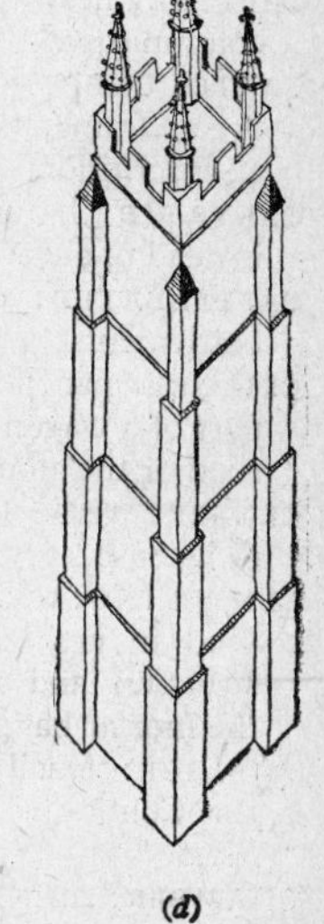

(*a*) (*b*) (*c*) (*d*)

Fig. 4

(Fig. 4*d*). *Diagonal Buttress:* one placed against the right angle formed by two walls, and more or less equiangular with both (Fig. 4*b*). *Flying Buttress:* arch or half arch transmitting the thrust of a vault or roof from the upper part of a wall to an outer support or buttress. *Setback Buttress:* angle buttress set slightly back from the angle (Fig. 4*c*).

CABLE MOULDING: moulding imitating a twisted cord.

CAMBER: slight rise or upward curve of an otherwise horizontal structure.

CAMPANILE: isolated bell tower.

CANOPY: ornamental covering above an altar, pulpit, niche, etc.

CAP: in a windmill the crowning feature.

CAPITAL: head or top part of a column (q.v.).

CARTOUCHE: tablet with an ornate frame, usually enclosing an inscription.

CARYATID: human figure used instead of a column.

CASTELLATED: decorated with battlements.

CEILURE: panelled and adorned part of a wagon-roof above the rood or the altar.

CENSER: vessel for the burning of incense.

CENTERING: wooden framework used in arch and vault construction and removed when the mortar has set.

CHALICE: small cup used in the Communion service or at Mass.

CHAMFER: surface made by cutting across the square angle of a stone block, piece of wood, etc., at an angle of 45° to the two other surfaces.

CHANCEL: that part of the E end of a church in which the altar is placed, usually applied to the whole continuation of the nave E of the crossing.

CHANCEL ARCH: arch at the W end of the chancel.

CHANTRY CHAPEL: chapel attached to, or inside, a church endowed for the saying of Masses for the soul of the founder or some other individual.

CHEVET: French term for the E end of a church (chancel, ambulatory, and radiating chapels).

CHEVRON: sculptured moulding forming a zigzag.

CHOIR: that part of the church where divine service is sung.

CIBORIUM: box or container for the consecrated bread. Also used to mean a baldacchino (q.v.).

CINQUEFOIL: *see* Foil.

CLAPPER BRIDGE: bridge made of large slabs of stone, some built up to make rough piers and other longer ones laid on top to make the roadway.

CLASSIC: here used to mean the moment of highest achievement of a style.

CLASSICAL: here used as the term for Greek and Roman architecture and any subsequent styles copying it.

CLERESTORY: upper storey of the nave walls of a church, pierced by windows.

COADE STONE: artificial (cast) stone made in the late C18 and the early C19 by Coade and Seely in London.

COB: walling material made of mixed clay and straw.

COFFERING: decorating a ceiling with sunk square or polygonal ornamental panels.

COLLAR-BEAM: *see* Roof.

COLONNADE: range of columns.

COLONNETTE: small column.

COLUMNA ROSTRATA: column decorated with carved prows of ships to celebrate a naval victory.

COMPOSITE: *see* Orders.

CONSOLE: bracket (q.v.) with a compound curved outline.

COPING: capping or covering to a wall.

CORBEL: block of stone projecting from a wall, supporting some horizontal feature.

CORBEL TABLE: series of corbels, occurring just below the roof eaves externally or internally, often seen in Norman buildings.

CORINTHIAN: *see* Orders.

CORNICE: in classical architecture the top section of the entablature (q.v.). Also for a projecting decorative feature along the top of a wall, arch, etc.

COVE, COVING: concave undersurface in the nature of a hollow moulding but on a larger scale.

COVER PATEN: cover to a Communion cup, suitable for use as a paten or plate for the consecrated bread.

CRADLE ROOF: *see* Wagon-roof.

CRENELLATION: *see* Battlement.

CREST, CRESTING: ornamental finish along the top of a screen, etc.

CROCKET, CROCKETING: decorative features placed on the sloping sides of spires, pinnacles, gables, etc. in Gothic architecture, carved in various leaf shapes and placed at regular intervals.

CROCKET CAPITAL: *see* Fig. 5.

Fig. 5

CROSSING: space at the intersection of nave, chancel, and transepts.

CRUCK: big curved beam supporting both walls and roof of a cottage.

CRYPT: underground room usually below the E end of a church.

CUPOLA: small polygonal or circular domed turret crowning a roof.

CURTAIN WALL: connecting wall between the towers of a castle.

CURVILINEAR: *see* Tracery.

CUSHION CAPITAL: *see* Block Capital.

CUSP: in tracery (q.v.) the small pointed member between two lobes of a trefoil, quatrefoil, etc.

DADO: decorative covering of the lower part of a wall.

DAGGER: tracery motif of the Dec. style. It is a lancet shape rounded or pointed at the head, pointed at the foot and cusped inside (*see* Fig. 6).

Fig. 6

DAIS: raised platform at one end of a room.

DEC ('DECORATED'): historical division of English Gothic architecture covering the first half of the C14.

DEMI-COLUMNS: columns half sunk into a wall.

DIAPER WORK: surface decoration composed of square or lozenge shapes.

DOG-TOOTH: typical E.E. ornament consisting of a series of four-cornered stars placed diagonally and raised pyramidally (Fig. 7).

Fig. 7

DOMICAL VAULT: *see* Vault.

DONJON: *see* Keep.

DORIC: *see* Orders.

DORMER (WINDOW): window placed vertically in the sloping plane of a roof.

DRIPSTONE: *see* Hood-mould.

DRUM: circular or polygonal vertical wall of a dome or cupola.

E.E. ('EARLY ENGLISH'): historical division of English Gothic architecture roughly covering the C13.

EASTER SEPULCHRE: recess with tomb-chest usually in the wall of a chancel, the tomb-chest to receive an effigy of Christ for Easter celebrations.

EAVES: underpart of a sloping roof overhanging a wall.

EAVES CORNICE: cornice below the eaves of a roof.

ECHINUS: quarter round moulding carved with egg and dart pattern, used in classical architecture.

EMBATTLED: *see* Battlement.

EMBRASURE: small opening in the wall or parapet of a fortified building, usually splayed on the inside. *See* Loop.

ENCAUSTIC TILES: earthenware glazed and decorated tiles used for paving.

ENGAGED COLUMNS: columns attached to, or partly sunk into, a wall.

ENGLISH BOND: *see* Brickwork.

ENTABLATURE: in Classical architecture the whole of the horizontal members above a column (that is architrave, frieze, and cornice) (*see* Fig. 11).

ENTASIS: very slight convex deviation from a straight line; used on Greek columns and sometimes on spires to prevent an optical illusion of concavity.

ENTRESOL: *see* Mezzanine.

EPITAPH: hanging wall monument.

ESCUTCHEON: shield for armorial bearings.

EXEDRA: the apsidal end of a room. *See* Apse.

EXTRADOS: outer surface of an arch.

FAIENCE: decorated glazed earthenware.

FAN TRACERY: *see* Tracery.

FAN VAULT: *see* Vault.

FERETORY: place behind the High Altar, where the chief shrine of a church is kept.

FESTOON: carved garland of flowers and fruit suspended at both ends.

FILLET: narrow flat band running down a shaft or along a roll moulding.

FINIAL: in Gothic architecture the top of a pinnacle, gable, or bench-end carved into a leaf or leaf-like form.

FLAGON: jug for the wine used in the Communion service.

FLAMBOYANT: properly the latest phase of French Gothic architecture where the window tracery takes on wavy undulating lines.

FLÈCHE: slender wooden spire on the centre of a roof (also called Spirelet).

FLEMISH BOND: *see* Brickwork.

FLEURON: decorative carved flower or leaf.

FLUSH WORK: Decorative use of flint in conjunction with dressed stone so as to form pattens: tracery, initials, etc.

FLUTING: vertical channelling in the shaft of a column.

FLYING BUTTRESS: *see* Buttress.

FOIL: lobe formed by the cusping (q.v.) of a circle or an arch. Trefoil, quatrefoil, cinquefoil, multifoil, express the number of leaf shapes to be seen.

FOLIATED: carved with leaf shapes.

FOSSE: ditch.

FOUR-CENTRED ARCH: *see* Arch.

FRATER: refectory or dining hall of a monastery.

FRESCO: wall painting on wet plaster.

FRIEZE: middle division of a classical entablature (q.v.) (*see* Fig. 11).

FRONTAL: covering of the front of an altar.

GALILEE: chapel or vestibule at the W end of a church enclosing the porch. Also called Narthex (q.v.).

GALLERY: in church architecture upper storey above an aisle, opened in arches to the nave. Also called Tribune (q.v.) and often erroneously Triforium (q.v.).

GARGOYLE: water spout projecting from the parapet of a wall or tower; carved into a human or animal shape.

GAZEBO: lookout tower or raised summer house in a picturesque garden.

'GEOMETRICAL': *see* Tracery.

'GIBBS' SURROUND: of a doorway or window. A surround with alternating larger and smaller blocks of stone, quoinwise, or intermittent large blocks, sometimes with a narrow raised band connecting them up the verticals and along the extrados of the arch (Fig. 8).

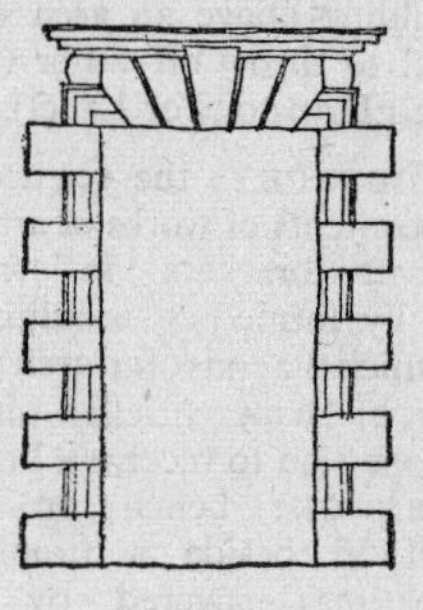

Fig. 8

GROIN: sharp edge at the meeting of two cells of a cross-vault.

GROINED VAULT: *see* Vault.

GROTESQUE: fanciful ornamental decoration: *see* also Arabesque.

HAGIOSCOPE: *see* Squint.

HALF-TIMBERING: *see* Timber Framing.

HALL CHURCH: church in which nave and aisles are of equal height or approximately so.

HAMMER-BEAM: *see* Roof.

HANAP: large metal cup, generally made for domestic use, standing on an elaborate base and stem; with a very ornate cover frequently crowned with a little steeple.

HEADERS: *see* Brickwork.

HERRINGBONE WORK: brick, stone, or tile construction where the component blocks are laid diagonally instead of flat. Alternate courses lie in opposing directions to make a zigzag pattern up the face of the wall.

HEXASTYLE: having four detached columns.

HIPPED ROOF: *see* Roof.

HOOD-MOULD: projecting moulding above an arch or a lintel to throw off water (also called Dripstone or Label).

ICONOGRAPHY: the science of the contents of works of art.

IMPOST: brackets in walls, usually formed of mouldings, on which the ends of an arch rest.

INDENT: shape chiselled out in a stone slab to receive a brass.

INGLENOOK: bench or seat built in beside a fireplace, sometimes covered by the chimney breast, occasionally lit by small windows on each side of the fire.

INTERCOLUMNATION: the space between columns.

IONIC: *see* Orders (Fig. 11).

JAMB: straight side of an archway, doorway, or window.

KEEL MOULDING: moulding whose outline is in section like that of the keel of a ship.

KEEP: massive tower of a Norman castle.

KEYSTONE: middle stone in an arch.

KING-POST: *see* Roof (Fig. 13).

LABEL: *see* Hood-mould.

LABEL STOP: ornamental boss at the end of a hood-mould (q.v.).

LANCET WINDOW: slender pointed-arched window.

LANTERN: in architecture, a small circular or polygonal turret with windows all round crowning a roof (*see* Cupola) or a dome.

LANTERN CROSS: churchyard cross with lantern-shaped top usually with sculptured representations on the sides of the top.

LEAN-TO ROOF: roof with one slope only, built against a higher wall.

LESENE OR PILASTER STRIP: pilaster without base and capital.

LIERNE: *see* Vault (Fig. 20).

LINENFOLD: Tudor panelling ornamented with a conventional representation of a piece of linen laid in vertical folds. The piece is repeated in each panel.

LINTEL: horizontal beam or stone bridging an opening.

LOGGIA: recessed colonnade (q.v.).

LONG AND SHORT WORK: Saxon quoins (q.v.) consisting of stones placed with the long sides alternately upright and horizontal.

LOUVRE: opening, often with lantern (q.v.) over, in the roof of a room to let the smoke from a central hearth escape.

LOZENGE: diamond shape.

LUNETTE: tympanum (q.v.) or curved opening in a vault.

LYCH GATE: wooden gate structure with a roof and open sides placed at the entrance to a churchyard to provide space for the reception of a coffin. The word lych is Saxon and means a corpse.

MACHICOLATION: projecting gallery on brackets constructed on the outside of castle towers or walls. The gallery has holes in the floor to drop missiles through.

MAJOLICA: ornamented glazed earthenware.

MANSARD: *see* Roof.

MERLON: *see* Battlement.

METOPE: in classical architecture of the Doric order (q.v.) the space in the frieze between the triglyphs (Fig. 11).

MEZZANINE: low storey placed between two higher ones.

MISERERE: *see* Misericord.

MISERICORD: bracket placed on the underside of a hinged choir stall seat which, when turned up, provided the occupant of the seat with a support during long periods of standing (also called Miserere).

MODILLION: small bracket of which large numbers (modillion frieze) are often placed below a cornice (q.v.) in classical architecture.

MOTTE: steep mound forming the main feature of C11 and C12 castles.

MOUCHETTE: tracery motif in curvilinear tracery, a curved dagger (q.v.) (Fig. 9).

Fig. 9

MULLION: vertical post or upright dividing a window into two or more 'lights'.

NAILHEAD: E.E. ornamental motif, consisting of small pyramids regularly repeated (Fig. 10).

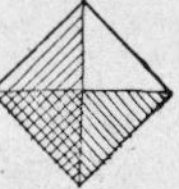

Fig. 10

NARTHEX: enclosed vestibule or covered porch at the main entrance to a church (*see* Galilee).

NEWEL: central post in a circular or winding staircase; also the principal post when a flight of stairs meets a landing.

OBELISK: lofty pillar of square section tapering at the top and ending pyramidally.

OGEE: *see* Arch (Fig. 1*c*).

ORATORY: small private chapel in a house.

ORDER: (1) *of a doorway or window:* series of concentric steps receding towards the opening; (2) *in classical architecture:* column with base, shaft, capital, and entablature (q.v.) according to one of the following styles: Greek Doric, Roman Doric, Tuscan Doric, Ionic, Corinthian, Composite. The established details are very elaborate, and some specialist architectural work should be consulted for further guidance (*see* Fig. 11).

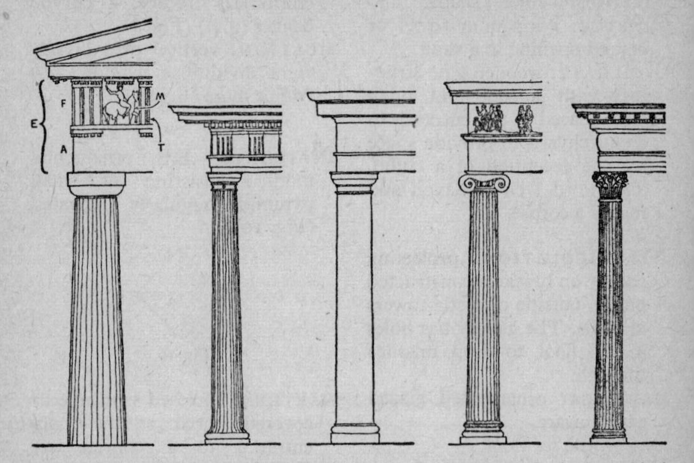

Fig. 11 – Orders of Columns (Greek Doric, Roman Doric, Tuscan, Ionic, Corinthian)
E, Entablature; F, Frieze; A, Architrave; M, Metope; T, Triglyph

ORIEL: *see* Bay Window.

OVERHANG: projection of the upper storey of a house.

OVERSAILING COURSES: series of stone or brick courses, each one projecting beyond the one below it.

PALIMPSEST: (1) *of a brass:* where a metal plate has been re-used by turning over and engraving on the back; (2) *of a wall painting:* where one overlaps and partly obscures an earlier one.

PALLADIAN: architecture following the ideas and principles of Andrea Palladio, 1518–80.

PANTILE: tile of curved S-shaped section.

PARAPET: low wall placed to protect any spot where there is a sudden drop, for example on a bridge, quay, hillside, housetop, etc.

PARGETTING: plaster work with patterns and ornaments either in relief or engraved on it.

PARVISE: room over a church porch. Often used as a schoolhouse or a store room.

PATEN: plate to hold the bread at Communion or Mass.

PATERA: small flat circular or oval ornament in classical architecture.

PEDIMENT: low-pitched gable (q.v.) used in classical, Renaissance, and neo-classical architecture above a portico and above doors, windows, etc. It may be straight-sided or curved segmentally. *Open Pediment:* one where the centre portion of the base is left open. *Broken Pediment:* one where the centre portion of the sloping sides is 'broken' out.

PENDANT: boss (q.v.) elongated so that it seems to hang down.

PENDENTIF: concave triangular spandrel used to lead from the angle of two walls to the base of a circular dome. It is constructed as part of the hemisphere over a diameter the size of the diagonal of the basic square (Fig. 12).

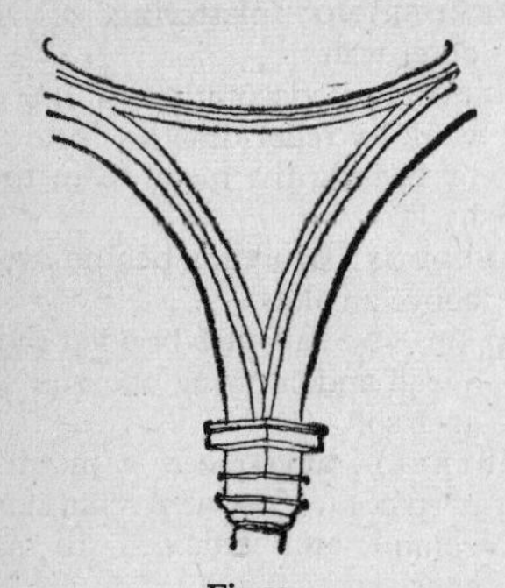

Fig 12.

PERP (PERPENDICULAR): historical division of English Gothic architecture roughly covering the period from 1350 to 1530.

PIANO NOBILE: principal storey of a house with the reception rooms; usually the first floor.

PIAZZA: square open space surrounded by buildings, in C17 and C18 English sometimes used to mean a long colonnade or loggia.

PIER: strong, solid support, frequently square in section or of composite section (compound pier).

PIETRA DURA: ornamental or scenic inlay by means of thin slabs of stone.

PILASTER: shallow pier attached to a wall.

PILLAR PISCINA: free-standing piscina on a pillar.

PINNACLE: ornamental form crowning a spire, tower, buttress, etc., usually of steep pyramidal, conical, or some similar shape.

PISCINA: basin for washing the Communion or Mass vessels, provided with a drain. Generally set in or against the wall to the S of an altar.

PLAISANCE: summer-house, pleasure house near a mansion.

PLATE TRACERY: *see* Tracery.

PLINTH: projecting base of a wall or column, generally chamfered (q.v.) or moulded at the top.

POPPYHEAD: ornament of leaf and flower type used to decorate the tops of bench or stall-ends.

PORTCULLIS: gate constructed to rise and fall in vertical grooves; used in gateways of castles.

PORTE COCHERE: porch large enough to admit wheeled vehicles.

PORTICO: centre-piece of a house or a church with classical detached or attached columns and a pediment. A portico is called *prostyle* or *in antis* according to whether it projects from or recedes into a building. In a portico *in antis* the columns range with the side walls.

POSTERN: small gateway at the back of a building.

PREDELLA: in an altar-piece the horizontal strip below the main representation, often used for a number of subsidiary representations in a row.

PRESBYTERY: the part of the church lying E of the choir. It is the part where altar is placed.

PRINCIPAL: *see* Roof (Fig. 13).

PRIORY: monastic house whose head is a prior or prioress, not an abbot or abbess.

PROSTYLE: with free-standing columns in a row.

PULPITUM: stone rood screen in a major church.

PURLIN: *see* Roof (Figs. 13, 14).

PUTTO: small naked boy.

QUADRANGLE: inner courtyard in a large building complex.

QUARRY: in stained-glass work, a small diamond or square-shaped piece of glass set diagonally.

QUATREFOIL: *see* Foil.

QUEEN-POSTS: *see* Roof (Fig. 14).

QUOINS: dressed stones at the angles of a building. Sometimes all the stones are of the same size; more often they are alternately large or small.

RADIATING CHAPELS: chapels projecting radially from an ambulatory or an apse.

RAFTER: *see* Roof.

RAMPART: stone wall, or wall of earth surrounding a castle, fortress, or fortified city.

RAMPART-WALK: path along the inner face of a rampart.

REBATE: channel or small recess cut into a piece of wood or stone longitudinally to receive the edge of some member that is to be secured in it. The depth of the channel is equal to the thickness of the member to be let into it.

REBUS: pun, a play on words. The literal translation and illustration of a name for artistic and heraldic purposes (Belton=bell, tun).

REEDING: decoration with parallel convex mouldings touching one another.

REFECTORY: Dining hall; *see* Frater.

RENDERING: plastering of an outer wall.

REPOUSSÉ: decoration of metal work by relief designs, formed by beating the metal from the back.

REREDOS: structure behind and above an altar.

RESPOND: half-pier bonded into a wall and carrying one end of an arch.

RETABLE: altar-piece, a picture or piece of carving, standing behind and attached to an altar.

RETICULATION: *see* Tracery (Fig. 19).

REVEAL: that part of a jamb (q.v.) which lies between the glass or door and the outer surface of the wall.

RIB VAULT: *see* Vault.

ROCOCO: latest phase of the Baroque style, current in most Continental countries between *c.* 1720 and *c.* 1760.

ROMANESQUE: that style in architecture which was current in the C11 and C12 and preceded the Gothic style (in England often called Norman).

ROOD: cross or crucifix.

ROOD LOFT: singing gallery on the top of the rood screen, often supported by a coving.

ROOD SCREEN: *see* Screen.

ROOD STAIRS: stairs to give access to the rood loft.

ROOF: *Hipped:* roof with sloped instead of vertical ends. *Mansard:* roof with a double slope, the lower slope being larger and steeper than the upper. *Saddleback:* tower roof shaped like an ordinary gabled timber roof. The following members have special names: *Rafter:* roof-timber sloping up from the wall plate to the ridge. *Principal:* principal rafter, usually corresponding to the main bay divisions of the nave or chancel below. *Wall Plate:* timber laid longitudinally on the top of a wall. *Purlin:* longitudinal member laid parallel with wall plate and ridge beam some way up the slope of the roof. *Tie-beam:* beam connecting the two slopes of a roof across at its foot, usually at the height of the wall plate, to prevent the roof from spreading. *Collar-beam:* tie-beam applied higher up the slope of the roof. *Strut:* upright timber connecting the tie-beam with the rafter above it. *King-post:*

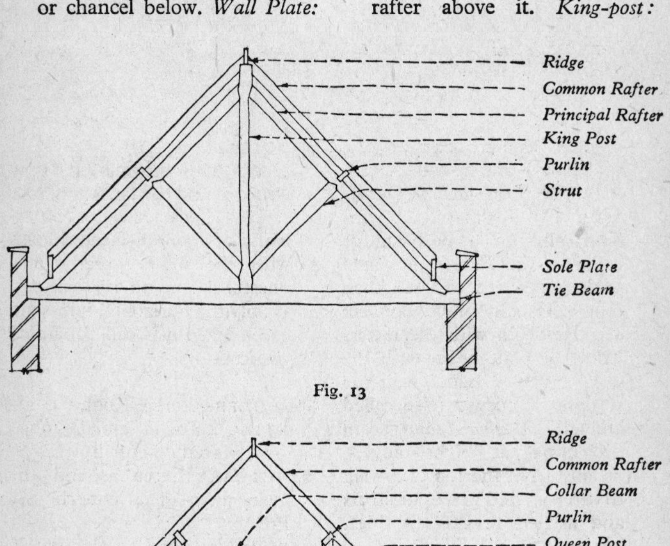

Fig. 13

Fig. 14

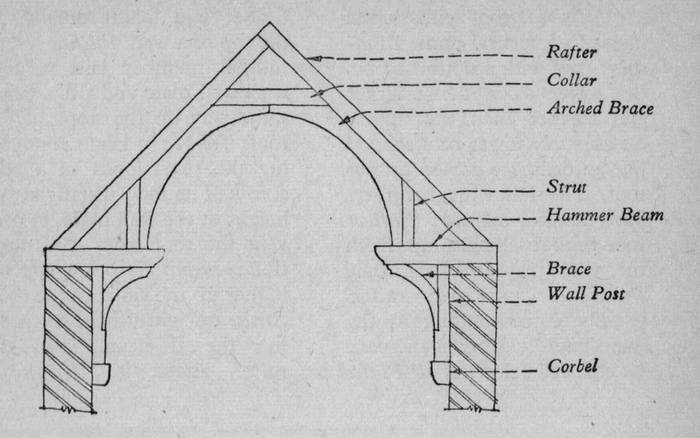

Fig. 15

upright timber connecting a tie-beam and collar-beam with the ridge-beam. *Queen-posts:* two struts placed symmetrically on a tie-beam or collar-beam. *Braces:* inclined timbers inserted to strengthen others. Usually braces connect a collar-beam with the rafters below or a tie-beam with the wall below. Braces can be straight or curved (also called arched). *Hammer-beam:* beam projecting at right angles, usually from the top of a wall, to carry arched braces or struts and arched braces (*see* Figs. 13, 14, 15).

ROSE WINDOW (or WHEEL WINDOW): circular window with patterned tracery arranged to radiate from the centre.

ROTUNDA: building circular in plan.

RUBBLE: building stones, not square or hewn, nor laid in regular courses.

RUSTICATION: Ashlar-work of blocks with the margins only wrought and the faces rough or specially rock-faced: or ashlar-work of smooth-faced blocks with the joints greatly emphasized (smooth rustication). If only the horizontal joints are emphasized it is called banded rustication.

SADDLEBACK: *see* Roof.

SALTIRE CROSS: equal-limbed cross placed diagonally.

SANCTUARY: area around the main altar of a church (*see* Presbytery).

SARCOPHAGUS: elaborately carved coffin.

SCAGLIOLA: material composed of cement and colouring matter to imitate marble.

SCALLOPED CAPITAL: development of the block capital (q.v.) in which the single semicircular surface is elaborated into a series of truncated cones (Fig. 16).

Fig. 16

SCARP: artificial cutting away of the ground to form a steep slope.

SCREEN: *Parclose screen:* screen separating a chapel from the rest of a church. *Rood screen:* screen at the W end of a chancel. Above it on the rood beam was the rood (q.v.).

SCREENS PASSAGE: passage between the entrances to kitchen, buttery, etc., and the screen behind which lies the hall of a medieval house.

SEDILIA: seats for the priests (usually three) on the S side of the chancel of a church.

SEGMENTAL ARCH: *see* Arch.

SET-OFF: *see* Weathering.

SEXPARTITE: *see* Vaulting.

SGRAFFITO: pattern incised into plaster so as to expose a dark surface underneath.

SHAFT-RING: ring round a circular pier or a shaft attached to a pier.

SILL: lower horizontal part of the frame of a window.

SLATEHANGING: the covering of walls by overlapping rows of slates, on a timber substructure.

SOFFIT: *see* Archivolt.

SOLAR: upper drawing-room of a medieval house.

SOPRAPORTE: painting above the door of a room, usual in the C17 and C18.

SOUNDING BOARD: horizontal board or canopy over a pulpit. Also called Tester.

SPANDREL: triangular surface between one side of an arch, the horizontal drawn from its apex, and the vertical drawn from its springer, also the surface between two arches.

SPIRE: tall pyramidal or conical pointed erection often built on top of a tower, turret, etc. *Broach Spire:* spire which is generally octagonal in plan rising from the top or parapet of a square tower. A small inclined piece of masonry covers the vacant triangular space at each of the four angles of the square and is carried up to a point along the diagonal sides of the octagon. *Needle Spire:* thin spire rising from the centre of a tower roof, well inside the parapet.

SPIRELET: *see* Flèche.

SPLAY: chamfer, usually of the jamb of a window.

SPRINGING: level at which an arch rises from its supports.

SQUINCH: arch or system of concentric arches thrown across the angle between two walls to support a superstructure, for example a dome (Fig. 17).

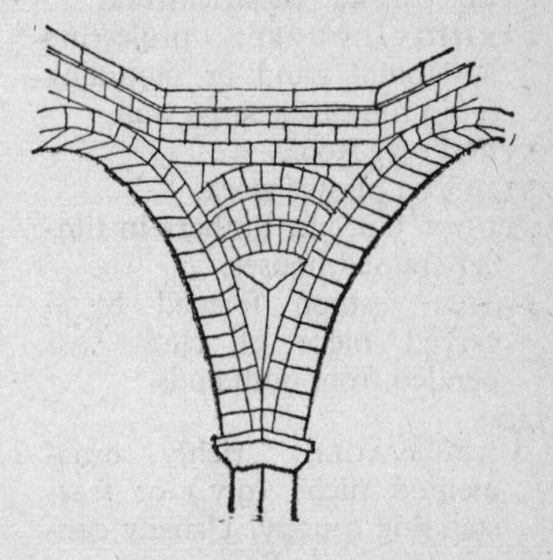

Fig. 17

SQUINT: hole cut in a wall or through a pier to allow a view of the main altar of a church from places whence it could not otherwise be seen (also called Hagioscope).

STALL: carved seat, one in a row, made of wood or stone.

STEEPLE: the tower or spire of a church.

STIFF-LEAF: E.E. type of foliage of many-lobed shapes (Fig. 18).

Fig. 18

STILTED: *see* Arch.

STOUP: vessel for the reception of holy water, usually placed near a door.

STRAINER ARCH: arch inserted across a room to prevent the walls from leaning.

STRAPWORK: C16 decoration consisting of interlaced bands, and forms similar to fretwork or cut and bent leather.

STRETCHERS: *see* Brickwork.

STRING COURSE: projecting horizontal band or moulding set in the surface of a wall.

STRUT: *see* Roof.

STUCCO: plaster work.

STUDS: Upright timbers in timber-framed houses.

SWAG: festoon formed by a carved piece of cloth suspended from both ends.

TABERNACLE: richly ornamented niche (q.v.) or free-standing canopy. Usually contains the Holy Sacrament.

TAZZA: shallow bowl on a foot.

TERMINAL FIGURES (TERMS, TERMINI): upper part of a human figure growing out of a pier, pilaster, etc., which tapers towards the base.

TERRACOTTA: burnt clay, unglazed.

TESSELATED PAVEMENT: decorative floor or wall covering made up of tesserae or small coloured cubes of stone, fitted into a bed of cement.

TESTER: *see* Sounding Board.

TETRASTYLE: having four detached columns.

THREE-DECKER PULPIT: pulpit with Clerk's Stall and Reading Desk placed below each other.

TIE-BEAM: *see* Roof (Figs. 13, 14).

TIERCERON: *see* Vault (Fig. 20).

TILEHANGING: *see* Slatehanging.

TIMBER-FRAMING: method of construction where walls are built of timber framework with the spaces filled in by plaster or brickwork. Sometimes the timber is covered over with plaster or boarding laid horizontally.

TOMB-CHEST: chest-shaped stone coffin, the most usual medieval form of funeral monument.

TOUCH: soft black marble quarried near Tournai.

TOURELLE: turret corbelled out from the wall.

TRACERY: intersecting ribwork in the upper part of a window, or used decoratively in blank arches, on vaults, etc. *Plate tracery:* early form of tracery where decoratively shaped openings are cut through the solid stone infilling in the head

(*a*)

(*b*)

(*c*)

(*d*)

Fig. 19

of a window. *Bar tracery:* intersecting ribwork made up of slender shafts, continuing the lines of the mullions of windows up to a decorative mesh in the head of the window. *Geometrical tracery:* tracery consisting chiefly of circles or foiled circles. *Intersected tracery:* tracery in which each mullion of a window branches out into two curved bars in such a way that every one of them runs concentrically with the others against the arch of the whole window. The result is that every light of the window is a lancet and every two, three, four, etc., lights together form a pointed arch (Fig. 19*a*). *Reticulated tracery:* tracery consisting entirely of circles drawn at top and bottom into ogee shapes so that a net-like appearance results (Fig. 19*b*). *Panel tracery:* tracery forming upright straight-sided panels above lights of a window (Fig. 19, *c* & *d*).

TRANSEPT: transverse portion of a cross-shaped church.

TRANSOME: horizontal bar across the opening of a window.

TRANSVERSE ARCH: *see* Vaulting.

TRIBUNE: *see* Gallery.

TRICIPUT, SIGNUM TRICIPUT: sign of the Trinity expressed by three faces belonging to one head.

TRIFORIUM: arcaded wall passage or blank arcading facing the nave at the height of the aisle roof and below the clerestory (q.v.) windows. (*See* Gallery.)

TRIGLYPHS: blocks with vertical grooves separating the metopes (q.v.) in the Doric frieze (Fig. 11).

TROPHY: sculptured group of arms or armour, used as a memorial of victory.

TRUMEAU: stone mullion (q.v.) supporting the tympanum (q.v.) of a wide doorway.

TURRET: very small tower, round or polygonal in plan.

TUSCAN: *see* Order.

TYMPANUM: space between the lintel of a doorway and the arch above it.

UNDERCROFT: vaulted room, sometimes underground, below a church or chapel.

VAULT: *Barrel vault: see* Tunnel vault. *Cross-vault: see* Groined vault. *Domical vault:* square or polygonal dome rising direct on a square or polygonal bay, the curved surfaces separated by groins (q.v.). *Fan vault:* vault where all ribs springing from one springer are of the same length, the same distance from the next, and the same curvature. *Groined vault* or *Cross-vault:* vault of two tunnel vaults of identical shape intersecting each other at right angles. *Lierne:* tertiary rib, that is, rib which does not spring either from one of the main springers or the central boss. *Quadripartite vault:* one wherein one bay of vaulting is divided into four parts. *Rib vault:* vault with diagonal ribs projecting along the groins. *Ridge-rib:* rib along the longitudinal or transverse ridge of a vault. *Sexpartite vault:* one wherein one bay of quadripartite vaulting is divided into two parts transversely so that each bay of vaulting has six parts. *Tierceron:* secondary rib, that is, rib which issues from one of the main springers or the central boss and leads to a place on a ridge-rib. *Transverse arch:* arch separating one bay of a vault from the next. *Tunnel vault* or *Barrel vault:* vault of semicircular or pointed section (Fig. 20).

VAULTING SHAFT: vertical member leading to the springer of a vault.

VENETIAN WINDOW: window with three openings, the central one arched and wider than the outside ones.

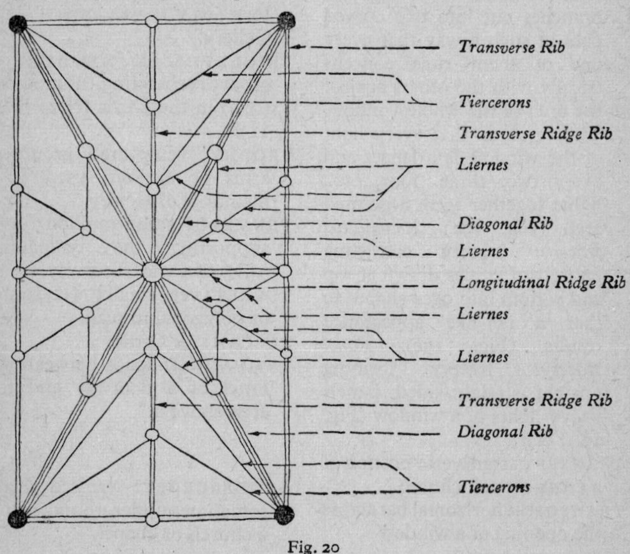

Fig. 20

VERANDAH: open gallery or balcony with a roof on light, usually metal, supports.

VESICA: Oval with pointed head and foot.

VESTIBULE: ante-room or entrance hall.

VILLA: according to Gwilt (1842) 'a country house for the residence of opulent persons'.

VITRIFIED: made similar to glass.

VOLUTE: spiral scroll, one of the component parts of an Ionic column (*see* Orders).

VOUSSOIR: wedge-shaped stone used in arch construction.

WAGON-ROOF: roof in which by closely set rafters with arched braces the appearance of the inside of a canvas tilt over a wagon is achieved. Wagon-roofs can be panelled or plastered (ceiled) or left uncovered.

WAINSCOT: timber lining to walls.

WALL PLATE: *see* Roof.

WATERLEAF: leaf shape used in later C12 capitals. The waterleaf is a broad, unribbed, tapering leaf curving up towards the angle of the abacus and turned in at the top (Fig. 21).

Fig. 21

WEATHER-BOARDING: overlapping horizontal boards, covering a timber-framed wall.

WEATHERING: sloping horizontal surface on sills, buttresses, etc., to throw off water.

WEEPERS: small figures placed in niches along the sides of some medieval tombs (also called Mourners).

WHEEL WINDOW: *see* Rose Window.

INDEX OF PLATES

INDEX OF ARTISTS

STOKE-ON-TRENT
PUBLIC
LIBRARIES

INDEX OF PLACES

The references in brackets indicate the square in which the place will be found on the map preceding the title-page

NOTES

NOTES

NOTES

NOTES